W9-BCR-533

Keys to College Success

Fifth Edition

Surry Community College

■ ■ ■

ACA 111: College Student Success
ACA 122: College Transfer Success

Kendall Hunt
publishing company

Cover image © Slavojub Pantelic, 2009. Used under license from Shutterstock, Inc.

Kendall Hunt
publishing company

www.kendallhunt.com
Send all inquiries to:
4050 Westmark Drive
Dubuque, IA 52004-1840

Copyright © 2001, 2003, 2005, 2007, 2009 by Surry Community College

ISBN 978-0-7575-6784-1

Kendall/Hunt Publishing Company has the exclusive rights to reproduce this work,
to prepare derivative works from this work, to publicly distribute this work,
to publicly perform this work and to publicly display this work.

All rights reserved. No part of this publication may be reproduced,
stored in a retrieval system, or transmitted, in any form or by any
means, electronic, mechanical, photocopying, recording, or otherwise,
without the prior written permission of the copyright owner.

Printed in the United States of America
10 9 8 7 6 5 4 3 2 1

Contents

Chapter 4 Learning Style/Instructional Style   115

Chapter 5 Reading Critically and Note Taking   137

Chapter 9 Transferring to a Four-Year College or University 283

KEYS TO COLLEGE SUCCESS

Fourth Edition

Textbook Developed by College Faculty and Staff:

Christina Connell, English Instructor

Anne Marie Hardy, Counselor, Director of Career Services

Dr. Candace Holder, Distance Education Director

Lisa Mabe, Director of Early Childhood Education

Sara McMillen, Mathematics Instructor

Cherise Millsaps, Reading Instructor

Brian Webb, Associate Dean of Enrollment Management

Scott Wilson, Coordinator of Transfer Advising

Connie Wolfe, Dean of Arts and Sciences

Dr. Susan Worth, Division Chair of Mathematics, College Student Success Coordinator

Dr. David Wright, Associate Dean of Learning Resources

Alan Unsworth, Reference and Web Services Librarian

■ ACA 111   College Student Success Syllabus

Instructor _____ **Office Number** _____

Phone Number _____ **Ext.** _____ **E-Mail** _____

Office Hours _____

Course Description: This course introduces the college's physical, academic, and social environment and promotes the personal development essential for success. Topics include campus facilities and resources; policies, procedures, and programs; critical and creative thinking; study skills; and life management issues such as health, self-esteem, motivation, goal setting, and communication. Upon completion, students should be able to function effectively within the college environment to meet their educational objectives.

Prerequisites/Corequisites: None
Credit Hours: 1
Contact Hours: 1

Required Textbooks: *Keys to College Success.* Surry Community College's current academic catalog.

Course Objectives: Upon completion of this course, you should be able to:

1. Make an effective transition to college. You will learn:
   a. About the college's policies and regulations
   b. About the location of college resources and how to use them

2. Understand yourself better. You will learn:
   a. More about your goals (academic, career, life)
   b. More about who you are (personality, interest, values, life style expectations)
   c. About critical thinking
   d. About your learning style
   e. More about time management
   f. More about personal wellness

3. Apply learning skills more effectively. You will learn:
   a. To be more aware of your learning skills and abilities
   b. How to develop specific learning skills (test taking, note taking, study techniques)
   c. How to develop communication skills (oral and written)

Attendance Policy: You are expected to be present and on time for all class meetings. Extenuating circumstances or emergencies will be handled on an individual basis.

Cooperative Learning and Teaching Component: Numerous activities in College Student Success will use cooperative learning and teaching techniques. A student's participation in these activities will affect the class participation grade.

Writing Component: Some of the assignments in College Student Success will be writing activities. The goal of these writing activities is to assist you in clarifying your thoughts and effectively communicating them. All written assignments should be neat, legible, and free of spelling errors. All written assignments will be evaluated using SCC's Writing Rubric which assesses the Intellectual Standards of clarity, precision, relevance, depth, breadth, logic, significance, and fairness.

Academic Integrity Statement: Students are expected to rely on their own knowledge when completing any graded activity. Cheating in any form will not be tolerated and may result in the loss of academic credit for the course.

Disability Statement: If you are a student who is disabled as defined under the Americans with Disabilities Act and requires assistance or support services, please seek assistance through Student Development.

Career Exploration Project: Students will be required to complete a mandatory project which integrates career exploration with several of SCC's general education learning outcomes. A detailed description of the project follows on the next several pages.

Group Presentations: Students will be required to participate in a group presentation of one of the textbook chapters. A detailed description follows on the next several pages.

Grading Policy:

1. Attendance   =   16 maximum points
2. Class Participation   =   16 maximum points
3. Career Exploration Project   =   26 maximum points
4. Group Presentations of ACA Chapters   =   10 maximum points
5. Other Assignments   =   32 maximum points
                                                      _____
                                                      100 total points

Grading Scale:

A = 90–100 points

B = 80–89 points

C = 70–79 points

D = 60–69 points

F = Below 60

Daily Schedule and Assignment Deadlines: Your instructor will provide a handout containing a daily schedule of readings, activities, and assignments, including specific due dates for major class assignments.

◼ ACA 122 College Transfer Success Syllabus

Instructor _____ Office Number _____

Phone Number _____ Ext. _____ E-Mail _____

Office Hours _____

Course Description: This course provides information and strategies necessary to develop clear academic and professional goals beyond the community college experience. Topics include the CAA, college culture, career exploration, gathering information on senior institutions, strategic planning, critical thinking, and communications skills for a successful academic transition. Upon completion, students should be able to develop an academic plan to transition successfully to senior institutions. *This course has been approved to satisfy the Comprehensive Articulation Agreement for transferability as a pre-major and/or elective course requirement.*

Prerequisites/Corequisites: None
Credit Hours: 1
Contact Hours: 1

Required Textbooks: *Keys to College Success.* Surry Community College's current academic catalog.

Course Objectives: Upon completion of this course, you should be able to:

1. Make an effective transition to college. You will learn:
    a. About Surry Community College policies and regulations
    b. About the location of SCC resources and how to use them
    c. About the Comprehensive Articulation Agreement (CAA)
    d. About successful transfer to senior institutions

2. Understand yourself better. You will learn:
    a. More about your goals (academic, career, life)
    b. About critical thinking
    c. About your learning style
    d. About time management

3. Apply learning skills more effectively. You will learn:
    a. To be more aware of your learning skills and abilities
    b. How to develop specific learning skills (test taking, note taking, study techniques)
    c. How to develop communication skills (oral and written)

Attendance Policy: You are expected to be present and on time for all class meetings. Extenuating circumstances or emergencies will be handled on an individual basis.

Cooperative Learning and Teaching Component: Numerous activities in College Transfer Success will use cooperative learning and teaching techniques. A student's participation in these activities will affect the class participation grade.

Writing Component: Some of the assignments in College Transfer Success will be writing activities. The goal of these writing activities is to assist you in clarifying your thoughts and effectively communicating them. All written assignments should be neat, legible, and free of spelling errors. All written assignments will be evaluated using SCC's Writing Rubric, which assesses the Intellectual Standards of clarity, precision, relevance, depth, breadth, logic, significance, and fairness.

Academic Integrity Statement: Students are expected to rely on their own knowledge when completing any graded activity. Cheating in any form will not be tolerated and may result in the loss of academic credit for the course.

Disability Statement: If you are a student who is disabled as defined under the Americans with Disabilities Act and requires assistance or support services, please seek assistance through Student Development.

Career Exploration Project: Students will be required to complete a mandatory project that integrates career exploration with several of SCC's general education learning outcomes. A detailed description of this project follows on the next several pages.

Group Presentations: Students will be required to participate in a group presentation of one of the textbook chapters. A detailed description follows on the next several pages.

Strategic Plan for Transfer Success Project: Students will be required to complete a mandatory project that asks them to research transfer institutions, create a transfer timeline, and prepare for transfer by explaining the skills needed to be successful at a four-year college or university. A detailed description of this three-part project is located in Chapter 9 of this textbook.

Grading Policy:

1. Attendance	=	16 maximum points
2. Class Participation	=	16 maximum points
3. Career Exploration Project	=	26 maximum points
4. Group Presentations	=	10 maximum points
5. Strategic Plan for Transfer	=	22 maximum points
6. Other Assignments	=	10 maximum points
		100 total points

Grading Scale:

A = 90–100 points

B = 80–89 points

C = 70–79 points

D = 60–69 points

F = Below 60

Daily Schedule and Assignment Deadlines: Your instructor will provide a handout containing a daily schedule of readings, activities, and assignments, including specific due dates for major class assignments.

■ ACA 111 and ACA 122 Syllabus Component: Career Exploration Project

The guide that follows should help you complete the Career Exploration Project. You should talk with family and friends, go on informational interviews, and do library and Internet research.

Overview

Surry Community College is a learning college that focuses on specific learning outcomes: critical thinking, communication (writing, speaking, and reading), information literacy, and quantitative literacy.

Since the instructors at Surry will expect you to be familiar with these outcomes, your Career Exploration Project will include several learning outcomes. This assignment will primarily assess critical thinking, reading, and writing. Skills involving the other learning outcomes may also be utilized to produce the final project, and you may be working both collaboratively as well as independently in completing it.

Purpose

- ■ to explore careers
- ■ to practice research skills
- ■ to improve writing skills
- ■ to improve thinking skills

Procedure

Your instructor will guide you through this project, so be sure to follow the specific guidelines and schedules set by him/her. The following information provides a general overview of the procedure you will use to complete all phases of the project.

- ■ **Read Chapter 2 and visit the Career Services Center.** Chapter 2 will help you identify appealing occupations that suit your strengths and personality and discover your occupational values. Next, you choose one career you are considering, and visit the Career Services Center for information on that career. This step may be done collaboratively or independently. Visit the Bureau of Labor Statistics Web site to find information online, and look for "Occupation" on the left side of the screen.
- ■ **Complete a written summary of your career.** The guidelines for this summary are described later in this project.
- ■ **Conduct library research.** You will visit the Learning Resources Center, and during this visit you should locate library resources in **About Your Career.** Be sure to appropriately document all sources as you gather your project research materials. You will need to have a *minimum* of three sources, one of which must come from your library research, one from your Career Services Center research, and one informational interview of an individual employed in the career field. Copy all your sources, if possible and submit a copy with your final project.

- **Complete a written Article Analysis and Evaluation,** which analyzes and evaluates one article from your sources. The guidelines for the Article Analysis and Evaluation are discussed later in this project. When you submit your Article Analysis and Evaluation paper, you must submit a copy of the article you used. Your instructor will give you the specific guidelines for this paper. You should select an article that represents the opinion of professionals in the career field you have selected. The article should be related to an issue or concern within that field. The assignment requires that you apply critical thinking concepts as you read carefully and think critically about this article (see critical thinking and reading rubrics). It also asks you to write the analysis and evaluation, keeping in mind the standards for good writing as outlined in the writing rubric. Your instructor will assess your analysis and evaluation using the critical thinking, reading, and/or writing rubric. Your instructor will ask you to assess/evaluate either your paper or someone else's, using one or more of the rubrics.
- **Complete a written Career Report** in which you discuss all relevant aspects of the career you chose using information from the research you collected. Additional guidelines for the Career Report are discussed later in the project. The Career Report will be assessed by your instructor using the writing rubric.

ACA Learning Outcomes Project Requirements

The following assignments must be turned in as a part of this project:

I. Three sources, one from the library, one from Career Center, and one interview. Provide instructor copies, if possible.
II. Career Summary
III. Article Analysis and Evaluation
IV. Career Report

Interview

Conduct an interview with someone who works in your chosen career. Be sure to ask all the questions so you get a full picture of the occupation.

Questions to Consider While Working on the Project

Do I have three source(s) of information? (One source has to be a person already working in the occupation you have chosen to explore.)

What does someone in this type of work actually do? What are the tasks, responsibilities, risks, and physical demands of this occupation?

What skills are required? Put a star beside those skills you already have.

What is the work environment, including workload, pace, people? How does it look, sound, and smell?

What is the work schedule: hours/weeks, hours/day, overtime expected, travel?

What training, education, or other qualifications (licenses, registration, certification) do you need for the occupation?

Where is this training offered?

What are the earnings or salary range?

What is the employment outlook or the future of this occupation?

What are the possibilities for advancement or promotion?

What are related occupations?

What are sources of additional information (books, schools, people)?

Career Summary

Assignment

Write a brief summary of the career you have selected to explore for this project, including the information that follows.

This summary will be submitted to your instructor as part of your grade for this project and should be as precise as you can make it at this point: You will use it to guide your research, so the more precise it is, the better.

Your summary should include the following:

1. A *title:* Use your particular field of interest

2. A *paragraph* that briefly explains the field you have chosen, why you are interested in it, specific questions you have at this point, particular areas of focus within the career field, etc.

3. A *list* of possible research avenues: Web sites, interviews, books, job shadowing, etc.

■ Article Analysis and Evaluation

Assignment

Locate at least one article related to the career you are researching. Write a paper that analyzes and evaluates this article according to the guidelines provided.

Remember to select an article that represents the opinion of professionals in the career field you have selected. The article should be related to an issue or concern within that field. Do not use an article that merely gives general information about your career.

Requirements

Your final paper should be three pages, typed and double-spaced in twelve-point font with standard margins.

Writing Your Analysis and Evaluation

Using the Elements of Thought and Intellectual Standards as outlined by Richard Paul and Linda Elder, answer the questions in paragraph form, including at least one paragraph per question. The Elements of Thought and the Intellectual Standards are discussed extensively in Chapter 3. In each numbered question use the statement to think about how you would discuss the information contained in the article. The statements apply to the Elements of Thought, and the questions listed after apply to the Intellectual Standards that relate to that Element. Conclude your analysis using the information in the conclusion section.

1. The main purpose of this article is . . . *(Here, you are trying to state as accurately as possible the author's purpose for writing the article. What was the author trying to accomplish?)*

    a. Is the purpose well-stated?

    b. Is it clear and justifiable (fair)?

2. The key question that the author is addressing is . . . *(Your goal is to figure out the key question that was in the mind of the author when he or she wrote the article. What was the key question the article addressed?)*

    a. Is the question at issue well-stated or clearly implied?

    b. Is it clear and unbiased?

    c. Does the expression of the question do justice to the complexity of the matter at issue?

    d. Are the question and purpose directly related to each other?

3. The most important information in this article is . . . *(You want to identify the key information the author used, or presupposed, in the article to support his or her main arguments. Here you are looking for facts, experiences, and data the author is using to support his or her conclusions.)*

    a. Does the writer cite relevant evidence, experiences, and information essential to the issue?

    b. Is the information accurate and directly relevant to the question at issue?

    c. Does the writer address the complexities of the issue?

4. The main inferences/conclusions in this article are . . . *(You want to identify the most important conclusions the author comes to and presents in the article.)*

a. Do the inferences and conclusions the author makes follow clearly from the information relevant to the issue, or does the author jump to unjustifiable conclusions?

b. Does the author consider alternative conclusions where the issue is complex?

c. Does the author use a sound line of reasoning to come to logical conclusions, or can you identify flaws in the reasoning somewhere?

5. The key concepts we need to understand in this article are . . . *(To identify these concepts, ask yourself: What are the most important ideas that you would have to understand to understand the author's line of reasoning? Then elaborate briefly on what the author means by those concepts.)*

a. Does the writer clarify key concepts when necessary?

b. Are the concepts used justifiable?

6. The main assumptions underlying the author's thinking are . . . *(Ask yourself: What is the author taking for granted that might be questioned? The assumptions are generalizations that the author does not think he or she has to defend in the context of writing the article, and they are usually unstated. This is where the author's thinking logically begins.)*

a. Does the writer show sensitivity to what he or she is taking for granted or assuming (insofar as those conclusions might reasonably be questioned)?

b. Or does the writer use questionable assumptions without addressing problems that might be inherent in those assumptions?

7. If we take this line of reasoning seriously, the implications are . . . *(What consequences are likely to follow if people take the author's line of reasoning seriously? You should follow the logical implications of the author's position. You should include implications that the author states, if you believe them to be logical, but you should do your best thinking to determine what you think the implications are.)*

a. Does the writer show sensitivity to the implications and consequences of the position he or she is taking?

b. Are those implications logical?

8. The main points of view presented in this article are . . . *(The main question you are trying to answer here is: What is the author looking at, and how is he or she seeing it?)*

a. Does the author show sensitivity to alternative relevant points of view or lines of reasoning?

b. Does he or she consider and respond to objections framed from the other relevant points of view?

9. Conclude your analysis and evaluation with a paragraph about how this article specifically relates to your career choice.

a. What are your reactions to the issue or concern discussed in the article as it relates to your career choice.

b. How might this affect you?

(Template is taken from Richard Paul and Linda Elder's *Critical Thinking: Tools for Taking Charge of Your Learning and Your Life,* 2001, pp. 166–169.)

Career Report

Assignment

Write a report that describes your chosen career and explains why you are interested in that career. Your audience for this report is a group of students (like your classmates) who are thinking about various career choices. In writing this report, you will synthesize the research you have done.

Visit the Academic Support Center on the second floor of the library or call 386-3460 for assistance in writing this report.

Requirements

Your final paper should be three pages, typed and double-spaced in twelve-point font with standard margins.

Writing the Report

Follow this template to help you develop your written report:

1. Decide on an important overall point you want to make about your career. This is your thesis; in the beginning of your paper, you will *state* it. Think of the thesis as the "umbrella idea" for this paper: Everything you write in this paper should fall under that umbrella. (If something you include doesn't seem to fall under that umbrella, then it is irrelevant.)

2. *Elaborate* on that point. Develop your thesis by discussing what you have learned about the following aspects of the career:

   - Job requirements (education, skills, certifications, etc.)
   - Job tasks, duties, responsibilities
   - Opportunities for advancement
   - Salary
   - The job market
   - Typical day
   - Challenges/downsides
   - Rewards
   - Why you chose this career

3. *Exemplify* these aspects. Use examples from the research you have collected.

4. Formulate reasonable objections or questions related to your thesis. What problems might you have in this career? Anticipate what others might say about your career and your thesis: What would someone object to or question about your chosen career or about your particular thesis? For example, someone might question why you would choose a career with a low salary. How would you respond? You might acknowledge that this particular career does not usually earn a high salary, and explain why salary is not as important a consideration as your reader might think.

Note: For additional help with writing a college-level paper, see the *Student Guide to Writing Well at SCC.* You can obtain a free copy in the Academic Support Center, or your instructor may obtain copies for the class.

Aca 111 and ACA 122 Syllabus Component: Group Presentations of ACA Chapters

Purpose

- Work with other classmates to give an informative and dynamic group presentation dealing with a chapter from the ACA book
- Incorporate the different learning styles during presentation
- Use the speaking outcome rubric to assess the presentations
- Learn about reading critically, note taking, test taking, time management, and wellness and apply that learning to your life

How Many Points?

Your instructor will assign you to a group. This project can earn you 10 final course grade points or one-tenth of your final grade. It is a group project, which means everyone in the group is expected to participate and will receive the same number of points.

However, each member will be asked to submit a confidential evaluation of each person in the group. It is possible for a member to receive fewer points than other group members if there is a serious discrepancy in workload. The goal is for all group members to contribute equally.

How Will You Prepare for Your Presentation?

Your instructor will assign your group one of the following chapters:

Learning Style/Instructional Style
Reading Critically and Note Taking
Test Taking
Time Management
Wellness

You should read all that the book has to offer on your assigned topic. You may want to use research avenues that are not found in the ACA book. For example, the Internet may provide valuable resources. However, make sure that you think critically about Internet sources. Be sure that you are using credible, reliable sources. After obtaining background information and thinking about your own past experiences related to the topic, within your group you will start working on a way to present the material to the class. Since you only have fifty minutes to present, you must make decisions about what you deem as the most important and interesting material to include that is related to your topic.

You must incorporate the different learning styles during your presentation. Therefore you will have to do more than just research your assigned topic. This book includes a chapter that discusses learning and instructional styles. Pretend that your audience will include students of all the different learning styles. You must present your topic in a way that uses each of the learning styles. If you do this effectively, chances are you will promote successful student learning. You will realize as you research the learning styles that simply reading from the book will not be an option for your presentation!

What Are Some More Expectations for This Presentation?

After the presentations, you will be evaluated by your classmates. Your classmates will be using the Speaking Outcome Rubric which is found in this book. It would be to your benefit to read the details of this rubric before you present so that you are aware of the differences between a presentation that is exemplary and a presentation that is unsatisfactory. Think about ways to be informative yet also interesting. Students will remember presentations that involve some creativity. You may include songs, posters, PowerPoint presentations or whatever it takes to get your point across during this presentation. Think about an effective opening, smooth transitions and a decisive ending.

How Will This Be Graded?

Your group project earns 10 points toward your final grade. Keep in mind that your instructor may be influenced by the student evaluations. The following paragraphs describe a few benchmarks in the 1–10 scale.

A **"10" presentation** will involve all group members equally and will be extraordinarily informative, interesting, and innovative. The creative elements will not overpower the precise information that is shared; rather, they will be effectively and appropriately integrated with the information. The information shared will be relevant, accurate, and clear. The presentation will flow smoothly; it will be clear that the group has been rehearsing—we will see a well-oiled machine up there! (There will be no awkward moments when everyone is looking at everyone else in the group and thinking "what comes next?"). The presentation will also open and close effectively (No "Well, that's about it" conclusions!). All of the different instructional and learning styles will be incorporated.

*Summary: A "perfect" presentation catches our attention and holds it. Every aspect is exemplary: the information, the delivery, the organization, the creativity, and the supplemental materials. When the group finishes, we wish that it wasn't over, and we remember what they shared.

In a **"5" presentation**, there may be inequities—not all group members may be equally involved. The presentation is not as well organized as a "10," but some organization is evident. The presentation may be average all around: not especially interesting, not especially informative, and not especially innovative. Another possibility: The presentation might be quite innovative but lack the relevance, accuracy, and clarity of a higher-scoring presentation (too much "fluff" and not enough substance, in other words). If handouts are distributed, there may be problems with clarity and correctness. Some of the different instructional and learning styles may not be included.

*Summary: An average presentation "underwhelms" its audience. We remember little about what was presented, more about how it was presented.

A **"1" presentation** lacks organization and depth of information and may also present inaccurate information. No attempt is made to make the presentation interesting or innovative. The group presents contradictory or irrelevant information. Information may even be repeated. The presentation may last only a few minutes (not enough info to present) or it may go on for 50 minutes (rambling). Group members aren't aware of what each other is supposed to be doing up front. Few, if any, of the instructional and learning styles are included.

*Summary: A poor presentation confuses its audience. Materials are nonexistent or poorly done. Group members seem disinterested and/or extremely nervous, and we wonder why they put us through the discomfort of watching this unfold. We just want it to be over!

CHAPTER 1
Surry Community College

This chapter contains material adapted from *The Community College: A New Beginning*, third edition by Linda S. Aguilar, Sandra J. Hopper, and Therese M. Kuzlik, copyright © 2001 by Kendall/Hunt Publishing Company; from *Building Success* by Bill Osher and Joann Ward, copyright © 2000 by Bill Osher and Joann Ward; and from *Practical Approaches for Building Study Skills and Vocabulary* by Gary Funk et al, copyright © 1996 by Kendall/Hunt Publishing Company. Adapted and reprinted with permission from Kendall/Hunt Publishing Company. Further reproduction is prohibited.

■ Surry Community College

Letter from the President of Surry Community College
Deborah Friedman, Ed.D.

Dear College Student,

We are grateful that you have selected Surry Community College to pursue your degree, diploma, or certificate. While you are here, we want to help you succeed in attaining your educational goals by offering this ACA class. This course focuses on topics such as career exploration, college services, critical thinking, study skills, and time management to ensure you have access to the tools needed for achievement. It provides learning resources that will assist in developing an individual academic plan that addresses your unique interests, talents, and needs, for maximum college success.

The faculty and staff of Surry Community College are dedicated, caring professionals who have a sincere interest in your academic success. They will do what they can to ensure that you will achieve, but your responsibility is to become an "active learner." Being an "active learner" requires knowing how to learn, and this is one of the essential course objectives in the ACA class. You have already made choices about becoming an active participant in your educational process. It is now time to utilize some of the many resources available for active learning at Surry Community College.

It is important to understand that college courses are presented at a fast pace and consequently, it is necessary to attend each class. By being present in class, you will not only have the direct benefit of the instructor, but also the classroom discussions with fellow students. It is equally important to understand that by participating in these class discussions, as well as doing homework assignments and meeting with your instructors during their office hours when additional assistance is needed, you will enhance your learning process. Do not let yourself get behind in any class when there are many learning resources in place to assist in your academic process.

Your decision to continue your education is the right choice for a better future. It is appropriate to value education at a time when our global economy is requiring us to continue learning in order to remain current in the workplace. Therefore, learn all you can from your ACA class on how to be a successful college student and put those techniques into practice immediately to achieve your educational goals.

We extend our best wishes as you "Learn it. Do it."

Sincerely,

Deborah Friedman, Ed.D.
President

■ Welcome!

Success begins with a question. What must I do in order to succeed? Your decision to attend Surry Community College (SCC) this semester suggests that you have asked that question. It also suggests that you have begun to answer it. Realizing the importance of a college education is the first step on your path to success.

This course is required of entering freshmen and designed to help you make the best of our facilities, our services, our staff, and our instruction. The ACA course reflects our student-focused approach to teaching and learning. Each instructor's goal is to introduce you to the skills, both academic and personal, necessary to be a successful student, both here and now and for a lifetime.

Students will be given activities that explore such issues as time management, career options, personal values, study skills, learning styles, diversity, and writing skills. Ultimately, the purpose of this course, as well as your college degree, is to prepare you for all the exciting challenges and opportunities that lie ahead.

So, welcome to your Student Success course. May your time here with us be both challenging and rewarding.

■ Surry Community College's History

Surry Community College offers a pleasing landscape, a harmonious blend of natural and architectural beauty. But the campus's visual appeal is not its most distinguishing feature. Indeed, the state system is filled with equally attractive college campuses. None, however, enjoy the unity and commitment of the SCC family. This family includes all those—past and present—who share a common vision for Surry County—a vision of opportunity for all willing to seize it. And it was out of this vision that SCC was born.

In 1960, the Mount Airy Lions Club appointed a committee to study the possibility of creating a commuters' college, a school where high school graduates could continue their education while living at home. After the idea was introduced, it quickly gained favor throughout the county. Representatives from all major civic organizations in the county joined the college movement/the push for a local college. By May 1963, county officials had presented an application for a comprehensive community college to the State Board of Education. This application was approved in January 1964; and by 1965, the first eager students began their higher education journey in the rented and borrowed facilities that were the first SCC campus. From this modest beginning, the college eventually grew to its current campus.

■ Facilities, Services, and Resources

The Campus

Now that you are an official student, there are some things you should know about your college. Your college has many resources to help you with a wide variety of needs. The campus itself is a resource. The buildings and grounds are maintained so that you will have an accessible place to study and attend classes. There are parking lots for staff, students, and visitors. The campus has a bookstore where you can buy textbooks, school supplies, clothes with the college logo, greeting cards, and other items. A campus map will help you find your way around. There is a campus police officer and other conveniences such as copy machines.

Food services on campus range from vending machines to a full service cafeteria. The cafeteria serves a variety of meal options. Student Development and the Business Office can help with general information, payment for everything from tuition to traffic tickets and access to your records. It is extremely important that you know where things are on campus and where to go when you need a specific service. The best way to become familiar with the campus is to explore it.

As you think about the many challenges that lie ahead, it's easy to feel overwhelmed. How are you going to cope with everything? In particular, how are you going to cope with everything all by yourself? We have some good news for you. While it's true that your destiny is in your hands, you don't really have to prepare for your future all by yourself.

Imagine that scattered around your campus are several large boxes with cash. Whenever your funds run low, you're free to drop by one of these handy mini-banks and help yourself. That's right, all you have to do is scoop up enough fives and tens to keep you in cheeseburgers and books for another month.

You'd expect these financial "free lunch" dispensers to get a lot of use, wouldn't you? Who could possibly be so dense as to miss out on such an opportunity? Yet agencies giving out thousands of dollars worth of services are often passed over by the majority of college students.

Ah, but that's different, you say. Money is money. Deans and counselors are somehow less appealing. Maybe so, but reflect for a moment on what money really is. You can't eat it or wear it. It doesn't even burn well enough to keep you warm. However, you can trade it for food, clothing, fuel, books, tuition, legal or medical advice, tutoring, psychotherapy, or any of a dozen other services. Further, as your array of skills grows, any number of employers will pay you lots of money so that you can choose to buy whichever goods and services your heart desires.

As you gear up for your future, don't pass up free help. Take advantage of every opportunity and resource in your environment, which will advance you toward your goals. Most high achievers do. Most students are surprised when they learn about all the services that are available to them. We recommend that you carefully review your college catalog and start using your campus resources. If SCC does not offer a service that you need, see if you can find it elsewhere. Remember that it's up to you to get whatever helps you succeed. Nobody is going to rescue you.

CAMPUS LOCATOR MAP & LEGEND

A— STUDENT DEVELOPMENT
BUSINESS OFFICE/CASHIER
TEACHING AUDITORIUM
KNIGHTS' GRILL

B— AUTO BODY

C— COMPUTER SERVICES
BOOKSTORE
ENGLISH

E— COMPUTER INFORMATION SYSTEMS
ELECTRONICS
DISTANCE EDUCATION
CERAMICS STUDIO

F— EMERGENCY SERVICES TRAINING

G— GREENHOUSE (Horticulture)

H— PRESIDENT'S OFFICE
INSTRUCTIONAL ADMINISTRATION
PUBLIC AFFAIRS
HEALTH SCIENCES
LEARNING CENTER
MATHEMATICS
DEVELOPMENTAL STUDIES
COSMETOLOGY

J— CLASSROOMS
CONTINUING EDUCATION
HUMANITIES AND SOCIAL SCIENCES

K— ENGINEERING TECHNOLOGIES

M— VITICULTURE & ENOLOGY

P— PHYSICAL EDUCATION

R— LEARNING RESOURCES CENTER (Library)

S— MACHINIST TECHNOLOGY
WELDING

T— SCIENCES/SCIENCE LECTURE
SURRY EARLY COLLEGE HIGH SCHOOL

V— BUSINESS TECHNOLOGIES
ELECTRICAL/INDUSTRIAL MECHANICS
AUTOMOTIVE MECHANICS
CONSTRUCTION TECHNOLOGY

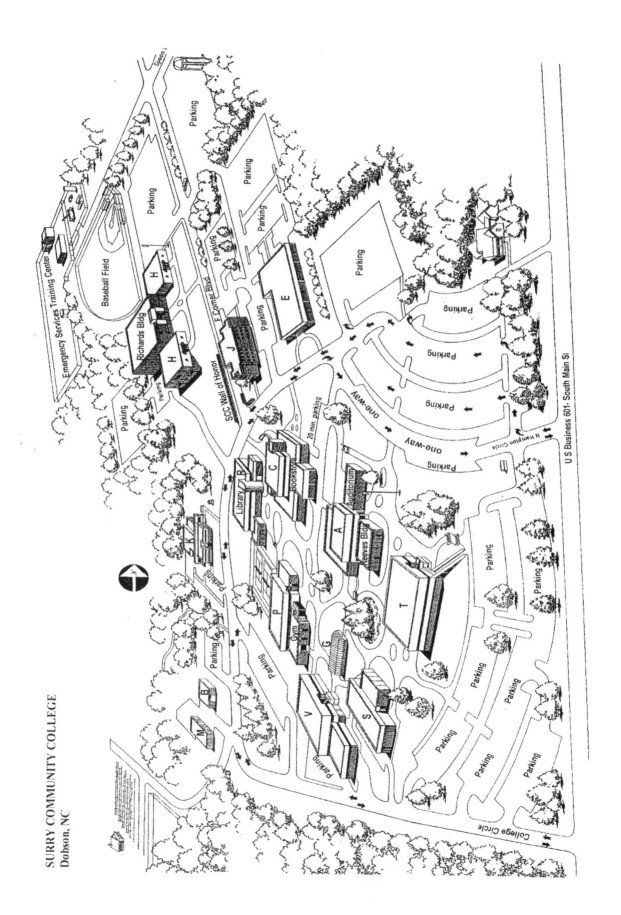

SURRY COMMUNITY COLLEGE
Dobson, NC

■ Library Services

The Library is your one-stop place for information. If you walk into the building to check out a book or use a computer to search databases, the library staff will help you make your search for information successful. The library catalog and databases are accessible from any campus location as well as from your home (with your campus login).

Librarians are trained to help you find the best information when you are preparing a class assignment. Library web pages are also organized under subjects to direct you to some of the best Internet sources.

You will use an interactive learning module to learn more about the information resources available through the SCC Library.

■ The Library

"The student who is successful will be able to manage information."

Library services have changed over the past several years with the advent of many more online services, online and distance education, and the students' need for instant information.

Several components comprise basic library services:

- Print resources
- Online databases
- Subject/research guides
- Internet sources

Each of these resources can satisfy information needs and together they provide a complete picture for any assignment or project. You will learn to use these information resources through training and hands-on examples. ACA students will find a Web-based tutorial designed to provide tools to identify and understand information resources available through the Library.

Log into BLACKBOARD or MOODLE and complete the first module **BEFORE** attending the ACA class tour and instruction. Be prepared with your library card and your module scorecard for your class Library visit.

—The Library Staff

■ The College Catalog

Here is another storehouse of useful information. In fact, your college catalog is generally the actual legal contract that you have with your college or university. If you are ever uncertain about an exact rule or regulation, it is likely covered in your catalog. Keep your catalog from each year that you are in college. Why? Because over time, degree requirements change and rules are modified. Generally, you may graduate based on *any* catalog during the time you are enrolled continuously at a college. So, if you enroll in 1998 and in 2001 the requirements for the degree you've just spent two years working on change, you can opt to graduate under the 1998 catalog. This can be VERY important if the rest of "getting on with your life" is based on a specific graduation date, or if you find you might have to wait a year for a required course to be taught again!

Granted, the catalog is not exactly a page-turner, but you can save a lot of time and trouble if you use this resource regularly. Almost every day, students ask us questions that they could easily answer themselves by checking their catalogs. Consider Jennifer who is particularly keen on double-checking rules and regulations. She should be. She had to leave town just before her graduation. Several months later, she learned that she had not been granted a degree because she was short three courses. (There had been a miscommunication about her requirements.) But it was she, not her advisor, that had to pay the extra tuition to make up her work.

The following forms and activities included in this chapter are designed to make you familiar with the layout of the Surry Community College Catalog as well as the information contained within the catalog. Following the activity, there are two important forms you must sign and return to your ACA instructor. Be sure to read the forms carefully before you sign them. If there is a policy mentioned on the form that you do not understand or you want more information about, ask your instructor or someone in Student Development before signing the form.

■ Important Student-Related Policies

Policies regulating student behaviors are necessary on any college campus. When you register for one or more classes at SCC, you must agree to abide by all of its policies, as documented by your signature on the front of this form. Complete copies of these policies are available in the Student Development Office. Listed below are summaries of some of the most important ones. Please consult the Vice President for Student Development for additional information and/or clarification of any policies.

Drug-Free Student: Drug use and abuse by students has become an immediate concern in our society. Drug users may endanger other students and the college educational environment. Therefore, it is the policy of Surry Community College that the manufacture, distribution, dispensation, possession or use of a controlled substance is prohibited while on college grounds. Use of any drug authorized by medical prescription from a registered physician is not considered a violation of this rule. However, students will be held strictly accountable for their behavior while under the influence of prescribed medicines.

Information Technology Acceptable Use: Electronic information technology systems are essential tools for learning and research. It is the policy of the college that the facilities be used ethically and legally, in accordance with applicable licenses and contracts, and according to their intended use for educational purposes in support of the college's mission and goals. Examples of specific activities that are not permitted include:

- Sending or displaying offensive messages, pictures or materials.
- Using obscene language.
- Harassing, insulting or attacking others.
- Damaging electronic components, computers, computer systems, or networks including knowingly transferring viruses.
- Violating copyright laws or using others' passwords.
- Trespassing in others' files, folders or storage areas of any kind.
- Intentionally wasting limited resources. (Internet time, supplies, etc.)

- Using the network for commercial, political or any unlawful purposes.
- Loading personal software on computers.
- **Connecting to inappropriate internet sites, such as pornography, hate groups, and other similar sites.**

Sexual Harassment: All employees and students are guaranteed the right to work and learn in an environment free from sexual harassment. This behavior is considered a form of discrimination based on sex, and as such is prohibited by Title IX of the Educational Amendments of 1972, which prohibits sex discrimination against students and employees in educational institutions receiving federal funds.

Prohibition of Weapons on Campus: No person, whether student, employee, or visitor, may possess or carry, whether openly or concealed, any weapon on any campus or other educational property of Surry Community College.

Unlawful Demonstrations, Violence, or Force: Recognizing the right of dissent, criticism, and protest, it is the policy of the college to give full and prompt attention to such expression presented in a lawful manner. However, the use of unlawful violence, disturbances, demonstrations, force, the occupying or damaging of property or intimidation will not be tolerated.

Campus Security: Federal regulations require that colleges inform all students about past occurrences of such acts as murder, rape, robbery, aggravated assault, burglary, motor vehicle theft, manslaughter, arson, forcible and nonforcible sexual offense, and hate crimes. The annual Campus Security/Crime Reports for the most recent three calendar years are available at http://www.surry.edu/.

Graduation Rate Disclosure Data: Graduation data are available in the Office of Planning, Research and Assessment, H-218.

Voter Registration: Voter Registration Application/Update forms are available in the Testing Center, located in A-204 of the Reeves Building. For additional information, contact Ms. Laura Bracken, Special Programs Coordinator.

■ ACA 111 Activity: SCC Catalog

1. You need a copy of your transcript sent to a prospective employer. What office do you contact to get a copy? What is the procedure?

2. You need to use a computer for word processing. Where can you go? What restrictions might apply?

3. The weather is bad. How do you find out if classes are canceled or delayed? If classes are not canceled, but conditions where you live are terrible, what do you do?

4. You feel someone is harassing you, and you want the harassment to stop. Whom should you notify?

5. You lost your job and you need financial assistance. Where should you go for help?

6. You locked your keys in your car. Where do you go for help?

7. Course registration for the spring is January 6, but you can't pay your tuition until January 10. Whom should you see? What are the repercussions of not paying?

8. You're having academic problems in Mat140. Where do you go for help? What academic assistance services are available?

9. Who is your advisor and what is his/her responsibility?

10. What GPA is required for the Dean's List?

11. What are the various degrees offered at SCC? What are the differences between them?

12. Who is responsible for monitoring your program of study toward graduation?

13. What does the grade "I" stand for? How is this grade treated on your record? How do you have an "I" replaced with a final grade?

14. Suppose you receive a grade and you are sure it is wrong, who do you contact? If not satisfied, who is next in the Chain of Command?

15. What is the Course Repeat Policy? How does this policy affect your GPA?

16. What is the procedure for withdrawing from classes? When can a student withdraw and under what conditions?

17. How will grades of D or F be treated on your SCC transcript? How will they be treated at colleges and universities to where you may transfer?

18. Look up the course BIO 111. Is there a pre-requisite? During which terms is the course typically taught?

19. You received extra tutoring in high school because you have a learning disability. Where do you go to request extra services?

◼ ACA 122 Activity: SCC Catalog

1. You need a copy of your transcript sent to a prospective transfer institution. What office do you contact to get a copy? What is the procedure?

2. You need to use a computer for word processing. Where on campus can you go? What restrictions might apply?

3. You feel someone is harassing you, and you want the harassment to stop. Whom should you notify?

4. You find yourself in a bind and need financial assistance to complete your associate degree at Surry. Where should you go for help?

5. You're having academic problems in your English class. Where do you go for help? What academic services are available?

6. Who is your advisor and what is his or her responsibility?

7. You aren't sure if you want an Associate in Arts or an Associate in Science before you transfer—what is the difference?

8. You know you need to take at least one literature class as part of your associate degree. What does ENG 131 cover, and are there any prerequisites or corequisites you need to follow when registering for the course?

9. Who is responsible for monitoring your program of study toward graduation?

10. What does the grade "I" stand for? How is this grade treated on your record? How do you have an "I" replaced with a final grade?

11. Suppose you receive a grade and you are sure it is wrong. Whom do you contact? If you are not satisfied, who is next in the chain of command?

12. You placed into MAT 080, a developmental studies course. What grade do you have to earn in the class to be eligible for the next course? Will the course credits be counted in your total toward graduation? When should you enroll in MAT 080?

13. What is the procedure for withdrawing from classes? When can a student withdraw and under what conditions?

14. How will grades of "D" or "F" be treated on your SCC transcript? How will they be treated at colleges and universities where you might transfer?

15. Look up BIO 111. Is there a prerequisite? During which semesters is the course typically taught?

16. You're a transfer student, and a friend suggests you take BUS 151: People Skills with him. Should you sign up? Why/why not?

Name: _____ Date: _____

◼ SCC Policies, Rules, and Regulations Form

DIRECTIONS: Complete and sign this form, tear out the form, and submit it to your instructor. Instructors: Please submit completed forms to the Office of Student Development. This document is to comply with the Consumer Information Act.

ACA POLICY FORM

Please print your full name as it appears on your student records.

Name _____ Student ID# _____

I have received information and feel that I have a basic knowledge and understanding of the following policies, rules, and regulations:

- ◼ Campus Security Act Information
- ◼ Registration and Drop/Add Information
- ◼ Financial Aid Information
- ◼ Student Success Services Available at SCC
- ◼ Regulations for Parking and Campus Safety
- ◼ Graduation Rates

- ◼ Sexual Harassment
- ◼ Voter Registration Information
- ◼ Information Technology Use Policy
- ◼ Drug-Free Environment Policy
- ◼ SCC Career Center Services
- ◼ Graduation Requirements

Note: SCC reserves the right to use random drug testing for all students involved in labs, shop, physical activity or any college sponsored extracurricular activities. The school also reserves the right to test any student whose impaired behavior may be a danger to themselves or to students around them.

_____   _____
Student Signature   **Date**

Instructor: _____

Name: _____ Date: _____

Information Literacy and Technology Form

DIRECTIONS: Complete and sign this form, tear out the form, and submit it to your instructor. Instructors: Please submit completed forms to the Office of Student Development.

Information Technology Acceptable Use Policy

Electronic Information Technology Systems at Surry Community College are essential and indispensable tools for learning, research and administration. It is the policy of the college that the facilities be used ethically and legally, in accordance with applicable licenses and contracts, and according to their intended use in support of the college's mission and goals. The systems are provided by the college for the use of students, faculty, and staff. It is expected that all users of these systems will do so responsibly, respecting the rights of other users, maintaining the integrity of the physical facilities and adhering to all applicable laws and regulations. Access to electronic systems is a privilege that is granted by the college and comes with a responsibility to respect the rights of other users and the rights of the college at all times.

The following are examples of specific activities which are not permitted:

- Sending or displaying offensive messages, pictures or materials.
- Using obscene language.
- Harassing, insulting or attacking others.
- Damaging electronic components, computers, computer systems, or networks including knowingly transferring viruses.
- Violating copyright laws or using others' passwords.
- Trespassing in others' files, folders or storage areas of any kind.
- Intentionally wasting limited resources. (Internet time, supplies, etc.)
- Using the network for commercial, political or any unlawful purposes.
- Loading personal software on computers.
- **Connecting to inappropriate internet sites, such as pornography, hate groups, and other similar sites.**

Electronic information systems include, but are not limited to, terminals, computers, computer peripherals, communication devices, telephones and telecommunications equipment, fax machines, computer data networks, video equipment, tapes or video networks, photocopying machines, computer software, supporting documentation, supplies, storage media, support facilities and energy sources. Electronic systems are limited to those leased, rented, owned by, or loaned to the college **wherever located.**

Violation of this policy should be reported to the appropriate area supervisor. Violations may result in suspension of privileges to access the information technology involved, initiation of college disciplinary procedures, or in extreme cases, criminal prosecution under federal or state law. Before attempting any activity about which you are in doubt, or if you have questions about this policy, consult your local area supervisor, appropriate dean or vice president.

The signature below acknowledges that I understand this Information Technology Acceptable Use Policy and agree to abide by the rules set forth herin.

_____   _____
Signature of User   **Date**

_____   _____
Print Full Name as it appears on Student Records   **Student ID No.**

Instructor: _____

Plagiarism: What Is It? Why Is It Wrong? How Can You Avoid It?

Introduction

Let's introduce the topic of plagiarism with a brief scenario.

It's 10:00 at night, and you have an essay assignment due in less than 24 hours. You're worried about your grade because you are not confident of your writing skills. You turn to the computer for help with research on, say, the importance of Martin Luther King, Jr., to the civil rights movement. Google presents you with an array of relevant sites. At the bottom of the page is an article from *Time* that addresses the topic.

It takes you a minute and a half to copy the text, add the heading your instructor requires, and have it ready to turn in. You think, "This will get me a good grade."

What's wrong with this scenario?

Here's the problem: you did not think, "This will get me a zero for the assignment—or possibly for the course." But that is what is likely to happen because copying words without giving credit to their source is plagiarism.

Look carefully at the definition of plagiarism in the Surry Community College Catalog:

> *Plagiarism is offering the work of another person as one's own without proper acknowledgement. Examples of plagiarism include copying a source (whether it's phrases, sentences, or paragraphs) verbatim without using quotation marks; quoting or paraphrasing a source without including a citation; failing to give credit for a source's ideas; inaccurately citing and listing bibliographic information; and purchasing papers on the Internet to submit (in part or in whole) under one's own name.*

The SCC Catalog also states that the consequences of plagiarism are determined by each instructor as outlined in the course syllabus.

The consequences are serious because plagiarism is plainly wrong.

Why Is Plagiarism Wrong?

Plagiarism is wrong for several reasons.

Plagiarism is wrong, first of all, because someone other than you has worked hard to produce the words that you have appropriated. Another person has contributed the intellectual effort of thinking, drafting, revising, and editing the composition. If you submit the same words or ideas as your own, you have stolen the work as much as if you broke into someone's home and stole a TV or computer. That is why using phrases, sentences, paragraphs, or ideas taken from another person and acting as though they are your own is unethical and unacceptable in the academic setting or in the wider world.

What if a friend or classmate agrees to let you copy his or her work? This, also, is cheating because you are still lying to your instructor about authorship when you turn it in under your own name.

Plagiarism is also wrong because it means you have not done the work that was assigned. You have not learned what the assignment was intended to teach; you have not demonstrated your commitment to learning the material needed for mastery of the subject; you have failed to think critically about the question or topic your instructor has presented. By avoiding the work designed to help you achieve mastery of the subject, you are harming yourself.

How to Avoid Plagiarism

Knowing that plagiarism is wrong and that it has serious consequences, you need to learn how to avoid it. The first step is to understand thoroughly what plagiarism looks like, so let's look at an example of plagiarism.

Here is the text of an internet source with information about the antidepressant drug Prozac:

> The antidepressant Prozac (fiuoxetine) has been approved by the FDA to treat children and adolescents ages 7 to 17 for depression and obsessive-compulsive disorder (OCD).

And here is what a student wrote:

> This article describes using the antidepressant Prozac for pediatric use. This drug can treat children and adolescents ages 7 to 17 for depression and obsessive-compulsive disorder.

The question in your mind may be, "What should the student have done instead?" Here's the answer:

> This article describes using the antidepressant Prozac for pediatric use. This drug can "treat children and adolescents ages 7 to 17 for depression and obsessive-compulsive disorder" (FDA 3).

Notice that two important things have changed. First, the words taken from the source have been placed in quotation marks. Second, the source is credited in parentheses immediately after the quotation. Is this enough? Not quite.

The source in parentheses also has to be listed at the back of the essay in an alphabetical list of works cited. The works cited entry for the example presented above looks like this:

> "Prozac for Pediatric Use." FDA Consumer. Mar/Apr 2003, Vol. 37, Issue 2. Health Source-Consumer Edition. Surry Community College Learning Resource Center, Dobson, NC. 21 February 2007 <http://search.ebscohost.com>.

The citation gives the reader all the information needed to locate the article, check the information, and learn more about the topic.

One other point needs to be made. The text inside the quotation marks must be exactly the same as the original. Do not change spelling, punctuation, capitalization, or any aspect of the text you are quoting. The quotation marks are a promise that the text between them is identical to the original.

Many websites offer examples of correct and incorrect use of sources. You will find a few of them listed under "Special Problems" below.

Citation Formats

There are several standard formats for citing sources. The citation above is in MLA (Modern Language Association) format. Other common formats are APA (American Psychological Association), Chicago, and Turabian. Examples are readily available for each format in the SCC Library and on-line. Your instructor will tell you which format to use.

What should you do if you are in doubt about how or whether to credit a source? Ask your instructor before turning in the assignment. If for some reason you are unable to ask your instructor, it is better to cite too often than not to cite at all.

Review

Notice that there are three steps involved in using a source:

1. Use lead-ins to indicate paraphrase or summary (see below); use quotation marks when copying words verbatim.

2. Identify the source in the text.

3. Include detailed information on each source in the bibliography or works cited list.

Remember that critical thinking is original thinking. Do your best to produce thoughtful, original responses to assignments. That way you will avoid plagiarism and benefit from your college experience. In addition, you will practice skills that will translate into the workplace while maintaining a high standard of ethics.

Special Problems

Does a paraphrase or summary avoid plagiarism?

A paraphrase substitutes your own terms for those in the source. Paraphrases are about equal in length to the original. Paraphrasing does not excuse you from citing the original. In fact, paraphrasing can look like an attempt to avoid detection while using a source, so be careful to indicate when you are paraphrasing. Use lead-in statements such as, "According to . . ." or "The author of this report states that . . ." or "To paraphrase the FDA. . . ." These lead-ins tell the reader that you are adapting source material.

A summary condenses the ideas in the source. Summaries can vary in length from a few sentences to a paragraph or more. If you decide to include a phrase or sentence from the original in your summary, put it in quotation marks and cite it. Also cite the source you are summarizing even if you do not include quotations. You can use lead-in phrases with summaries as well as with paraphrases.

What is "common knowledge" and do you need to cite it?

"Common knowledge" refers to facts readily available from many sources. A typical example of common knowledge is the date of birth of a person. The date can be found in many sources and readily checked from public records. Another example is the capital city of a country or state, which can be found in encyclopedias, almanacs, and on maps. Such facts do not need to be cited.

What if you find identical text on several websites?

Frequently you will find identical text on several websites that pertain to the same topic. It is difficult to determine which site had the text first. In any case, you may not copy the text into your writing without crediting it. Consult your instructor as to how to handle the problem of which site to credit. Typically, if you do research using books, periodicals, and the SCC Library databases, you will not face this issue.

What if I forget that some words in my notes are copied from a source?

Accidental plagiarism is still plagiarism. It is your responsibility to be scrupulously careful while doing research. As you take notes and create drafts for your assignments, use quotation marks whenever you copy text. You may also want to highlight quotations to make them stand out so that you don't omit quotation marks while revising and editing. The bottom line is that forgetfulness and sloppy notetaking do not excuse plagiarism.

Where can I find additional information?

Numerous websites offer advice on citing sources correctly and avoiding plagiarism.

Visit the links available from the SCC Library website section called "Citing and Writing."

http://www.umuc.edu/distance/odell/cip/vail/home.html: The University of Maryland website offers a tutorial on avoiding plagiarism. VAIL stands for Virtual Academic Integrity Laboratory and includes examples illustrating the difference between quoting, paraphrasing, and summarizing.

http://library.duke.edu/research/plagiarism: By visiting this site which presents Duke University's policy regarding plagiarism, you will see that SCC is not the only institution that takes the issue seriously. It also contains excellent commentary on some of the reasons people (not only students) take the risk of committing plagiarism—and the embarrassing results.

http://owl.english.purdue.edu/owl: Purdue University's Online Writing Laboratory (OWL) provides an excellent presentation of a variety of formats for citing sources. The website also includes detailed sections on composition and grammar.

http://www.depts.drew.edu/composition/Avoiding_Plagiarism.htm: On Drew University's website you will find examples of correct and incorrect use of sources along with advice on avoiding accidental plagiarism.

Prevention

You do not need to plagiarize. What should you do to prevent plagiarism? Remove the temptation to plagiarize by becoming a diligent student.

- Allow yourself plenty of time to complete assignments.
- Do your research carefully and record complete works cited information as you take notes from the source.
- When you have questions, ask your instructor or visit the Academic Support Center.

Use writing or research assignments as opportunities to exercise your critical thinking skills. Produce work that you are proud to call your own. Maintain high standards of ethics for yourself and your fellow students. Prevention of plagiarism is your responsibility.

■ Advising and Registration

This section discusses two important processes: advising and registration. First we will describe the differences between advising and registration and what each process involves. Then we will look at activities, plans and questions to prepare you for your pre-registration session with your faculty advisor each semester. You will also want to look over all of the certificate, diploma and degree opportunities at SCC that are detailed in your SCC Catalog to make sure you are accomplishing the learning and skill outcomes you want.

The advising period is generally the two to three weeks prior to registration. During this period you may discuss registration plans, transfer requirements, and any other concerns that you have. You will have time to ask questions about policies and any other topics you wish to bring up. You will need to schedule an appointment with your faculty advisor for the advising period. Many advisors post appointment opportunities on their door. Faculty office numbers, phone extensions, and email addresses are listed in the back of your SCC catalog. An important part of your learning will be to attempt to complete a schedule prior to your appointment. Your faculty advisor will then review your schedule and make suggestions or changes. When the two of you agree on your schedule, your faculty advisor will enter your schedule into the computer. Your next step will be to pay in the Business Office during posted payment days.

On the following pages you will find forms you and your advisor may choose to use for advising and registration.

1. The Student Registration Form is for your use in developing your schedule. You should take this form to your advising appointment. During this session your advisor should help you develop an educational plan much like the example on the next page and answer any questions you may have.

2. Your advisor will want you to have completed a student registration form and educational plan like the ones included in this text. Before going to your advising appointment:

   A. Fill out the top of the Student Registration Form.

   B. Have available a list of the courses you are presently taking.

   C. List the courses you are considering for the next term. (A sample of a properly completed Educational Plan is included.).

Advising Questions

1. Who is your faculty advisor? Did you meet with your faculty advisor to plan your initial schedule? If not, schedule an appointment during the semester to get to know your advisor and to introduce yourself.

2. Is your advisor an instructor in the major or program you are considering?

3. What are some of the areas in which you see your advisor assisting you?

4. What are your responsibilities in regard to the advising process?

5. Have you given any thought to your schedule for next semester?

■ Example of a Student's Educational Plan

Name _____

The following schedule is planned for a major in ___ History—College Transfer ___

Schedule This Semester Fall Sem 2005 Yr	
Course	**Hours**
ENG 111	3.0
HIS 121	3.0
BIO 111	4.0
ACA 111	1.0
MAT 080	4.0
PED 110	2.0
Total Semester Hours:	**17.0**

Schedule Plan for Fall Sem 2006 Yr	
Course	**Hours**
SPA 111	3.0
HIS 131	3.0
PSY 150	3.0
ECO 251	3.0
CIS 110	3.0
Total Semester Hours:	**15.0**

Schedule Plan for Spring Sem 2006 Yr	
Course	**Hours**
ENG 113	3.0
HIS 122	3.0
BIO 112	4.0
MAT 171	3.0
COM 231	3.0
Total Semester Hours:	**16.0**

Schedule Plan for Spring Sem 2007 Yr	
Course	**Hours**
SPA 112	3.0
HIS 132	3.0
SOC 210	3.0
POL 120	3.0
HUM 110	3.0
Total Semester Hours:	**15.0**

Schedule Plan for Summer (if needed) 2006	
Course	**Hours**
ENG 241	3.0
MAT 172	3.0
Total Semester Hours:	**6.0**

SURRY COMMUNITY COLLEGE
STUDENT REGISTRATION FORM

Fall Semester ☐   Spring Semester ☐   Summer Semester ☐   Date: _____

To help us report accurate State and Federal demographic information, please complete entire registration form.

Name: _____   Student ID No. _____

Street Address: _____ City: _____ State: _____ Zip: _____

Has your address changed since last registration: ☐ Yes   ☐ No

Telephone Numbers: Home # _____   Work # _____

Curriculum: _____   ☐ Degree ☐ Diploma ☐ Certificate

Have you changed programs since your last registration?   ☐ Yes   ☐ No

---

Please check items that pertain to you so we can notify you of services available at SCC. Completion of these items is optional.

I have the following economic concerns:
- _____ None
- _____ Family
- _____ Receiving a Pell Grant to attend college
- _____ Receiving public assistance (AFCD, school lunch, etc.)
- _____ Adult homemaker preparing for paid employment
- _____ Single parent (unmarried, or separated with one or more minor children)
- _____ WorkFirst participant
- _____ Receiving JTPA/OJT

I have the following educational concerns
- _____ None
- _____ Documented learning impairment
- _____ Hearing impairment
- _____ Speech/language impairment
- _____ Severe visual impairment
- _____ Orthopedic impairment
- _____ Other physical impairment
- _____ Limited English speaking ability
- _____ Native language is not English
- _____ Vocational Rehabilitation

CLASS SCHEDULE

☼☼ **At this point, consult with your faculty advisor or counselor to complete your class schedule.**

Course No Prefix	No	Sec No	Course Title	Credit Hours	Mon	Tue	Wed	Thur	Fri	Sat	Room

_____   _____
Advisor's Signature   **Student's Signature**
I have read the information on the next page and agree to
abide by all Surry Community College policies.

■ Activity: Understanding Your Advisor's Role

This form explains the advisor/advisee relationship. Fill in the information below and obtain your advisor's signature on the line at the bottom of the page.

Advisor: **Office #:**

Phone: (336) 386-   **Office Hours:**

My role as your advisor: I am here to guide you through the registration process and to offer any advice I can. I am the one who officially enters your schedule into the system to register you for classes. When you meet with me, you should already have developed a schedule of classes you want to take; I will look over it to make sure everything is okay. After the first semester, you must bring the completed schedule to me, and we will review it together. Each semester around advising time, sign up for an appointment on the schedule posted on my door.

Your role: You are ultimately responsible for your schedule—you need to read the academic catalog to determine what classes you need to take and in what order. I am here always to help by answering questions, and I will do so gladly. If I don't know the answers, we'll work together to find them.

_____

Advisor's Signature

■ Extracurricular Activities

Besides learning in the classroom, you will learn from other experiences. Taking advantage of these opportunities is important. You will need to have some fun—all of the learning and related stress should be balanced with recreation and relaxing. How do you do that? First, get involved in something that interests you! There are clubs, organizations, and groups for many interests. Your college catalog will give you the specifics. Student Development is a good place to begin your search.

Student Activities and Student Organizations

Clubs, athletics, and organizations can be found in many areas of interest which offer students many extracurricular activities. You may find clubs or organizations with any of the following affiliations: departmental, professional, political, honors, service, social, and sports. Within these categories, you can find a range that is hard to imagine. Surely, there's something of interest to you.

You might investigate a number of groups on campus for the sole purpose of extracurricular activities, personal development, making new friends, or just having fun. The athletic department, the wellness area, service clubs, awareness groups, music and theater groups, and honor societies can all add a little spice to your life. If you are interested in politics, student government may be the avenue for you. It is an excellent training ground for teamwork and leadership and will look terrific on any resume. A number of honor societies invite students with high GPA's and/or specific majors to become members.

You may have the opportunity to participate in a service learning project. This comes in various forms but the concept is that you have a combination of volunteering (or working) in the community and classroom learning. There are several ways SCC approaches this: cooperative education, practicums, apprenticeships, volunteering, etc. The positive reasons to take advantage of these opportunities include gaining work experience before graduating, "trying out" a career before graduating, giving valuable services to your community, and learning and improving skills which are best learned outside the classroom.

You should make the effort to get involved in something on campus in which you have an interest. Your experience will then be more enjoyable, and you will be meeting more people who share your interests. If you are an adult coming back to college, you will probably find activities, organizations, or special programs for you. There are many students in the same situation as you—returning to school, work, raising families, and all that goes along with being a nontraditional student. Explore different programs and take advantage of those programs of interest to you.

Getting Involved on Campus

Reasons to Join a Campus Organization

1. *Meet people* with interests and ideas similar to yours. Also meet people who are different.

2. *Gain experience.* College is the ideal place to try things you might never do otherwise.

3. *Improve communication skills.* Giving an impromptu speech at a club meeting will prepare you for speaking up in class.

4. *Improve your resume.* Employers and graduate schools usually prefer well-rounded individuals to people with straight A's with no extra curricular activities.

5. *Meet advisors* who generally are instructors or staff of college.

6. *There's more to life than just working.* If you spend all of your time studying, what are you going to do later in life?

Things to Ask Before Choosing an Organization

1. *What am I already interested in?*

2. *What do I still want to learn?*

3. *How much time can I commit?* Find out when the group meets and how often. Determine if you can work your schedule around it.

4. *What's the cost?* Some groups charge fees. If dues are high, is there a payment plan?

5. *What's required for membership?* Must you attend a certain number of meetings, maintain a certain grade point average, take a special class to qualify for membership?

What If You Can't Find the Right Organization for You?

1. *Start one.* Ask the Student Activities Director for guidelines on starting a new group. Circulate the word to other students, post on bulletin boards and newsletters.

2. *Set goals* for your group, even if it's small at first.

3. *Plan* how your group is to be funded. Check with Activities Director on fundraising ideas.

■ Activity: Clubs and Organizations

Surry Community College will seem like your "home" for the next couple of years. It will profit you to become involved in the college because the more you put into it, the more you will get back. Much of your time and energy as well as some of your money will be spent here. Your involvement in the college will have a direct impact on your happiness and perhaps your success. Through involvement, you will most likely make friends with people who will become your future fellow workers and colleagues. So, get involved!

Assignment: Research five clubs and organizations that interest you. Complete the Chart below.

Organization	President of Organization	Major Project of Organization

■ Career Services Center

You may want to find out more about your chosen career or you may want to get help choosing a career. If so, the Career Services Center is the place. Resources such as a career library, computer-assisted career guidance, and individual career counseling and assessments can help you explore career options and discover your career choices. Assistance with job-seeking skills, including resume preparation help and interviewing tips and techniques, is also available here. Several events are sponsored by the center, including an annual Employment Fair.

Service learning, cooperative education (gaining college credit while working), and volunteer opportunities are also housed in the Career Services Center.

For further assistance, please visit the Career Services Center in the A Building.

■ The Academic Support Center

College can be pretty daunting. You hand in a paper to your teacher, and she hands it back to you covered in so much red ink you think her pen must have exploded while she was grading it. What does it all mean? Well, it's very simple. It means you need help. Do you ever wish your teacher would just sit down with you and explain what all those marks mean? There's someone who can do that. At the Academic Support Center, we help students with all subjects, from English to Mathematics to Psychology. We select tutors from some of the brightest students at Surry Community College, and train them to help their fellow students. Here, maybe this Question and Answer section will help . . .

Q: Is there free food?
A: No. Sorry.

Q: I've got a paper due next week in my English class, and I have no idea where to start. Can you help me?
A: Sure. All you have to do is tell us what the teacher assigned you to do, and we'll point you in the right direction.

Q: Sounds good. How much will it cost me?
A: Nothing. Tutors are paid by Surry Community College, so you don't have to pay a cent. We do the same work that paid, professional tutors do, and you get it for free. Good deal.

Q: If I give you 20 bucks, will you write the paper for me?
A: No. We'll help you in every way we can, but sorry, we don't write papers for students. And for just 20 bucks? Are you trying to insult us?

Q: My teacher gave me my paper back, and it looks like a paintball target. What do I do?
A: Well, some teachers will offer you a second chance to revise your paper by bringing it to the Academic Support Center. You make an appointment, bring us the paper, and we go over the errors with you. We discuss how to correct them, and show you how to make it a stronger paper.

Q: Cool. Are you sure there's no free food?

A: I'm sure. Stop asking.

Q: I'm making great grades in English, but I have no idea what I'm doing in my math class. What do I do?

A: For more in-depth subjects like math and various sciences, we assign you a personal tutor, someone you can get to know and become comfortable with. They work with you one-on-one to help you understand the really difficult concepts.

Q: I can remember the first time I saw the Beatles on Ed Sullivan, but I'm really lost on that whole "I before E except after C" rule. What can I do?

A: Come down and see us. We understand that the longer you've been out of school, the harder it is to remember all the little rules. At the Academic Support Center, we applaud anyone going back to school after a long break, and we'll do everything we can to help out.

Q: I like my paper the way it is, and the only reason I'm coming to the Support Center is because my teacher made me. What if I don't want to make any changes?

A: You don't have to. But then again, it never hurts to have someone take a look at your paper. Proofreading is an important step, and it's a lot more effective when you get someone to take a fresh look at your paper. Sometimes it's really easy to miss those small misteaks . . . oops.

Q: I really need some help in biology. What can you do?

A: Give you a tutor. Your own personal tutor will help you study, will work with you on key concepts, and will go over your tests and assignments. Kind of like a personal trainer for your brain. We'll find one who really knows what they're doing and will help you study everything from binomial nomenclature to biochemistry. Just don't ask us to dissect the frog. You can do that on your own time.

Q: I have an online course that I'm really having trouble with. Is there anything you can do?

A: Our tutors can also assist you with navigating Moodle and even tutor you in whatever course you're taking. Isn't that nice of us? :-)

Q: Okay, I've decided to get some help with my studies. What do I need to bring to be prepared?

A: A good rule of thumb would be to bring to your tutoring sessions whatever you would bring to class. Also, if you need help on a specific assignment, please bring any information you have on the assignment. It's easiest for us to help you if we know just what your instructor expects.

Q: Okay, I am convinced I need help in math (not to mention chemistry, accounting, and psychology!). Who do I contact to get a tutor?

A: Come to the Academic Support Center and fill out a yellow "request for tutoring" form. Once you've filled it out, you can give it to any ASC staff member on the second floor of the library.

Q: Well, I just want to bring in a paper. What if I don't want weekly tutoring?

A: Good question! We do walk-ins and one-time appointments for reading and English only. You can come by to sign up for a time when an English tutor is working, or you can stop by and see if anyone is available to help you right then.

If you've read this far, I'm guessing that you're really interested in getting some outside help. Here at the Academic Support Center, you can think of us as a life preserver in a sea of confusion. We can't teach you how to swim, but we can make it a little easier to stay afloat. Just stop by the second floor of the library, and see what we're all about. Our operating hours are from 8 a.m. to 6 p.m. Monday through Thursday, and from 8 a.m. to 2 p.m. on Fridays. Our summer hours are different, but are always posted on the door. We hope you'll come by!

■ Distance Education

Distance education students have a variety of reasons for pursuing learning at a distance. Some students have time constraints, long commuting distances, or financial problems. Some students take distance education courses in order to gain knowledge that may otherwise be unavailable to them or to come in contact with students from different social, cultural, economic, and experimental backgrounds. As a result, distance learners have the opportunity to acquire new knowledge and social skills, including the ability to communicate and collaborate with widely dispersed peers whom they may never have seen.

Successful distance education learners take responsibility for their own learning. They are self-disciplined, organized, and motivated. They know that assignments must be completed by specified dates. They know that if they miss assignment deadlines and fall behind in their work that they probably will not successfully complete the course. The ideal distance learner is:

- Computer literate
- Mature
- Independent/Self-motivated
- Self-directed/Focused
- Disciplined/Organized
- Able to Study Independently
- Dependable/Responsible
- Studious/Above Average
- Able to Read and Write Well
- Able to Think Critically and Solve Problems
- Timely in Keeping Assignments Current
- Dedicated/Committed/Goal Oriented

SCC Distance Education Brings the College to You

SCC students can expand their horizons with college classes in the privacy of their own home . . . on days and at times convenient for them. The Distance Education program shares the same goals, objectives, skills, and competencies as all educational opportunities at SCC. Students are offered full-service access to learning resources, program advisement, and financial aid information. Internet courses are delivered online by a learning management system. Students must follow specific procedures for registering for Distance Education programs. Specific program information is available online at http://www.surry.edu.

Tips for a Successful Distance Education Experience

■ Tools

- Before enrolling in a distance education course, you must have access to the tools necessary to complete assignments. A word processor can help to organize work and communicate thoughts clearly and is required when taking online classes.
- Students taking distance education courses at SCC are required to meet specific equipment and software minimums. Minimal hardware and software requirements are found on the Distance Education website.

■ Schedule

- You should set aside a regularly scheduled study time. This time should be when you are mentally fresh and able to devote at least one hour to your work. Think of the hour as "reserved time."

■ Where to Study

- It is easier to focus in an appropriate environment for study. Find a place that is free from distractions, possibly the library or a separate room in your house.

■ Reading Skills

- You must be able to read and comprehend material. Reading skills can be developed by concentrating on what you read and by taking frequent pauses to organize and review the materials in your mind. At the end of a study session, review everything read, making special notes of important points. Reading a computer screen can be hard on the eyes; it may be necessary to print copies of reading assignments and communications from the instructor.

■ Communication Skills

- Speaking into a microphone on a video or conference call can be intimidating, but communication skills are an important part of any assignment—on the job, at home, and at school. Pay careful attention to instructions and be certain to understand what is being asked. It often helps to develop a brief outline before responding to questions, whether they are submitted in writing, via e-mail, by spoken word or on video/audio tape. Organization, grammar, and appropriate style are important.

Source: http://www.petersons.com/distancelearning/code/articles/study by Virtual Learning Ink Press.

◼ Activity: Identifying Requirements of Participating in the Distance Education Program

1. Using the Internet, go to the SCC home page at http://www.surry.edu and click on the Distance Education link. Then choose the "Students" link. Which link would you choose to find out about taking a degree completely online?

2. Listed on the left side of the screen of the Distance Education home page are buttons that provide information about the program. Click on the "Students" link. Next choose "Apply Now" button. Determine the steps that a student taking Distance Education courses for the first time would take to register for a course. List the steps.

3. From the "Students" link, what link describes the software and equipment requirements for taking an Internet course?

4. All students taking an Internet course are required to use a free SCC student e-mail account. What is the format for your student e-mail username and password?

5. SCC uses a learning management system such as Moodle to deliver Internet courses and to provide information to students in traditional courses. To learn more about this program, complete the online orientation. You will be required to take two quizzes, setup your SCC e-mail account, use the e-mail account to submit an attachment to the director of distance education, and submit a form verifying you have successfully completed the orientation.

   Start by finding your username and password required for logging in. The information can be found at www.surry.edu.

CHAPTER 2

Self-Discovery, Career Exploration, and Job Readiness

If you don't know where you are going, you will probably end up somewhere else.

David Campbell

Introduction

Career development is a lifelong process. Steps in the process include knowing yourself, learning about various occupations and the education and training required for those occupations, and building employability skills. Values are qualities that are important to you, principles by which you live and which give your life meaning. Your values make you unique and often act as motivators. Values are fundamental to the way you view yourself and your world and help you to develop a lifestyle. Clarifying and prioritizing your values is another way of knowing yourself and knowing what you want out of life and choosing a career path that is compatible with what you want to contribute to and get out of life. In other words, before deciding on what you want to do with your life, it is important to know who you are.

Have you thought through what is most meaningful to you? Is it financial security, recognition, or health? Is having plenty of time to spend with family and friends important to you? Would you rather spend time working in order to become wealthy? Do you want to have power over people and things? What do you value in other people? The answers to the previous questions will invariably affect the educational, personal, and career choices that you make throughout life.

Your values will affect the emphasis you place on studying, how you perform on the job, and how you live your life. Various studies have shown that individuals tend to be more satisfied and productive when life goals, behavior, college major, and career choice are consistent with personal values. In this chapter, you will examine your personal values, as well as determine which are most important in your life. This information and basic awareness can help you to make the best, most appropriate choices for your life.

Knowing Yourself (Self-Discovery Assessment)

You might begin the self-discovery process by taking inventory or assessing your personality traits, your likes and dislikes, interests, skills, and values. As your life experiences change, so will you. It is important for you to know about various inventories or self-assessment instruments available to you so that you can assess or re-assess yourself from time to time. The activity on the following page is one such assessment.

■ Values, Interests, Abilities, and Personality Should All Play a Part in Career Selection

Visit the SCC Career Services Center, create a "portfolio," and complete the following two activities. Career Services staff will provide you with instructions.

Activity I: Self-Discovery/Career Exploration

Complete an assessment. Print out your results, write a brief synopsis, and bring to class.

Activity II: Career Research

Research a career. Write a paragraph including reasons you narrowed your options to this career. Be sure to be clear, logical, and precise. Provide as much depth and breadth as possible for you at this point. Print out the information you obtain about your chosen career. Bring your paragraph and the printed information to class.

I used the following resources from the SCC Career Services Center. (Must have at least one.)

_____

_____

_____

Mandatory Career Services Staff Signature/Date

■ Tips for Filling Out an Application Form

- ■ Read the instructions and examples and follow them carefully.
- ■ Print or write neatly so the finished form can be easily read. Use a pen or type your information.
- ■ Be complete. If a question does not apply to you, write none or draw a line in the blank to show that you didn't overlook it.
- ■ Be accurate. Read everything on the application carefully before you start to fill out the blanks. This will help you write accurate answers. Be sure your spelling is correct. Refer to your personal information form to double-check details.
- ■ Be sure you understand the application form. If you don't know a word or abbreviation, ask the person who gave you the application form to explain it.
- ■ List all types of education, experience, on-the-job-training, or hobbies that have given you skills for any type of work.
- ■ Describe your previous work experience accurately and completely. Employers are looking for applicants with skills, abilities, and experience. Be sure to list the different types of machines and equipment you have operated or can operate.
- ■ Include any special license or membership in a trade union on the application form.
- ■ Remember to take your personal information form or other important papers you prepared. These papers will save time and will help you fill out your application completely and accurately.

■ Getting Hired: A Cover Letter Is Your First Line of Attack

A retiring consultant on executive recruiting recently wrote, "I strongly object to your constant references to a cover letter. It implies it is an ordinary transmitted letter. I always call it a marketing letter," which it must be. "The sender is marketing himself from the first sentence to the last. Why not call it what it really is, a marketing letter?"

The letter-writer is right. A letter introducing a resume is much more than an ordinary letter.

I talk about "marketing" or "sales" letters when discussing letters sent to employers or network contacts that do not include resumes.

What is much more important than the name you call a letter introducing a resume is the content, form, and accuracy of the letter.

Here are some rules to follow:

- ■ Always print your letters on quality paper. Be sure to include the date it was written.
- ■ Use an accepted format for business letters. You can get a guide from many books at your public library.
- ■ Check carefully for typos and misspelled words. Be tough on yourself and allow no errors.
- ■ In the first paragraph, clearly state why you are sending your resume. If you are responding to an advertised job opening, identify the ad, the date run, and the publication.
- ■ In the second paragraph, sell yourself by referring to specific experience, training or education that qualifies you for the job opening or job objective, but do not repeat everything in your resume.
- ■ Close by asking for action. State when you will follow up with a telephone call to ask for a mutually convenient in-person interview.

■ Your Resume

FULL NAME

Street Address
City, State, Zip Code
Telephone Number with Area Code

_____

_____

_____

_____

JOB OBJECTIVE

State Position Desired or Career Field.

_____

EDUCATION

List Schools, Years Attended, and Degrees Earned. Start with the Most Recent; Include the Start and End Dates for Each.

_____

_____

_____

_____

WORK EXPERIENCE

List Work and Military Experience. Start with the Most Recent and Include the Beginning and Ending Dates.

(List 3 past job experiences, start with present or most recent.)

Month & Year Began _____   to   Job Title _____

Month & Year Ended _____   Company Name _____

                                           City, State _____

Month & Year Began _____   to   Job Title _____

Month & Year Ended _____   Company Name _____

                                           City, State _____

Month & Year Began ____   to   Job Title _____

Month & Year Ended ____   Company Name _____

                                           City, State _____

OCCUPATIONAL SKILLS

List Special Skills, Such as the Ability to Speak Another Language, Computer Skills, or Artistic Ability.

_____

_____

_____

_____

AWARDS/HONORS

List Awards and Honors (Academic, Athletic, or Community Service). Include the Year the Honor Was Received.

_____

_____

INTERESTS

This Optional Section Can Include Hobbies, Such as Skiing, Playing the Piano, and Gardening.

_____

_____

REFERENCES: Available upon Request

List below 3 or 4 References. Include Name, Position, Street Address, City, State, Zip Code, and Telephone. Be Sure to Ask Permission of Each Reference First.

Name: _____

Title: _____

Street: _____

City, State, Zip: _____

(Area Code) Phone: _____

Name: _____

Title: _____

Street: _____

City, State, Zip: _____

(Area Code) Phone: _____

Name: _____

Title: _____

Street: _____

City, State, Zip: _____

(Area Code) Phone: _____

Name: _____

Title: _____

Street: _____

City, State, Zip: _____

(Area Code) Phone: _____

How To Make a Good Impression On a Prospective Employer

1. Study your qualifications, abilities and training. Be prepared to present the information briefly and clearly.

2. Be certain that you're really interested in the type of work for which you're applying.

3. Before the interview, learn as much as possible about the firm. Be prepared to ask questions concerning the company and the position for which you're applying.

4. Be prompt, and allow time before your scheduled appointment to complete an application form.

5. Be clean, neat and dressed appropriately for the job you're seeking.

6. Avoid taking anyone with you to a job interview. The employer only wants to talk with you.

7. Answer all the employer's questions accurately, honestly, and promptly.

8. Be able to give a continuous record of all your jobs, dates of employment, wages received, job descriptions and your reasons for leaving. Also, be able to give the names of at least three reliable references.

9. When an employer asks, point out the value derived from your training and past experiences which will help you do the job you're seeking.

10. Be polite and courteous. Speak distinctly, with confidence and enthusiasm.

11. Don't criticize others, including past employers and associates. Avoid mention of your personal, domestic or financial problems. The employer is only interested in you and your ability to do the job for which you're applying.

12. Don't be discouraged if you're nervous or if you don't feel that you've presented yourself well during your first interview. Employers will understand and make allowances. Continue setting up job interviews and improve your presentation each time.

■ Most Frequently Asked Interview Questions

1. Why don't you tell me about yourself?

2. Why should I hire you?

3. What are your major strengths?

4. What are your major weaknesses?

5. What sort of pay do you expect to receive?

6. How does your previous experience relate to the jobs we have here?

7. What are your plans for the future?

8. What will your former employers (or references) say about you?

9. Why are you looking for this sort of position and why here?

■ Handling Tough Interview Questions

The employer's purpose in interviewing you is to learn more about you than your job application or resume reveals. There is no script or standard set of questions which an interviewer follows. If you are not properly prepared, they may stump you. Stay alert and be ready for the "tough" questions.

Answer Suggestions for "Tough Questions" Asked in Interviews

"What can I do for you today?"

Employers do not really want a straight answer to this question. They already know that you are applying for a job. Suggested responses should therefore tell the employer what you can do for them.

"Well, actually I'm here to let you know of my varied training and experience in drafting."

"I'm here to talk about your need for an experienced driver."

"What kind of work are you looking for?"

Be as specific as you can with this particular employer. If you are applying for a specific job, say so. If not, you may want to respond with:

"I would like a job in which I will be able to produce for the company and grow along with it."

"I have always done well in food preparation jobs, so I would be willing to discuss such a job with you which has career potential."

"Why did your last job end?"

If the answer reflects a positive situation, don't hesitate to answer fully. However, if this response would elicit a negative response from the employer, choose selectively what you say and leave out minute details. Explain just the basic facts.

"I felt my career potential was limited with that company, so I left to seek work that had more advancement opportunities."

"My employer and I both felt I would be happier in another work environment which requires me to work against deadlines, so I was released to seek other work."

"Can you explain why you've been out of work for so long?"

No problem if you have a valid reason; i.e., raising a family, or returning to school, however, if you were just traveling, or not looking for work very seriously, it's more difficult.

"I felt that before I settled into a career job I had better get some personal travel out of the way. So, I traveled all over the country as a sort of self-education. The travel bug is now out of my system and I'm ready to start on that career."

"I held many jobs before this long period of having no job. I decided I didn't want to settle for just any job again, so I pretty much stopped looking while I decided what I really wanted to do as a career. I did decide, and working for you fits my career plans very well."

"How did you get along with your former boss and coworkers?"

Never "bad mouth" a former employer or the people with whom you worked. New employers want to feel you are going to be able to get along and will be a loyal worker.

"Great bunch of people. We all got along just fine. It was a work environment where everyone cooperated and helped out everyone else."

"Well, I certainly have no complaints, and I'm sure they don't either."

"Do you know anything about our company?"

Hopefully, you will have done some homework and will know something about the company, but if you don't you should be prepared to say something other than "no," and indicate some interest in knowing more.

"What do you expect as a starting salary?"

Never mention a salary figure before the employer's range is known. To do so is to either overprice or underprice yourself. Once the employer mentions a figure, you agree with it. Negotiations, if there are to be any, should be attempted a couple of days later, when the "balance of power" between you and the employer is more to your favor, and the pressure of being in an interview is off. It is best to wait until you get a job offer before being too specific. Try to avoid a dollar amount if the question comes up too early in the interview.

"I am more interested in career potential than just the job of the moment right now, so I would be willing to consider whatever your firm usually pays new hires in this situation."

"I would be willing to accept whatever your company policy states."

"What do you hope to be doing five or ten years from now?"

Indicate ambition and confidence in your abilities, but be careful not to appear to be threatening the employer's own job.

"I would hope to be somewhat up the career ladder from this job, perhaps in a supervisory or design capacity."

"I would hope to still be employed here, in an advanced position which would take advantage of my knowledge, abilities and experience."

■ Questions You Can Ask During the Job Interview

It is very important that you learn as much as you can about the business and about the job for which you are applying. Think about questions you want to ask an employer before going to the interview.

EXAMPLES:

1. What is the nature of the work and duties required for this job?

2. Where would I work? What are the working hours.

3. Are there any special skills required for this job?

4. How long does it usually take for someone to learn the job? Is on-the-job training provided?

5. Does the job offer potential for advancement within the company?

6. What are the company's education and training policies?

7. Does the job offer health insurance or other benefits? (This should not be your first question.)

■ Dress Code for Job Seekers

Never underestimate the power of a first impression. The way you speak, the manner in which you carry yourself, and perhaps most importantly, the way you dress will give the prospective employer a snapshot of you that could mean the difference between getting that job or staying unemployed.

Use the following guidelines when deciding how to dress for a job interview:

1. Daily bathing and personal hygiene are necessities. Offensive body odor is the quickest way not to get a job.

2. Hair should be kept neat and clean. Beards, mustaches, and sideburns should be neatly trimmed.

3. The amount of makeup you wear should be appropriate for job seeking. Heavy perfume should be avoided.

4. Nails should be clean and trimmed, and should not be chipped. Limit nail polish to clear or light shades.

5. Jewelry should be minimal. Avoid large earrings and noisy bracelets.

6. It is not acceptable for any job seekers to wear T-shirts, printed T-shirts, sweatshirts, low cut tops, "see-through" clothing or caps.

7. Cleaned and pressed clothing is a necessity. Avoid wearing torn or patched clothing.

8. It is acceptable for job seekers to wear dungarees or blue jeans for some types of interviews (i.e., maintenance, custodial, factory work, construction) as long as they are not faded, patched, or extremely light.

9. Dress clothes such as suits, ties, dresses and stockings should be worn for some interviews (i.e., secretarial, office, sales, management, etc.).

10. Wear conservative colors and avoid loud, flashy colors for job seeking.

CHAPTER 3
Critical Thinking: Concepts and Tools

Introduction

Beyond college, critical thinking is helpful in being a good citizen and a productive member of society. Throughout history, critical thinkers have helped to advance civilization. Thoughts that were once widely accepted were questioned, and newer and more useful ideas came to be accepted. For example, it was once assumed that blood-sucking leeches were helpful in curing diseases. Some critical thinkers questioned this practice, and the science of medicine was advanced. It was not so long ago that women were not allowed to vote. Critical thinkers questioned this practice so that women could participate in a democratic society.

A lack of critical thinking can lead to great tragedy. The memoirs of Adolf Eichmann, who played a central role in the killing of six million Jews by the Nazis, have recently been published. Eichmann wrote:

> *From my childhood, obedience was something I could not get out of my system. When I entered the armed services at the age of 27, I found being obedient not a bit more difficult than it had been during my life at that point. It was unthinkable that I would not follow orders. Now that I look back, I realize that a life predicated on being obedient and taking orders is a very comfortable life indeed. Living in such a way reduces to a minimum one's own need to think.[1]*

If you can think critically, you can have the freedom to be creative and generate new ideas.

> *There are one-story intellects, two-story intellects, and three-story intellects with skylights. All fact-collectors who have no aim beyond their facts are one-story men. Two-story men compare, reason, generalize, using the labor of the fact-collectors as their own. Three-story men idealize, imagine, predict—their best illumination comes from above through skylights.*
> —Oliver Wendell Holmes

Use the information in this chapter to become a better critical thinker. And by the way, even though Oliver Wendell Holmes talks about men, women can be three-story intellects too.

This chapter contains material adapted from *College & Career Success*, 2nd edition by Marsha Fralick. Copyright © 2003 by Kendall/Hunt Publishing Company. Adapted and reprinted with permission of the publisher. Further reproduction is prohibited.

[1] Roger Cohen, "Nazi Leader's Notes Cite 'Obedience' as Reason for His Genocidal Actions," *The San Diego Union Tribune*, Friday, August 13, 1999.

▪ Why Critical Thinking?

The Problem:

Everyone thinks; it is our nature to do so. But much of our thinking, left to itself, is biased, distorted, partial, uninformed or down-right prejudiced. Yet the quality of our life and that of what we produce, make, or build depends precisely on the quality of our thought. Shoddy thinking is costly, both in money and in quality of life. Excellence in thought, however, must be systematically cultivated.

A Definition:

Critical thinking is that mode of thinking—about any subject, content, or problem—in which the thinker improves the quality of his or her thinking by skillfully taking charge of the structures inherent in thinking and imposing intellectual standards upon them.

The Result:

A well cultivated critical thinker:

- ▪ raises vital questions and problems, formulating them clearly and precisely;
- ▪ gathers and assesses relevant information, using abstract ideas to interpret it effectively.
- ▪ comes to well-reasoned conclusions and solutions, testing them against relevant criteria and standards;
- ▪ thinks open mindedly within alternative systems of thought, recognizing and assessing, as need be, their assumptions, implications, and practical consequences; and
- ▪ communicates effectively with others in figuring out solutions to complex problems.

Critical thinking is, in short, self-directed, self-disciplined, self-monitored, and self-corrective thinking. It presupposes assent to rigorous standards of excellence and mindful command of their use. It entails effective communication and problem solving abilities and a commitment to overcome our native egocentrism and sociocentrism.

▪ A Checklist for Reasoning

1. All reasoning has a PURPOSE.
   - ▪ Take time to state your purpose clearly.
   - ▪ Distinguish your purpose from related purposes.
   - ▪ Check periodically to be sure you are still on target.
   - ▪ Choose significant and realistic purposes.

2. All reasoning is an attempt to FIGURE something out, to settle some QUESTION, solve some PROBLEM.
   - ▪ Take time to clearly and precisely state the question at issue.

From *The Miniature Guide to Critical Thinking Concepts & Tools*, 3rd edition by Dr. Richard Paul and Dr. Linda Elder. Copyright © 2003 by The Foundation for Critical Thinking, www.criticalthinking.org. Reprinted with permission.

The Elements of Thought

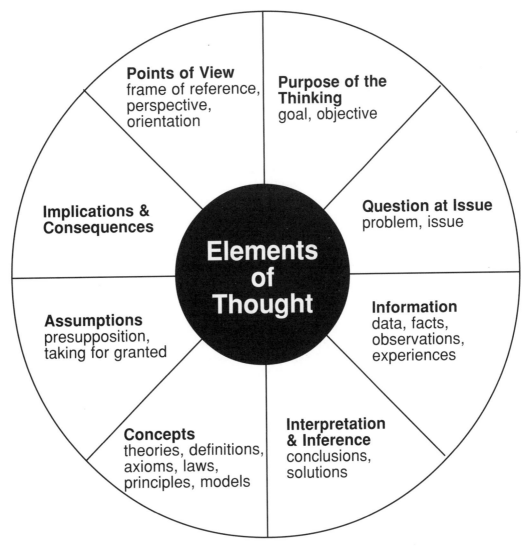

Points of View
frame of reference,
perspective,
orientation

Purpose of the Thinking
goal, objective

Implications & Consequences

Question at Issue
problem, issue

Elements of Thought

Information
data, facts,
observations,
experiences

Assumptions
presupposition,
taking for granted

Concepts
theories, definitions,
axioms, laws,
principles, models

Interpretation & Inference
conclusions,
solutions

Used with Sensitivity to Universal Intellectual Standards

Clarity ⟶ Accuracy ⟶ Depth ⟶ Significance
Precision
Relevance

- Express the question in several ways to clarify its meaning and scope.
- Break the question into sub-questions.
- Identify if the question has one right answer, is a matter of mere opinion, or requires reasoning from more than one point of view.

3. All reasoning is based on ASSUMPTIONS.
   - Clearly identify your assumptions and determine whether they are justifiable.
   - Consider how your assumptions are shaping your point of view.

From *The Miniature Guide to Critical Thinking Concepts & Tools*, 3rd edition by Dr. Richard Paul and Dr. Linda Elder. Copyright © 2003 by The Foundation for Critical Thinking, www.criticalthinking.org. Reprinted with permission.

4. All reasoning is done from some POINT OF VIEW.
   - ■ Identify your point of view.
   - ■ Seek other points of view and identify their strengths as well as weaknesses.
   - ■ Strive to be fairminded in evaluating all points of view.

5. All reasoning is based on DATA, INFORMATION AND EVIDENCE.
   - ■ Restrict your claims to those supported by the data you have.
   - ■ Search for information that opposes your position as well as information that supports it.
   - ■ Make sure that all information used is clear, accurate, and relevant to the question at issue.
   - ■ Make sure you have gathered sufficient information.

6. All reasoning is expressed through, and shaped by, CONCEPTS and IDEAS.
   - ■ Identify key concepts and explain them clearly.
   - ■ Consider alternative concepts or alternative definitions to concepts.
   - ■ Make sure you are using concepts—with care and precision.

7. All reasoning contains INFERENCES or INTERPRETATIONS by which we draw CONCLUSIONS and give meaning to data.
   - ■ Infer only what the evidence implies.
   - ■ Check inferences for their consistency with each other.
   - ■ Identify assumptions which lead you to your inferences.

8. All reasoning leads somewhere or has IMPLICATIONS and CONSEQUENCES.
   - ■ Trace the implications and consequences that follow from your reasoning.
   - ■ Search for negative as well as positive implications.
   - ■ Consider all possible consequences.

■ Questions Using the Elements of Thought

(in a paper, an activity, a reading assignment . . .)

Purpose:	What am I trying to accomplish? What is my central aim? My purpose?
Information:	What information am I using in coming to that conclusion? What experience have I had to support this claim? What information do I need to settle the question?
Inferences/Conclusions:	How did I reach this conclusion? Is there another way to interpret the information?
Concepts:	What is the main idea here? Could I explain this idea?
Assumptions:	What am I taking for granted? What assumption has led me to that conclusion?
Implications/Consequences:	If someone accepted my position, what would be the implications? What am I implying?
Points of View:	From what point of view am I looking at this issue? Is there another point of view I should consider?
Questions:	What question am I raising? What question am I addressing?

From *The Miniature Guide to Critical Thinking Concepts & Tools*, 3rd edition by Dr. Richard Paul and Dr. Linda Elder. Copyright © 2003 by The Foundation for Critical Thinking, www.criticalthinking.org. Reprinted with permission.

■ The Problem of Egocentric Thinking

Egocentric thinking comes from the unfortunate fact that humans do not naturally consider the rights and needs of others, nor do we naturally appreciate the point of view of others or the limitations in our own point of view. We become explicitly aware of our egocentric thinking only if trained to do so. We do not naturally recognize our egocentric assumptions, the egocentric way we use information, the egocentric way we interpret data, the source of our egocentric concepts and ideas, the implications of our egocentric thought. We do not naturally recognize our self-serving perspective.

As humans we live with the unrealistic but confident sense that we have fundamentally figured out the way things actually are, and that we have done this objectively. We naturally believe in our intuitive perceptions—however inaccurate. Instead of using intellectual standards in thinking, we often use self-centered psychological (rather than intellectual) standards to determine what to believe and what to reject. Here are the most commonly used psychological standards in human thinking.

"IT'S TRUE BECAUSE I BELIEVE IT." Innate egocentrism: I assume that what I believe is true even though I have never questioned the basis for many of my beliefs.

"IT'S TRUE BECAUSE WE BELIEVE IT." Innate sociocentrism: I assume that the dominant beliefs within the groups to which I belong are true even though I have never questioned the basis for many of these beliefs.

"IT'S TRUE BECAUSE I WANT TO BELIEVE IT." Innate wish fulfillment: I believe in, for example, accounts of behavior that put me (or the groups to which I belong) in a positive rather than a negative light even though I have not seriously considered the evidence for the more negative account. I believe what "feels good," what supports my other beliefs, what does not require me to change my thinking in any significant way, what does not require me to admit I have been wrong.

"IT'S TRUE BECAUSE I HAVE ALWAYS BELIEVED IT." Innate self-validation: I have a strong desire to maintain beliefs that I have long held, even though I have not seriously considered the extent to which those beliefs are justified, given the evidence.

"IT'S TRUE BECAUSE IT IS IN MY SELFISH INTEREST TO BELIEVE IT." Innate selfishness: I hold fast to beliefs that justify my getting more power, money, or personal advantage even though these beliefs are not grounded in sound reasoning or evidence.

Since humans are naturally prone to assess thinking in keeping with the above criteria, it is not surprising that we, as a species, have not developed a significant interest in establishing and teaching legitimate intellectual standards. It is not surprising that our thinking is often flawed. We are truly the "self-deceived animal."

■ Universal Intellectual Standards

And questions that can be used to apply them

Universal intellectual standards are standards which must be applied to thinking whenever one is interested in checking the quality of reasoning about a problem, issue, or situation. To think critically entails having command of these standards. To help stu-

From *The Miniature Guide to Critical Thinking Concepts & Tools*, 3rd edition by Dr. Richard Paul and Dr. Linda Elder. Copyright © 2003 by The Foundation for Critical Thinking, www.criticalthinking.org. Reprinted with permission.

dents learn them, teachers should pose questions which probe student thinking, questions which hold students accountable for their thinking, questions which, through consistent use by the teacher in the classroom, become internalized by students as questions they need to ask themselves.

The ultimate goal, then, is for these questions to become infused in the thinking of students, forming part of their inner voice, which then guides them to better and better reasoning. While there are a number of universal standards, we have elected to comment on the following:

Clarity:

Could you elaborate further on that point? Could you express that point in another way? Could you give me an illustration? Could you give me an example?

Clarity is a gateway standard. If a statement is unclear, we cannot determine whether it is accurate or relevant. In fact, we cannot tell anything about it because we don't yet know what it is saying. For example, the question "What can be done about the education system in America?" is unclear. In order to adequately address the question, we would need to have a clearer understanding of what the person asking the question is considering the "problem" to be. A clearer question might be "What can educators do to ensure that students learn the skills and abilities which help them function successfully on the job and in their daily decision-making?"

Accuracy:

Is that really true? How could we check that? How could we find out if that is true? A statement can be clear but not accurate, as in "Most dogs are over 300 pounds in weight."

Precision:

Could you give me more details? Could you be more specific? A statement can be both clear and accurate, but not precise, as in "Jack is overweight." (We don't know how overweight Jack is, one pound or 500 pounds.)

Relevance:

How is that connected to the question? How does that bear on the issue? A statement can be clear, accurate, and precise, but not relevant to the question at issue. For example, students often think that the amount of effort they put into a course should be used in raising their grade in a course. Often, however, "effort" does not measure the quality of student learning, and when that is so, effort is irrelevant to their appropriate grade.

Depth:

How does your answer address the complexities in the question? How are you taking into account the problems in the question? Is that dealing with the most significant factors?

From *The Miniature Guide to Critical Thinking Concepts & Tools*, 3rd edition by Dr. Richard Paul and Dr. Linda Elder. Copyright © 2003 by The Foundation for Critical Thinking, www.criticalthinking.org. Reprinted with permission.

A statement can be clear, accurate, precise, and relevant, but superficial (that is, lack depth). For example, the statement "Just Say No" which is often used to discourage children and teens from using drugs, is clear, accurate, precise, and relevant. Nevertheless, it lacks depth because it treats an extremely complex issue, the pervasive problem of drug use among young people, superficially. It fails to deal with the complexities of the issue.

Breadth:

Do we need to consider another point of view? Is there another way to look at this question? What would this look like from a conservative standpoint? What would this look like from the point of view of . . . ?

A line of reasoning may be clear, accurate, precise, relevant, and deep, but lack breadth (as in an argument from either the conservative or liberal standpoints which gets deeply into an issue, but only recognizes the insights of one side of the question).

Logic:

Does this really make sense? Does that follow from what you said? How does that follow? But before you implied this and now you are saying that, I don't see how both can be true.

When we think, we bring a variety of thoughts together into some order. When the combination of thoughts are mutually supporting and make sense in combination, the thinking is "logical." When the combination is not mutually supporting, is contradictory in some sense, or does not "make sense," the combination is "not logical."

Clarity	Could you elaborate further? Could you give me an example? Could you illustrate what you mean?
Accuracy	How could we check on that? How could we find out if that is true? How could we verify or test that?
Precision	Could you be more specific? Could you give me more details? Could you be more exact?
Relevance	How does that relate to the problem? How does that bear on the question? How does that help us with the issue?
Depth	What factors make this a difficult problem? What are some of the complexities of this question? What are some of the difficulties we need to deal with?
Breadth	Do we need to look at this from another perspective? Do we need to consider another point of view? Do we need to look at this in other ways?
Logic	Does all this make sense together? Does your first paragraph fit in with your last? Does what you say follow from the evidence?

From *The Miniature Guide to Critical Thinking Concepts & Tools*, 3rd edition by Dr. Richard Paul and Dr. Linda Elder. Copyright © 2003 by The Foundation for Critical Thinking, www.criticalthinking.org. Reprinted with permission.

Significance	Is this the most important problem to consider?
	Is this the central idea to focus on?
	Which of these facts are most important?
Fairness	Do I have any vested interest in this issue?
	Am I sympathetically representing the viewpoints of others?

■ Template for Analyzing the Logic of an Article

Take an article that you have been assigned to read for class, completing the "logic" of it using the template below. This template can be modified for analyzing the logic of a chapter in a textbook.

The Logic of "(name of the article)"

1. The main **purpose** of this article is _____.
   (State as accurately as possible the author's purpose for writing the article.)

2. The key **question** that the author is addressing is _____.
   (Figure out the key question in the mind of the author when s/he wrote the article.)

3. The most important **information** in this article is _____.
   (Figure out the facts, experiences, data the author is using to support her/his conclusions.)

4. The main **inferences**/conclusions in this article are _____.
   (Identify the key conclusions the author comes to and presents in the article.)

5. The key **concept(s)** we need to understand in this article is (are)

   _____. By these concepts the author means

   _____. (Figure out the most important ideas you would have to understand in order to understand the author's line of reasoning.)

6. The main **assumption(s)** underlying the author's thinking is (are)

   _____. (Figure out what the author is taking for granted [that might be questioned].)

7. a) If we take this line of reasoning seriously, the **implications** are

   _____. (What consequences are likely to follow if people take the author's line of reasoning seriously?)

   b) If we fail to take this line of reasoning seriously, the **implications**

   are _____. (What consequences are likely to follow if people ignore the author's reasoning?)

8. The main **point(s) of view** presented in this article is (are)

   _____. (What is the author looking at, and how is s/he seeing it?)

From *The Miniature Guide to Critical Thinking Concepts & Tools*, 3rd edition by Dr. Richard Paul and Dr. Linda Elder. Copyright © 2003 by The Foundation for Critical Thinking, www.criticalthinking.org. Reprinted with permission.

■ Criteria for Evaluating Reasoning

1. **Purpose:** What is the purpose of the reasoner? Is the purpose clearly stated or clearly implied? Is it justifiable?

2. **Question:** Is the question at issue well-stated? Is it clear and unbiased? Does the expression of the question do justice to the complexity of the matter at issue? Are the question and purpose directly relevant to each other?

3. **Information:** Does the writer cite relevant evidence, experiences, and/or information essential to the issue? Is the information accurate? Does the writer address the complexities of the issue?

4. **Concepts:** Does the writer clarify key concepts when necessary? Are the concepts used justifiably?

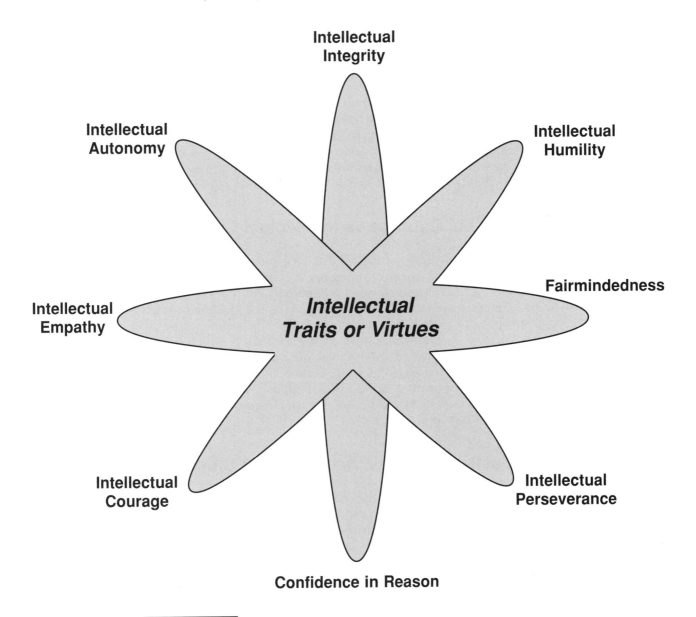

Intellectual Integrity

Intellectual Autonomy

Intellectual Humility

Fairmindedness

Intellectual Empathy

Intellectual Traits or Virtues

Intellectual Courage

Intellectual Perseverance

Confidence in Reason

From *The Miniature Guide to Critical Thinking Concepts & Tools*, 3rd edition by Dr. Richard Paul and Dr. Linda Elder. Copyright © 2003 by The Foundation for Critical Thinking, www.criticalthinking.org. Reprinted with permission.

5. **Assumptions:** Does the writer show a sensitivity to what he or she is taking for granted or assuming? (Insofar as those assumptions might reasonably be questioned?) Does the writer use questionable assumptions without addressing problems which might be inherent in those assumptions?

6. **Inferences:** Does the writer develop a line of reasoning explaining well how s/he is arriving at her or his main conclusions?

7. **Point of View:** Does the writer show a sensitivity to alternative relevant points of view or lines of reasoning? Does s/he consider and respond to objections framed from other relevant points of view?

8. **Implications:** Does the writer show a sensitivity to the implications and consequences of the position s/he is taking?

■ Essential Intellectual Traits

Intellectual Humility vs Intellectual Arrogance

Having a consciousness of the limits of one's knowledge, including a sensitivity to circumstances in which one's native egocentrism is likely to function self-deceptively; sensitivity to bias, prejudice and limitations of one's viewpoint. Intellectual humility depends on recognizing that one should not claim more than one actually knows. It does not imply spinelessness or submissiveness. It implies the lack of intellectual pretentiousness, boastfulness, or conceit, combined with insight into the logical foundations, or lack of such foundations, of one's beliefs.

Intellectual Courage vs Intellectual Cowardice

Having a consciousness of the need to face and fairly address ideas, beliefs or viewpoints toward which we have strong negative emotions and to which we have not given a serious hearing. This courage is connected with the recognition that ideas considered dangerous or absurd are sometimes rationally justified (in whole or in part) and that conclusions and beliefs inculcated in us are sometimes false or misleading. To determine for ourselves which is which, we must not passively and uncritically "accept" what we have "learned." Intellectual courage comes into play here, because inevitably we will come to see some truth in some ideas considered dangerous and absurd, and distortion or falsity in some ideas strongly held in our social group. We need courage to be true to our own thinking in such circumstances. The penalties for non-conformity can be severe.

Intellectual Empathy vs Intellectual Closemindedness

Having a consciousness of the need to imaginatively put oneself in the place of others in order to genuinely understand them, which requires the consciousness of our egocentric tendency to identify truth with our immediate perceptions of long-standing thought or belief. This trait correlates with the ability to reconstruct accurately the view-

From *The Miniature Guide to Critical Thinking Concepts & Tools*, 3rd edition by Dr. Richard Paul and Dr. Linda Elder. Copyright © 2003 by The Foundation for Critical Thinking, www.criticalthinking.org. Reprinted with permission.

points and reasoning of others and to reason from premises, assumptions, and ideas other than our own. This trait also correlates with the willingness to remember occasions when we were wrong in the past despite an intense conviction that we were right, and with the ability to imagine our being similarly deceived in a case-at-hand.

Intellectual Autonomy vs Intellectual Conformity

Having rational control of one's beliefs, values, and inferences. The ideal of critical thinking is to learn to think for oneself, to gain command over one's thought processes. It entails a commitment to analyzing and evaluating beliefs on the basis of reason and evidence, to question when it is rational to question, to believe when it is rational to believe, and to conform when it is rational to conform.

Intellectual Integrity vs Intellectual Hypocrisy

Recognition of the need to be true to one's own thinking; to be consistent in the intellectual standards one applies; to hold one's self to the same rigorous standards of evidence and proof to which one holds one's antagonists; to practice what one advocates for others; and to honestly admit discrepancies and inconsistencies in one's own thought and action.

Intellectual Perseverance vs Intellectual Laziness

Having a consciousness of the need to use intellectual insights and truths in spite of difficulties, obstacles, and frustrations; firm adherence to rational principles despite the irrational opposition of others; a sense of the need to struggle with confusion and unsettled questions over an extended period of time to achieve deeper understanding or insight.

Confidence in Reason vs Distrust of Reason and Evidence

Confidence that, in the long run, one's own higher interests and those of humankind at large will be best served by giving the freest play to reason, by encouraging people to come to their own conclusions by developing their own rational faculties; faith that, with proper encouragement and cultivation, people can learn to think for themselves, to form rational viewpoints, draw reasonable conclusions, think coherently and logically, persuade each other by reason and become reasonable persons, despite the deep-seated obstacles in the native character of the human mind and in society as we know it.

Fairmindedness vs Intellectual Unfairness

Having a consciousness of the need to treat all viewpoints alike, without reference to one's own feelings or vested interests, or the feelings or vested interests of one's friends, community or nation; implies adherence to intellectual standards without reference to one's own advantage or the advantage of one's group.

From *The Miniature Guide to Critical Thinking Concepts & Tools*, 3rd edition by Dr. Richard Paul and Dr. Linda Elder. Copyright © 2003 by The Foundation for Critical Thinking, www.criticalthinking.org. Reprinted with permission.

■ Three Kinds of Questions

In approaching a question, it is useful to figure out what type it is. Is it a question with one definitive answer? Is it a question that calls for a subjective choice? Or does the question require you to consider competing answers?

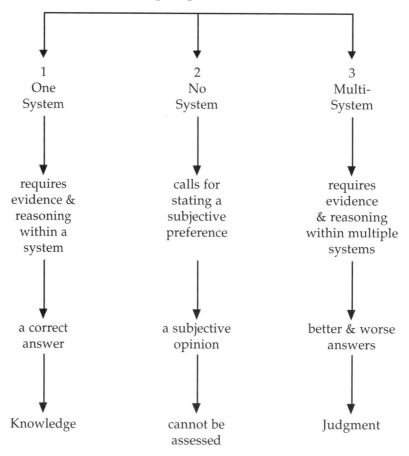

1 One System	2 No System	3 Multi- System
requires evidence & reasoning within a system	calls for stating a subjective preference	requires evidence & reasoning within multiple systems
a correct answer	a subjective opinion	better & worse answers
Knowledge	cannot be assessed	Judgment

■ A Template for Problem-Solving

To be an effective problem solver:

1. Figure out, and regularly re-articulate, your goals, purposes, and needs. Recognize problems as emergent obstacles to reaching your goals, achieving your purposes, and satisfying your needs.

2. Wherever possible take problems one by one. State the problem as clearly and precisely as you can.

3. Study the problem to make clear the "kind" of problem you are dealing with. Figure out, for example, what sorts of things you are going to have to do to solve it. Distinguish problems over which you have some control from problems over which you have no control. Set aside the problems over which you have no control. Concentrate your efforts on those problems you can potentially solve.

From *The Miniature Guide to Critical Thinking Concepts & Tools*, 3rd edition by Dr. Richard Paul and Dr. Linda Elder. Copyright © 2003 by The Foundation for Critical Thinking, www.criticalthinking.org. Reprinted with permission.

4. Figure out the information you need and actively seek that information.

5. Carefully analyze and interpret the information you collect, drawing what reasonable inferences you can.

6. Figure out your options for action. What can you do in the short term? In the long term? Recognize explicitly your limitations as far as money, time, and power.

7. Evaluate your options, taking into account their advantages and disadvantages in the situation you are in.

8. Adopt a strategic approach to the problem and follow through on that strategy. This may involve direct action or a carefully thought-through wait-and-see strategy.

9. When you act, monitor the implications of your action as they begin to emerge. Be ready at a moment's notice to revise your strategy if the situation requires it. Be prepared to shift your strategy or your analysis or statement of the problem, or all three, as more information about the problem becomes available to you.

■ A Checklist for Assessment

1. What are you assessing and why? (Be precise.)

2. Ask probing, evaluative questions (that reflect your purpose).

3. Specify the information you need to collect (to answer your question).

4. Decide on criteria or standards. (Are they practical, reasonable, and in line with your purpose?)

5. Be clear about what exactly you are trying to find out.

6. Are there any unintended negative consequences of your mode of evaluation?

7. Review your evaluation overall. Is it coherent, logical, realistic, and practical?

From *The Miniature Guide to Critical Thinking Concepts & Tools*, 3rd edition by Dr. Richard Paul and Dr. Linda Elder. Copyright © 2003 by The Foundation for Critical Thinking, www.criticalthinking.org. Reprinted with permission.

Critical thinkers routinely apply the intellectual standards to the elements of reasoning in order to develop intellectual traits.

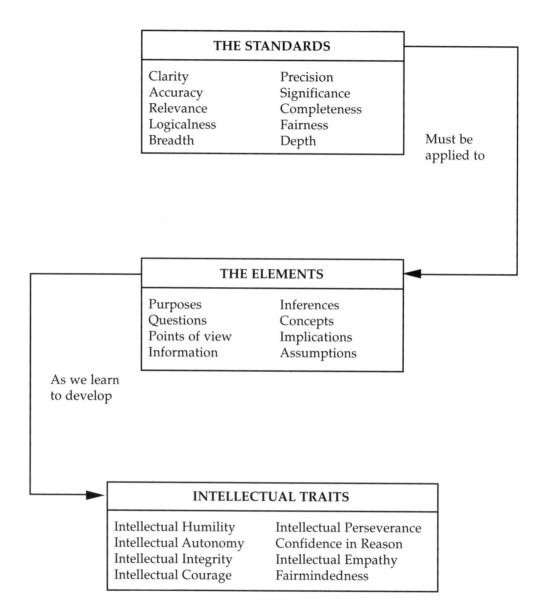

THE STANDARDS

Clarity   Precision
Accuracy   Significance
Relevance   Completeness
Logicalness   Fairness
Breadth   Depth

Must be applied to

THE ELEMENTS

Purposes   Inferences
Questions   Concepts
Points of view   Implications
Information   Assumptions

As we learn to develop

INTELLECTUAL TRAITS

Intellectual Humility   Intellectual Perseverance
Intellectual Autonomy   Confidence in Reason
Intellectual Integrity   Intellectual Empathy
Intellectual Courage   Fairmindedness

From *The Miniature Guide to Critical Thinking Concepts & Tools*, 3rd edition by Dr. Richard Paul and Dr. Linda Elder. Copyright © 2003 by The Foundation for Critical Thinking, www.criticalthinking.org. Reprinted with permission.

■ Stages of Critical Thinking Development

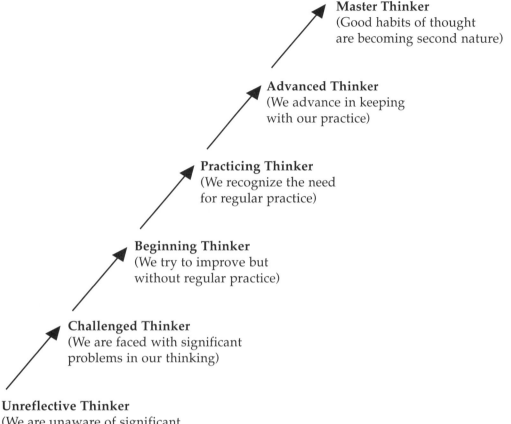

Master Thinker
(Good habits of thought
are becoming second nature)

Advanced Thinker
(We advance in keeping
with our practice)

Practicing Thinker
(We recognize the need
for regular practice)

Beginning Thinker
(We try to improve but
without regular practice)

Challenged Thinker
(We are faced with significant
problems in our thinking)

Unreflective Thinker
(We are unaware of significant
problems in our thinking)

■ Critical Thinking and Logic

You have probably heard someone say, "Everybody is entitled to his or her opinion." That may be true; your opinions reflect your interests, values, needs, and experiences, but not all opinions are equal. Would you rather have the opinion of a wise person or the opinion of a fool? What makes the wise person wise and the fool foolish? Which one do you want designing your car or running your government? How can you form wise opinions?

Critical thinkers—or wise people and problem solvers—share the following characteristics:

1. *Critical thinkers separate thought from feeling.* They are able to step away from their emotions and decide when to use their intellects.

    The baby in the tire commercial may make them feel warm and cozy, but they still check out the data before they decide which brand to buy.

2. *Critical thinkers gather the best evidence.* They know that the college library is a better source of information than the *National Enquirer,* that several good sources are better than one, and that direct evidence is better than hearsay.

From *The Miniature Guide to Critical Thinking Concepts & Tools,* 3rd edition by Dr. Richard Paul and Dr. Linda Elder. Copyright © 2003 by The Foundation for Critical Thinking, www.criticalthinking.org. Reprinted with permission.

If they want to know about Vietnam, they talk to Vietnam veterans and read books written by experts. If they want to know about nursing, they talk to nurses and nursing instructors and read professional publications.

3. *Critical thinkers separate fact from opinion.* Facts can be proved or disproved. Opinions are value judgements. Valid opinions are based on facts, on logic, or on the opinions of experts.

   '"Tiger Woods is a great golfer," and "Tiger Woods is cute," are both opinions. The first statement has greater validity because it is the opinion of Arnold Palmer and Jack Nicklaus, both experts on golf. "Tigers Woods won the 1997 Masters tournament," is a fact. It can be proved.

4. *Critical thinkers are skeptical.* Young children believe everything they hear (or read). Critical thinkers think for themselves and require good evidence. Even when they agree with an idea, they say, "Prove it!" Even more important, they are willing to examine their own ideas for error and self-correction.

   Columbus didn't really discover America, and Lincoln didn't really free the slaves. Don't take my word for it; check it out.

5. *Critical thinkers recognize biases, including their own biases, and make allowances.* Our beliefs and experiences make us all biased, but when we recognize our biases we can guard against being ruled by them. When we recognize other people's biases, we can "take what they say with a grain of salt."

   We don't expect the president of General Motors to drive a Honda.

6. *Critical thinkers don't over-simplify.* They are flexible and aware that most issues are many-sided. They are open-minded, objective, and willing to test their assumptions.

   It just may not be true that the world would be a better place if we required all people to marry before they have children and to stay married for life.

7. *Critical thinkers choose their wording carefully.* They know that using the wrong word or the wrong syntax (word order) can completely change meaning. If they aren't certain they know what they want to say, they look it up.

   Look up *uninterested* and *disinterested* and *sanguine* and *sanguinary* to get some good examples of the difference a few letters can make.

8. *Critical thinkers are logical.* The connections between their ideas make sense. They don't believe that washing cars causes rain—or that wanting to make a lot of money is enough to make them rich. Critical thinkers avoid some common logical fallacies (flaws in their thinking).

Fallacies in Reasoning

As critical thinkers, it is important to be able to recognize fallacies in reasoning.[2] Fallacies are patterns of incorrect reasoning. Recognizing these fallacies can help you to avoid them in your thinking and writing. You can also be aware when others are using these fallacies to persuade you. They may use these fallacies for their own purpose, such as power or financial gain.

Appeal to Authority. It is best to make decisions based on reviewing the information and arguments and reaching our own conclusions. Sometimes we are encouraged to rely on experts for a recommendation because they have specialized information. Obviously,

---

[2] Information on fallacies in reasoning was adapted from the Institute for Teaching and Learning and their interactive Web site called Mission Critical: http://www.sjsu.edu/depts/itl/index.html

we need to have trust in the experts to accept their conclusions. However, when we cite some person as an authority in a certain area when they are not, we make an appeal to a questionable authority. For example, when a company uses famous sports figures to endorse a product (a particular brand of athletic shoes or breakfast cereal, for example), they are appealing to a questionable authority. Just because the athletes are famous, they are not experts in the product they are endorsing. They are endorsing the product to make sales and earn money. Notice the commercials you see on TV. Many of them are appeals to a questionable authority.

Jumping to Conclusions. When we jump to conclusions, we make hasty generalizations. For example, if a college student borrows money from a bank and does not pay it back, the manager of the bank may conclude that all college students are poor risks and refuse loans to other college students.

Making Generalizations. We make generalizations when we say that all members of a group are the same:

- All lawyers are greedy.
- All blondes are airheads.

Your occupation does not determine whether or not you are greedy, and the color of your hair does not determine your intelligence. Such thinking leads to harmful stereotypes and reasoning fallacies. Instead of generalizing, think of people as unique individuals.

Attacking the Person Rather than Discussing Issues. To distract attention from the issues, we often attack the person. For example, during the Clinton administration, much time was spent attacking the person rather than discussing the issues. Rather than focusing attention on health care and education, attention was focused on real estate deals and extramarital affairs. Political candidates today are routinely asked about personal issues such as extramarital affairs and drug use rather than focusing on political issues. Of course personal integrity in politicians is important, but attacking the person can serve as a smokescreen to direct attention away from important political issues. Critical thinkers need to avoid reacting emotionally to personalities and need to use logical thinking to analyze the issues.

Appeal to Common Belief. Just because it is a common belief does not mean that it is true. At one time people believed that the world was flat and that when you got to the edge of the earth, you would fall off. If you were to survey the people who lived in that period in history, the majority would have agreed that the earth was flat. A survey just tells us what people believe. The survey does not tell us what is true and accurate.

Common Practice. Appealing to common practice is the "everyone else is doing it" argument. Just because everyone else does it, doesn't mean that it is right. Here are some common examples of this fallacy:

- It is okay to cheat in school. Everyone else does it.
- It is okay to speed on the freeway. Everyone else does it.
- It is okay to cheat on your taxes. Everyone else does it.

Appeal to Tradition. Appeal to tradition is a variation of "everyone else is doing it." The appeal to tradition is "we've always done it that way." Just because that is the way it has always been done, doesn't mean it is the best way to do it. With this attitude, it is very difficult to make changes and improve our ways of doing things. While tradition is very important, it is open to question. For example, construction and automotive technology have traditionally been career choices for men, but not for women. When women tried to enter or work in these careers, there was resistance by those who did not want to change traditions. This resistance limited options for women.

Two Wrongs. In this fallacy, it is assumed that it is acceptable to do something because other people are doing something just as bad. For example, if someone cuts you off on the freeway, you may assume that it is acceptable to zoom ahead and cut in front of their car. The "two wrongs" fallacy has an element of retribution and getting back at the other person. The old saying "two wrongs do not make a right" applies in this situation.

The Slippery Slope or Domino Theory. The slippery slope or domino theory is best explained with an example. If I fail the test, I will fail class. If I fail this class, I will drop out of college. My parents will disown me and I will lose the respect of my friends. I will not be able to get a good job. I will start drinking and end up homeless. In this fallacy, the consequences of our actions are remotely possible and negative and are assumed to be certain. This thinking assumes that if we allow one thing to happen, we will be unable to stop a disastrous chain of events. These dire consequences are given to influence the decisions and change behavior. In this situation, it is important to evaluate these consequences. One does not necessarily lead to the other. If you fail the test, you could study and pass the next test. As a child you were probably cautioned about many slippery slopes in life:

- Brush your teeth or your teeth will fall out.
- Do your homework or you will never get into college and get a good job.
- If you don't make an "A" in this course, you will never be able to finish your education and get a good job, and you will end up starving to death in the gutter.

Wishful Thinking. In wishful thinking an extremely positive outcome, however remote, is proposed as a distraction from logical thinking. For example, a new sports stadium may be proposed. Extremely positive outcomes may be given, such as progress, downtown redevelopment, recreation, professional sports teams, increased revenue and creation of jobs. On the other hand "slippery slope" advocates may see increased taxes, lack of parking and neglect of other important social priorities such as education and shelter for the homeless. Neither position is correct if we assume that the outcomes are certain and automatic. Outcomes need to be evaluated realistically.

Appeal to Fear or Scare Tactics. Sometimes people use an emotion such as fear to interfere with rational thinking. I once saw a political commercial that showed wolves chasing a person through the forest. It was clearly designed to evoke fear in those who watched it. The message was to vote against a proposition to limit lawyers' fees. The idea was that if lawyers' fees were limited, the poor client would be a victim of limited legal services. Lawyers wanted to have the freedom to charge whatever they chose. The proposition was defeated and lawyers retained the right to charge exorbitant fees, resulting in higher insurance costs for everyone. The commercial used scare tactics to interfere with rational thinking.

Appeal to Pity. In an appeal to pity, emotion is used to replace logic. It is what is known as a "sob story." Some appeals to pity are legitimate and are used to request charity and empathy. However, the sob story uses emotion in place of reason to persuade and is often exaggerated. College faculties often hear sob stories from students having academic difficulties. Here are some examples:

- Please don't disqualify me from college. I failed all my classes because I was emotionally upset when my grandmother died.
- Please don't fail me in this class. If you fail me, my parents will kick me out of the house and I will not be able to get health insurance.

■ Please don't give me a speeding ticket. I have to get home right away. My cat is sick.

Appeal to Loyalty. Human beings are social creatures who enjoy being attached to a group. This fallacy involves acting according to the group's best interests without considering whether the actions are good or bad, right or wrong. An example is the saying, "My country, right or wrong." Critical thinkers consider whether the actions are right or wrong and do not support ideas just to support a group with which they identify. We can feel this loyalty to our friends, family, school, communities, teams and favorite musicians.

Peer pressure is related to the loyalty fallacy. With peer pressure, members of the group act in a certain way because they think members of the group act that way. Another variation to the loyalty fallacy is called "bandwagon." It involves supporting the group ideas just to be part of the group. This emotion is powerful when the group is perceived to be powerful or "cool." In elections, people often vote for the candidate that is perceived to be the most popular. If everyone else is voting for the candidate, the candidate must be the best. This is not necessarily true.

Appeal to Prejudice. A prejudice is judging groups of people or things positively or negatively, even if the facts do not agree with the judgment. A prejudice is based on a stereotype in which all members of a group are judged to be the same. By appealing to a prejudice, speakers seek to gain support for their causes. Listen for the appeal to prejudice in "hate" speeches or literature directed against different ethnicities, genders or sexual orientations.

Appeal to Vanity. An appeal to vanity is also known as "apple polishing." Using this strategy, the goal is to get agreement by paying compliments. Students who pay compliments to teachers and then ask for special treatment are engaging in "apple polishing."

Post Hoc Reasoning or False Causes. Post hoc reasoning has to do with cause and effect. It explains many superstitions. If I play a good game of golf whenever I wear a certain hat, I may conclude that the hat causes me to play a good golf game. If I lose my lucky hat, I may not be able to play golf as well. The hat is a false cause (or post hoc) for playing a good game of golf. I may feel more comfortable wearing my lucky hat, but it is a secondary reason for playing a good game. I play a good game of golf because I practice good golf skills and develop my self-confidence. In scientific research, care is taken to test for false causes. Just because an event regularly precedes another event, it may not be the cause of it. For example, when the barometer falls, it rains. The falling barometer does not cause the rain. A drop in atmospheric pressure causes the rain. If falling barometers caused the rain, we could all be rainmakers by adjusting our barometers.

Joanne has not made a bad grade since she started eating Wheaties for lunch, so eating cereal in the middle of the day must make people smart.

Red Herring or Straw Man (or Woman). Watch for this fallacy during election time. With this strategy the politician creates an image of someone else's statements, ideas or beliefs, much as we create a scarecrow to scare away the birds from the garden. For example, politicians accuse their opponents of being liberals and raising taxes. Maybe that is only part of the story. Maybe their opponents also voted for many tax-saving measures. When politicians or anyone else uses the straw man (or woman) fallacy, they are falsifying or oversimplifying. Use your critical thinking to identify the straw men or women (political opponent) during the next election. Of course you don't have to be a politician to use this strategy. People often use this strategy when they spread gossip or rumors about someone they want to discredit.

Ms. Q said that I was not eligible for the promotion because my computer skills were not strong enough. Ms. Q is a stuck-up @#$% who is older than dirt.

Burden of Proof. Burden of proof simply refers to the person who should provide the evidence for the truth of a statement. Generally the person making the statement is the one who should provide the evidence of the truth of the statement. However, the speaker may attempt to shift the burden of proof to another person to distract attention. Here is an example of shifting the burden of proof from the popular TV show, *The X-Files*:

Scully: Your sister was abducted by aliens? Mulder, that's ridiculous!
Mulder: Well, until you can prove it **didn't** happen, you'll just have to accept it as true.

Mulder shifts the burden of proof to Scully. If she can't prove it didn't happen, it must be true. It is actually Mulder who needs to prove that what he says is true. It is not up to Scully to provide the evidence for or against the possibility of alien abduction. Mulder is making the claim, and he needs to provide the evidence of the truth of his statement.

False Dilemma. This fallacy is called the "either-or fallacy" or the "black-and-white fallacy" because you think that you have to choose one option or the other. It assumes that there are only two choices for dealing with a problem. It doesn't allow for other possibilities. For example, think about this statement:

■ *My country, love it or leave it.*
■ *If you want to be healthy, you have to eat broccoli every day.*

In this statement you are presented with two opposite choices: love it or leave it. Are these the only options? Maybe if I disagree with my country's policies, I could work to change them or exercise my right to vote for a different political leader. Maybe I could leave my country and still love it. Most social issues today are so complex that we need to examine many options to find the best answers. When students say that they need an "A" grade or will drop the class, they are using the false dilemma fallacy. It is possible to earn other grades and make progress toward graduation. Critical thinkers are not limited by either-or choices, but look to find creative solutions.

Viruses of the Mind. No, it's not a real virus; it just acts like one. Viruses of the mind refer to beliefs for which hard evidence is lacking.[3] These beliefs survive like viruses in that they need a host to ensure their survival. Some person or group believes the idea and promotes it. The ideas jump from person to person, much like a virus. An example is the Heavensgate cult:

It all seems perfectly ludicrous: 39 people don their new sneakers, pack their flight bags and poison themselves in the solemn belief that a passing UFO will whisk them off to Wonderland.[4]

Cults and new millennium doomsday forecasters spread unorthodox and sometimes harmful beliefs with great fervor. These thoughts are perpetuated through mind control techniques. With mind control, members of a group are taught to suppress emotion and accept the ideas of the group in exchange for a sense of belonging. These groups survive because they do not allow members to think critically or question the belief system. Mind control is the opposite of critical thinking. It is important to use critical thinking about beliefs for which there is no hard evidence.

---

[3] Geoffrey Cowley, "Viruses of the Mind: How Odd Ideas Survive," *Newsweek,* April 14, 1997, p. 14.
[4] Ibid.

Tips for Critical Thinking

1. Beware of your mind-set. A mind-set is a pattern of thought that you use like a habit. You develop these patterns of thinking based on your personal experiences, culture and environment. When the situation changes, your old mind-set may need to be changed.

2. Be willing to say, "I don't know." With this attitude you are open to explore new ideas. In today's rapidly changing world, it is not possible to know everything. Rather than trying to know everything, it is more important to be able to find the information you need.

3. Practice tolerance for other people's ideas. We all have a different view of the world based on our own experiences and can benefit from an open exchange of information.

   If there is any secret of success, it lies in the ability to get the other person's point of view and see things from his angle as well as from your own.

   —*Henry Ford*

4. Try to look for several answers and understand many points of view. Remember the false dilemma fallacy of reasoning? The world is not either-or, or black-and-white. Looking at all the possibilities is the first step in a creative solution.

5. Understand before criticizing. Life is not about justifying your point of view. It is important to understand and then offer your suggestions.

6. Realize that your emotions get in the way of clear thinking. We all have beliefs that are important to us. It is difficult to listen to a different point of view when someone questions your personal beliefs that you consider important. Open your mind to see all the alternatives. Then construct your reasonable view.

7. Examine the source and outlook of the message. If the material downplays the hazards of smoking to your health but is written by the tobacco industry, you will gain some insight about the message and motivation of the authors. Political announcements require that information about the person or organizations paying for the ad be provided. Knowing who paid for the advertisement helps you to understand the point of view that is being promoted.

8. Ask the question, "What makes the author think so?" In this way you can discover what premises the author uses to justify his or her position.

9. Ask the question, "So what?" Ask this question to determine what is important and how the author reached the conclusion.

Critical Thinking over the Internet

The Internet is revolutionizing the way we access and retrieve information today. Through the use of search engines, Web sites, electronic periodicals and online reference, it is possible to find just about any information you need. The Internet is also full of scams, rumors, gossip, hoaxes, exaggerations, and illegal activity. Anyone can put anything on the Internet. You will need to apply critical thinking to the information that you find on the Internet.

Author Reid Goldsborough offers suggestions for thinking critically over the Internet:[5]

The ability to think critically about information found on the Internet is a crucial component of SCC's Information Literacy Outcome.

- ■ Don't be fooled by appearance. It is easy to create a flashy and professional-looking web site. Everyone is jumping on the e-commerce bandwagon. Some products or services are legitimate, but some are scams.
- ■ Find out about the person or organization providing the information. There should be links to a home page that lists the author's background and credentials. You need to be skeptical if the author is not identified. If you cannot identify the person who authored the web site, find out what organization sponsored the site. Most of the Internet resources in this text are from educational or government sources. It is the goal of these organizations to provide the public with information.
- ■ Look for the reason the information was posted. What is the agenda? Keep this in mind when evaluating the information. It is the agenda of many web sites to sell a product or influence public opinion.
- ■ Look for the date that the information was created or revised. A good web site posts the date of creation or revision because links become outdated quickly.
- ■ Try to verify the information elsewhere, especially if the information does not match common sense or is at odds with what you believe. Verify the information through other web sites or your local library.

■ Success over the Internet

A web site called Mission Critical was developed to assist college teachers and students understand and apply concepts of critical thinking required in all college-level courses in California. It contains an interactive tutorial on the principles of critical thinking and has exercises to practice these concepts.

http://www.sjsu.edu/depts/itl/index.html

Visit Mindtools to learn more about techniques to think excellently:
http://www.mindtools.com/

To learn more about the core concepts of critical thinking, visit:
http://www.kcmetro.cc.mo.us/longview/ctac/corenotes.htm
http://www.criticalthinking.org/articles/index.cfm

---

[5] Reid Goldsborough, "Teaching Healthy Skepticism about Information on the Internet," *Technology and Learning*, January, 1998.

■ Activity: Critical Thinking Activity: Assisted Suicide

DIRECTIONS: The critical thinking exercises in this chapter are presented as a way to practice the process of critical thinking. These issues are **controversial** and complex. There are many different views and **there is no right answer;** there is only your reasonable view. Read the following summary of a news article on the topic of assisted suicide. Use the following worksheet to construct your reasonable view. You may want to discuss these issues with groups of students in your class.

The following is a summary of a news article about a man who killed his terminally ill wife.[6]

A man was ordered to face a murder trial for the killing of his wife who was suffering from Lou Gehrig's disease as well as severe heart disease. As a result of this disease, she could not talk or walk and had to be fed through a tube in her abdomen. One day, his wife managed to scrawl a note in which she asked her husband of 48 years to kill her. The husband was described as a loving spouse who was devoted to caring for his wife. The man gave his wife an injection of ground-up sleeping pills. The wife became unconscious after the sleeping pills were administered, but she did not die. The distraught husband carried his wife to the car where he attached a vacuum-cleaner hose to the exhaust pipe and ran it into the car. He also got into the car, along with the family pets, intending to kill his wife, himself and the pets. After 12 hours, the man woke up to find his wife and one of the family pets dead. The level of carbon monoxide in the wife's blood was not high enough to kill a healthy person, but enough to kill his frail wife.

The man was ordered to stand trial for killing his wife. His lawyer argued that it was a crime of "passion and compassion." The prosecution said that what the man did was illegal and that he should be sent to jail. Assisted suicide is a source of debate across the country. In Oregon, there is a law called "Death with Dignity."[7] This law allows a doctor to prescribe a lethal dose of barbiturates to patients who have less than six months to live. In 1999, twenty-seven people, who were mostly elderly cancer patients, died under this law.

Was the man described above guilty of murder? Should he go to jail? What were the man's values? Should laws be changed to allow assisted suicide? Look at the different points of view and examine your own values to construct your reasonable point of view.

---

[6] Harry Jones, "Man Ordered to Face Murder Trial in the Killing of His Invalid Wife," *The San Diego Union Tribune*, Thursday, January 13, 2000.

[7] "27 Died under Oregon Suicide Law," *The San Diego Union Tribune*, Thursday, February 24, 2000.

■ Activity: Critical Thinking Worksheet: Assisted Suicide

DIRECTIONS: Use the summary of the news article on assisted suicide to complete this worksheet. Discuss the issues with groups of students in your class. Remember that there is no right answer, only your reasonable view.

Checklist for Reasoning

1. Think about **purpose**.
2. State the **question**.
3. Gather **information**.
4. Check your **assumptions**.
5. Clarify your **concepts**.
6. Understand your **point of view**.
7. Watch your **inferences**.
8. Think through the **implications**.

---

1. What was the husband's purpose in killing his wife? What was the wife's purpose in writing the note? What are the lawyers' purposes?

2. What is the question we are trying to answer here? Is this question clear? Is it complex? What kind of question is this: Historical? Ethical? Political? Economic? Or . . . ? What information do we need to answer this question?

3. What other important questions are embedded in this issue?

4. Do we need to gather more information? (Have we left out any important information that we need to consider?) If so, what information do we need? Where could we find it?

5. How do we know this information is accurate?

6. What are we taking for granted? Are we assuming something we shouldn't? Why are we assuming this?

7. What did the husband assume? The defense attorney? The prosecution?

8. What idea(s) are the key players (husband, wife, defense, prosecution) using in their thinking about this issue? What are the main concepts here? How do we define those concepts? How would the key players define those concepts?

9. How are we looking at this situation? Is there another way to look at it that we should consider? Is our view the only reasonable view? What does our point of view ignore?

10. What is the viewpoint of the husband? The wife? The defense attorney? The prosecutor?

11. After carefully considering the information here, what could we conclude? Is the man guilty of murder? Should laws be changed to allow assisted suicide? Are those conclusions logical?

12. Are there other plausible conclusions we should consider? What conclusions did the husband, wife, defense attorney, and prosecutor reach?

13. Given all of the facts, what is the best possible conclusion? Why is it the best?

14. What are the implications and consequences of our conclusions? Of the wife's conclusions? The husband's? The defense attorney's? The prosecutor's?

***

After analyzing the issue, what is your reasonable conclusion? Was the husband guilty of murder? Should he go to jail? Should laws be changed to allow assisted suicide? State your final conclusion and explain your reasoning. Keep the intellectual standards (clarity, accuracy, precision, relevance, etc.) in mind as you write your answer.

■ Critical Thinking Activity: The Problem of Egocentric Thinking

1. What is egocentric thinking? Why is it a problem? Explain, in your own words, the concept of egocentrism. *Egocentrism is . . .*

2. Elaborate on your explanation: *In other words. . .*

3. Identify a situation you were recently in that, in looking back on the situation, you realize you were probably irrational. Go through each of the elements of your reasoning and determine where your thinking was egocentric. Try to be as honest as you possibly can, remembering that our egocentrism is always ready to deceive us. Complete the following statements:

   The situation was as follows (describe the situation):

   In this situation my purpose was . . .

   The key question I was posing was . . .

   The main information I used in my reasoning was . . .

   The key concepts I was using in my thinking were . . .

   The main assumptions I was using in my thinking were . . .

   The point of view from which I was reasoning was . . .

   The main conclusions I came to were . . .

   The implications that followed from my thinking were . . .

   Read through your responses to the statements above. In which areas of your thinking did you display egocentrism? (In other words, did you use information in an egocentric way? Was your purpose egocentric? What other elements of your thinking were irrational?) Explain your answers.

4. *Intellectual Traits*: Explain how a lack of one or more of the intellectual traits (intellectual humility, intellectual courage, intellectual empathy, fairmindedness, etc.) may have impacted your thinking about the situation you described in the previous question. Do you see any of the traits' opposites in your irrational thinking? For example, could closed-mindedness have played a role in that you were not being empathetic in considering another point of view? Could intellectual arrogance have played a role?

■ Critical Thinking Activity: Logic

Critical thinkers are logical. One of the standards for good thinking is logic: When we think, we bring a variety of thoughts together into some order. When the combination of thoughts is mutually supporting and makes sense in combination, the thinking is "logical." When the combination is not mutually supporting, is contradictory in some sense, or does not "make sense," the combination is not "logical."

As critical thinkers, it is important, then, to be able to recognize fallacies in reasoning. Fallacies are patterns of incorrect or illogical reasoning: When you add up the information used to reach a conclusion, it doesn't make sense.

Read through the fallacies in your ACA textbook. Look through magazines or watch television commercials to find advertisements that illustrate one or more of the fallacies. Advertisements are actually short arguments (often in visual form) with the ultimate objective of persuading you to buy a product or service. After you choose an advertisement, complete the following:

1. Write a description of the commercial or print advertisement. Be clear and precise in your description. If you choose a print advertisement, bring it with you to class.

2. Explain how the advertisement's argument is illogical. Identify and explain at least one fallacy at work in the ad. Use these questions to help you explain the advertisement's reasoning:

   ■ What is the advertisement trying to persuade you to do?

   ■ How does it make its argument? What information does the ad use? Is this information reliable, accurate? How do you know? (How would you find out?)

   ■ What are the key concepts in the ad? How would you define them? How are the concepts used to make the argument?

   ■ What are the assumptions? (What is taken for granted or presupposed?) Are they valid?

   ■ What is the ad's main conclusion? What reasons are given to support that conclusion? (Some reasons may be implied, not directly stated.) Is the conclusion logical, based on the reasons or evidence?

   ■ What is illogical about the reasoning in the advertisement? Does it rely on any fallacies to make its case?

3. Be prepared to explain your answers in class.

■ SCC Learning Outcomes and Rubrics

At Surry Community College, we want to help you improve your critical thinking skills. With the modern work environment requiring more thinking and problem solving than jobs of the past, individuals need to become more capable of reflective and critical thought. A common complaint is that entry-level employees lack the reasoning and critical thinking abilities needed to process and refine information. Our faculty will integrate critical thinking activities and projects into their teaching practices to better prepare you to function effectively in today's workforce and society. Ultimately, as a graduate of Surry Community College, you should be an effective problem solver—one who possesses and generates information to arrive at solutions.

In addition to critical thinking, we want to ensure that all SCC graduates gain several other core "learning outcomes." These college-wide learning outcomes are the learning goals identified as relevant for all Surry Community College students. The outcomes will be constantly reinforced throughout all curriculum courses, and you will be provided with opportunities to develop competency in each core outcome.

The college-wide learning outcomes are as follows:

> **Critical Thinking**: Students who graduate from Surry Community College should be able to think about their thinking in order to improve it. They should display competence in the cognitive skills and abilities that underlie critical thinking. Specifically, they should be able to (1) analyze thought by identifying, examining, and employing the essential elements of reasoning; (2) assess thought by applying intellectual standards; and (3) think ethically and fairly by cultivating intellectual traits. SCC students should be willing to adjust thinking and behavior based on the results of their reasoning.

> **Reading**: Students who graduate from Surry Community College should be able to read actively and analytically at the college level and should be able to synthesize and apply information across disciplines.

> **Writing**: Students who graduate from Surry Community College should be able to produce writing that is clear, precise, organized, incisive, and correct (according to the guidelines of Standard Written English) for a variety of purposes and audiences.

> **Speaking**: Students who graduate from Surry Community College should be able to speak in a manner that is clear, precise, coherent, perceptive, audience-aware, and correct in both small and large group settings.

> **Quantitative Literacy**: Students who graduate from Surry Community College should be able to apply college-level mathematical concepts and methods to understand, analyze, and communicate in quantitative terms.

> **Information Literacy**: Students who graduate from Surry Community College should be able to recognize when information is needed and have the ability to locate, evaluate, and effectively use the needed information.

Rubrics to assess all learning outcomes were developed by college faculty and staff. These rubrics appear on the following pages. Because these learning outcomes and their assessment play such an important role in your education at Surry Community College, you should become very familiar with them.

■ What Is a Rubric?

Pronounced RUE-brick, the word *rubric* comes from the Middle English word *rubrike*, which means "red ocher," and from the Latin *ruber*, which is the color red. Think of our English word *ruby*, a dark red gemstone. And think of the red pen students often associate with teachers' grading of their work—when teachers evaluate a student's work, sometimes they use a red pen so their comments and markings are easy to see.

We use the word *rubric* in education to refer to a **scoring device that differentiates levels of development in a specific area**. A rubric is a way to measure or assess your performance or development of a particular skill, such as your writing ability, your speaking ability, your thinking abilities, etc. A rubric, then, is much like the red-penned comments your teachers make when grading your work.

Rubrics help us assess or evaluate how well you demonstrate certain key skills. Instead of asking you to take a multiple-choice test on critical thinking, for example, we may ask you to **demonstrate** your thinking—to show us your thinking in action. The rubric we have developed to assess thinking helps us evaluate that demonstration.

A rubric communicates a precise explanation of "exemplary" or "satisfactory" or "unsatisfactory" work. A rubric can be scaled to a letter grade (such as an "A" or a "B") and can explain exactly why you earned a particular grade on a particular assignment. In other words, a rubric helps your instructor clarify exactly what an "A" means. A rubric shows you the target you are aiming for.

Your instructors at Surry may use modified versions of the rubrics included in this textbook. Whenever you are asked to complete a project or assignment (speech, paper, proposal, etc.), you should ask your instructor how the final product will be graded. He or she should be able to produce a rubric or a set of explanations that describe an excellent product, an above-average product, an average product, and so on.

How to Read a Rubric

When looking at the rubric, **first examine the categories used to organize the rubric**. With the speaking rubric, you will see the categories of "clear," "precise," "coherent," "perceptive," "audience-aware," and "correct." The critical thinking rubric is a little more complex. Look at the left-most, shaded column on the critical thinking "grid," and you see categories organized by element of thought: purpose, key question, point of view, etc. You will also see that the rubric is further organized across the top by performance level.

Second, review the explanations/descriptions for each performance level: "exemplary," "satisfactory," etc. For example, the speaking rubric gives a detailed description of an exemplary speech:

> The goal of the speech was clear. The speaker had high-quality and accurate information or material and used a variety of kinds of development with visual aids and/or vivid language to meet the audience's interests, knowledge, and attitudes. The introduction had an attention-getter; main points were easy to follow, coherent; the closure was solid. The language was appropriate, clear, vivid, and emphatic. Delivery was excellent!

You can go on to read similarly precise descriptions of a "satisfactory" speech, a "below satisfactory" speech, etc.

The same is true of the critical thinking rubric. Take a look at the brief descriptions at the bottom of the grid. Exemplary thinking is described as thinking that is:

> skilled, marked by excellence in clarity, accuracy, precision, relevance, depth, breadth, logicality, and fairness.

You can go on to read descriptions of "satisfactory" thinking and so on. Next, look at the column labeled "4—Exemplary": Fold or cover up the page so that all you see is that one column. Reading *down* the column will give you a more detailed description of excellent thinking:

> Demonstrates a clear understanding of the assignment's purpose
>
> Clearly defines the issue or problem; accurately identifies the core issues
> Appreciates depth and breadth of the problem
>
> Demonstrates fairmindedness toward the problem
>
> Identifies and evaluates relevant significant points of view, and so on.

This is a precise picture of good thinking. You can repeat the exercise with each column: Fold or cover the page so that only the "3—Satisfactory" column is visible. Now, read *down* the column to get a clear picture of satisfactory thinking.

You can also read *across* the rows to single out one element. For example, look at *concepts*: Reading across that row reveals the differences in performance related to a writer's understanding and use of concepts in his/her thinking. You can repeat this with each element.

Note: Use the same process to review the writing rubric: Examine the categories used to organize the rubric and review the descriptions for each performance level. Check with your instructor if you have questions about any of these rubrics.

How to Score a Product (Speech, Paper, etc.) Using the Rubrics

Each rubric asks you to first score individual categories before arriving at an overall final score.

Speaking: On the speaking "worksheet," the evaluator provides a score for each category using a 0–5 scale for each item. Five would be the most a speaker could earn for each category. For example, if you thought the speaker did an excellent job of stating the goal of the presentation, you would give the speaker five points. If the speaker did not state a purpose at all, then you would assign zero points for that item.

Add all of those scores to get the final, overall score of "exemplary," "satisfactory," etc.

Critical Thinking: On the critical thinking "worksheet," you score each category (each element of thought) using a 1–4 scale. For example, you would give the writer a score of four for "purpose" if you felt the writer demonstrated a clear understanding of the assignment's purpose, and did so with excellent precision and clarity, accuracy, etc. (review the explanations of 1–4 at the bottom of the worksheet).

Add the score for each category and then divide by the number of elements scored to get the final, overall score. The writing rubric follows the same scoring process.

The Benefits of Rubrics

With practice and careful attention, you can use rubrics to help you evaluate your own work, and your classmates' work before you ever submit it to your instructor. An educated person should be able to self-assess and self-correct—to identify his or her own strengths and weaknesses and to determine a plan for improving weak areas. After all, you won't always have an instructor hanging around to provide feedback and give you a grade. Rubrics help you learn the art of self-monitoring.

Rubrics will help you better understand your instructor's final evaluation of your work, too. If you don't understand why you earned the grade you did on a speech, paper, or project, respectfully ask your instructor for more feedback, so that you can learn from the experience to improve your skills. That's the ultimate goal of your education, right? You should learn from every assignment. Think of every assignment as a learning experience—not simply as a requirement to pass a course and earn a degree. Rubrics help you understand the target you were trying to hit and show you where you may have fallen short of that target.

Employers value graduates who can think well, speak well, write well, and read well. Surry Community College is committed to helping every student in every program improve and refine thinking and communication skills. Our rubrics show you what you should be aiming for, striving toward, as you work on improving these important life skills.

What follows are the outcome statements for each learning outcome, along with the actual rubrics and worksheets.

■ Critical Thinking Outcome

Students who graduate from Surry Community College will think about their thinking in order to improve it. They will display competence in the cognitive skills and abilities that underlie critical thinking. Specifically, they will be able (1) to analyze thought (their own and that of others) by identifying, examining, and employing the essential elements of reasoning; (2) to assess thought by applying intellectual standards; and (3) to think ethically and fairly by cultivating intellectual traits. SCC students will be willing to adjust thinking and behavior based on the results of their reasoning.

The following elements of reasoning and intellectual standards govern the critical thinking outcome:

Elements of Reasoning

- Purpose
- Key Question, Problem, or Issue
- Point of View
- Information
- Concepts
- Assumptions
- Interpretations and Inferences
- Implications and Consequences

Intellectual Standards

- Clarity
- Accuracy
- Precision
- Relevance
- Depth
- Breadth
- Logic
- Significance
- Fairness

Artifacts are to be evaluated to determine whether the student has satisfactorily demonstrated the cognitive skills comprised of the elements and standards as applicable in the context of the assignment. See the *critical thinking grid* for a detailed description of *exemplary, satisfactory, below satisfactory* and *unsatisfactory* artifacts.

4 *Exemplary* thinking is skilled, marked by excellence in clarity, accuracy, precision, relevance, depth, breadth, logicality, and fairness

3 *Satisfactory* thinking is competent, effective, accurate and clear, but lacks the exemplary depth, precision, and insight of a 4

2 *Unsatisfactory* thinking is inconsistent, ineffective; shows a lack of consistent competence: is often unclear, imprecise, inaccurate, and superficial

1 *Below Satisfactory* thinking is unskilled and insufficient, marked by imprecision, lack of clarity, superficiality, illogicality, inaccuracy, and unfairness

A Critical Thinker Can Do the Following:

———— demonstrate a clear understanding of the assignment's purpose

———— clearly define the issue or problem

———— accurately identify the core issues

———— appreciate depth and breadth of the problem

———— demonstrate fair-mindedness toward the problem

———— identify and evaluate relevant significant points of view

———— examine relevant points of view fairly, empathetically

———— gather sufficient, credible, relevant information: observations, statements, logic, data, facts, questions, graphs, themes, assertions, descriptions, etc.

———— include information that opposes as well as supports the argued position

———— distinguish between information and inferences drawn from that information

———— identify and accurately explain/use relevant key concepts

———— accurately identify assumptions (things taken for granted)

———— make assumptions that are consistent, reasonable, and valid

———— follow where evidence and reason lead in order to obtain defensible, thoughtful, logical conclusions or solutions

———— make deep rather than superficial inferences

———— make inferences that are consistent with each other

———— identify the most significant implications and consequences of the reasoning (whether positive and/or negative)

———— distinguish probable from improbable implications

Critical Thinking Grid

	4—Exemplary	3—Satisfactory	2—Below Satisfactory	1—Unsatisfactory
	If applicable, consistently does all or almost all of the following	If applicable, consistently does most or many of the following	If applicable, consistently does most or many of the following	If applicable, consistently does all or almost all of the following
Purpose	—Demonstrates a clear understanding of the assignment's purpose	—Demonstrates an understanding of the assignment's purpose	—Is not completely clear about the purpose of the assignment	—Does not clearly understand the purpose of the assignment
Key Question, Problem, or Issue	—Clearly defines the issue or problem; accurately identifies the core issues —Appreciates depth and breadth of problem —Demonstrates fair-mindedness toward problem	—Defines the issue; identifies the core issues, but may not fully explore their depth and breadth —Demonstrates fair-mindedness	—Defines the issue, but poorly (superficially, narrowly); may overlook some core issues —Has trouble maintaining a fair-minded approach toward the problem	—Fails to clearly define the issue or problem; does not recognize the core issues —Fails to maintain a fair-minded approach toward the problem
Point of View	—Identifies and evaluates relevant significant points of view —Is empathetic, fair in examining all relevant points of view —Distinguishes between source's point of view and student's point of view	—Identifies and evaluates relevant points of view —Is fair in examining those views —Clearly delineates between source's point of view and student's point of view	—May identify other points of view but struggles with maintaining fairmindedness; may focus on irrelevant or insignificant points of view; may fail to delineate between authors' perspective and student's	—Ignores or superficially evaluates alternate points of view —Cannot separate own vested interests and feelings when evaluating other points of view
Information	—Gathers sufficient, credible, relevant information: observations, statements, logic, data, facts, questions, graphs, themes, assertions, descriptions, etc. —Includes information that opposes as well as supports the argued position —Distinguishes between information and inferences drawn from that information	—Gathers sufficient, credible, and relevant information —Includes some information from opposing views —Distinguishes between information and inferences drawn from it	—Gathers some credible information, but not enough; some information may be irrelevant —Omits significant information, including some strong counter-arguments —Sometimes confuses information and the inferences drawn from it	—Relies on insufficient, irrelevant, or unreliable information —Fails to identify or hastily dismisses strong, relevant counter-arguments —Confuses information and inferences drawn from that information
Concepts	—Identifies and accurately explains/uses the relevant key concepts	—Identifies and accurately explains and uses the key concepts, but not with the depth and precision of a "4"	—Identifies some (not all) key concepts, but use of concepts is superficial and inaccurate at times	—Misunderstands key concepts or ignores relevant key concepts altogether

(continued)

■ Critical Thinking Grid (continued)

	4—Exemplary If applicable, consistently does all or almost all of the following	3—Satisfactory If applicable, consistently does most or many of the following	2—Below Satisfactory If applicable, consistently does most or many of the following	1—Unsatisfactory If applicable, consistently does all or almost all of the following
Assumptions	—Accurately identifies assumptions (things taken for granted) —Makes assumptions that are consistent, reasonable, valid	—Identifies assumptions —Makes valid assumptions	—May identify assumptions, but the assumptions identified are irrelevant, not clearly stated, and/or invalid	—Fails to identify assumptions —Makes invalid assumptions
Interpretations, Inferences	—Follows where evidence and reason lead in order to obtain defensible, thoughtful, logical conclusions or solutions —Makes deep rather than superficial inferences —Makes inferences that are consistent with one another	—Follows where evidence and reason lead to obtain justifiable, logical conclusions —Makes valid inferences, but not with the same depth as a "4"	—Does follow some evidence to conclusions, but inferences are more often than not unclear, illogical, inconsistent, and/or superficial	—Uses superficial, simplistic, or irrelevant reasons and unjustifiable claims —Makes illogical, inconsistent inferences —Exhibits closed-mindedness or hostility to reason; regardless of the evidence, maintains or defends views based on self-interest
Implications, Consequences	—Identifies the most significant implications and consequences of the reasoning (whether positive and/or negative) —Distinguishes probable from improbable implications	—Identifies significant implications and consequences and distinguishes probable from improbable implications, but not with the same insight and precision as a "4"	—Has trouble identifying significant implications and consequences; identifies improbable implications	—Ignores significant implications and consequences of reasoning

4 = Thinking is exemplary, skilled, marked by excellence in clarity, accuracy, precision, relevance, depth, breadth, logicality, and fairness

3 = Thinking is competent, effective, accurate and clear, but lacks the exemplary depth, precision, and insight of a 4

2 = Thinking is inconsistent, ineffective; shows a lack of consistent competence; is often unclear, imprecise, inaccurate, and superficial

1 = Thinking is unskilled and insufficient, marked by imprecision, lack of clarity, superficiality, illogicality, inaccuracy, and unfairness

Name: _____   Date: _____

■ Critical Thinking Worksheet

If applicable, score the element (1–4)	Element of Reasoning	Comments
	Purpose: Does the student demonstrate a clear understanding of the assignment's purpose?	
	Key Question, Problem, or Issue: Does the student clearly define the issue or problem, accurately identify the core issues, appreciate their depth and breadth?	
	Point of View: Does the student identify and evaluate relevant significant points of view? Does the student demonstrate fairmindedness toward the problem? Does the student distinguish between his/her point of view and the source's point of view?	
	Information: Does the student gather sufficient, credible, relevant information (statements, logic, data, facts, questions, graphs, assertions, observations, etc.)? Does the student include information that opposes as well as supports the argued position? Does the student distinguish between information and inferences drawn from that information?	
	Concepts: Does the student identify and accurately explain/use the relevant key concepts?	
	Assumptions: Does the student accurately identify assumptions (things taken for granted)? Does the student make assumptions that are consistent, reasonable, valid?	
	Interpretations, Inferences: Does the student follow where evidence and reason lead in order to obtain defensible, thoughtful, logical conclusions or solutions? Does the student make deep (rather than superficial) inferences? Are the inferences consistent?	
	Implications, Consequences: Does the student identify the most significant implications and consequences? Does the student distinguish probable from improbable implications?	

4 = Thinking is exemplary, skilled, marked by excellence in clarity, accuracy, precision, relevance, depth, breadth, logicality, and fairness

3 = Thinking is competent, effective, accurate and clear, but lacks the exemplary depth, precision, and insight of a 4

2 = Thinking is inconsistent, ineffective; shows a lack of consistent competence; is often unclear, imprecise, inaccurate, and superficial

1 = Thinking is unskilled and insufficient, marked by imprecision, lack of clarity, superficiality, illogicality, inaccuracy, and unfairness

■ Communication: Reading Outcome

OUTCOME STATEMENT: SCC graduates should be able to read actively and analytically at the college level and synthesize and apply information across disciplines.

RUBRIC: The Reading outcome consists of three major competencies (Comprehension, Analysis, and Synthesis). Achievement of the major competencies is determined by using a four-point scale. The SCC standard for proficiency is a score of "3-Satisfactory" or "4-Exemplary." Proficiency is determined by the following rubric guidelines:

Exemplary (4)	Exceeds the standard; response is excellent/skilled.
Satisfactory (3)	Meets the standard; response is competent/effective.
Below Satisfactory (2)	Approaches the standard; response shows lack of consistent competence.
Unsatisfactory (1)	Below the standard; response is unskilled and insufficient.

READING COMPETENCIES: The reading rubric measures the following skills. Students should be able to:

1. Comprehend ideas and supporting details of college-level reading materials by:
   a. identifying the key question the author is addressing
   b. identifying the author's main purpose for writing the text
   c. identifying the key concepts/theme of the text
   d. distinguishing between facts and opinions that may be presented in the text

2. Analyze college-level reading materials in order to interpret content by:
   a. identifying the main conclusions of the text
   b. identifying inferences that could be made from reading the text
   c. summarizing the point of view represented in the text
   d. identifying the implications/consequences of applying the text to real-life situations

3. Synthesize components of college-level reading materials by:
   a. explaining the relevance of textual evidence to the key concepts/theme
   b. using text evidence to explain author's tone, style, bias, or assumptions
   c. using text evidence to explain the logic of the author's argument

Name: _____ Date: _____

Reading Worksheet   ID Code _____   Score _____

If applicable, score the competency (1–4)	Reading Competencies	Comments
▯▯▯▯	**Comprehension:** Comprehends ideas and supporting details of college-level reading materials by: identifying the key question the author is addressing identifying the author's main purpose for writing the text identifying the key concepts/theme of the text distinguishing between facts and opinions that may be presented in the text	
▯▯▯▯	**Analysis:** Analyzes college-level reading materials in order to interpret content by: identifying the main conclusions of the text identifying inferences that could be made from reading the text summarizing the point of view represented in the text identifying the implications/consequences of applying the text to real-life situations	
▯▯▯	**Synthesis:** Synthesizes components of college-level reading materials by: explaining the relevance of textual evidence to the key concepts/theme using text evidence to explain author's tone, style, bias, or assumptions using text evidence to explain the logic of the author's argument	

4 = Exemplary: Exceeds the standard; response is excellent/skilled.
3 = Satisfactory: Meets the standard; response is competent/effective.
2 = Below Satisfactory: Approaches the standard; response shows a lack of consistent competence.
1 = Unsatisfactory: Below the standard; response is unskilled and insufficient.

■ Communication: Writing Outcome

OUTCOME STATEMENT: Students who graduate from Surry Community College should be able to produce writing that is clear, precise, organized, incisive, and correct (according to the guidelines of Standard Written English) for a variety of purposes and audiences.

To be more specific, students who graduate from SCC should be able to produce writing that is clear, accurate, precise, relevant, deep, broad, logical, meaningful, fair, and correct for a variety of purposes and audiences.

RUBRIC: This rubric uses a four-point scale. SCC has stated that it wants its students to be "exemplary" or "satisfactory" writers.

Exemplary:	4 = *All* the *applicable* standards are skillfully demonstrated; the writing is particularly marked by excellence in depth, insight, and expression
Satisfactory:	3 = *Most* of the applicable standards are competently and effectively demonstrated, but the writing lacks the exemplary depth and insight of a 4
Below Satisfactory:	2 = *Some* of the applicable standards are demonstrated, but there is a lack of consistent competence; writing is marked by mixed thinking and ineffective expression
Unsatisfactory:	1 = *A few* of the applicable standards are demonstrated, but poorly; writing is marked by a low level of reasoning and expression

TEN WRITING STANDARDS: These writing standards can be used to measure student writing.

Clear: understandable, concise
Do you know exactly what the writer means or could there be several ways to interpret the paper/paragraph/sentence? Does the writer need to refine word choice, add examples, or elaborate to clarify ideas?

Accurate: free of errors or distortions
Does the content conform to fact? Can the statements be verified or tested? Does the writer attempt to verify/test statements for the reader?

Precise: specific, exact to the necessary level of detail
Is the writing specific and focused? Is the wording exact?

Relevant: clearly connected to the matter at hand
Is all the information relevant to the paper's thesis and purpose? Does every paragraph, every sentence, example, etc., clearly connect to the paper's focus and purpose?

Deep: intellectually complex, open to multiple interrelationships and complexities
Has the writer addressed the complexities of the topic? Has the writer acknowledged related difficulties and dealt with them reasonably? Has the writer tried to get at the key issue? Has the writer oversimplified a complex situation, issue, problem, or question?

Broad: open to multiple relevant viewpoints (while still being focused)
Has the writer examined all the relevant concepts, issues, and perspectives? Has the writer accounted for/justified any necessary narrowing?

Logical: combining thoughts that are mutually supporting and that make sense in combination; free of contradictions and fallacies
Do the paper's conclusions follow logically from its points? Do the points follow logically from the evidence? Does the first paragraph fit in with the last? Does it all make

sense together? Is there a logical chain of reasons to support the point? Are there gaps in the reasoning? Are there fallacies?

Significant: notable, thoughtful, focused on the most important information and ideas
Has the writer considered the most important points, problems, questions, etc.? Is discussion absent that ought to be included? Does the writer address the prompt (if a prompt is given)? If the writer has addressed the prompt and is allowed or asked to choose a focus, is that focus meaningful?

Fair: not merely self-serving or one-sided; consistent with ethics
Does the writer sympathetically or fairly present the views of others? If the assignment calls for sources, has the writer acknowledged those sources clearly and fully and delineated between borrowed and original ideas? Does the writer ignore other perspectives? Does the writer rely on his/her biases to the exclusion of other viewpoints?

Correct: free from errors in grammar, punctuation, spelling, and usage; appropriate and effective in style, tone, and vocabulary; consistent in following requirements
Are grammar, punctuation, spelling, and usage correct? (Do those features conform to the rules of Standard Written English—and if they do not, have the rules been broken for effective reasons?) Are vocabulary, tone, and style effective and appropriate for the chosen purpose and audience? Does the writing follow the expected requirements?

(All but the last criterion are adapted from Richard Paul and Linda Elder's "Intellectual Standards," *The Miniature Guide to Critical Thinking Concepts and Tools*, pp. 7–9. Paul and Elder's questions have been modified and expanded to make them more appropriate for evaluating student writing.)

Name: _____   Date: _____

■ Writing Worksheet

Does the standard apply?	Writing Standard	Questions/Comments
	Clear: understandable, precise	Do you know exactly what the writer means?
	Accurate: free of errors or distortions	Does the content conform to fact?
	Precise: specific, exact to the necessary level of detail	Does the writer need to add details or be more exact?
	Relevant: clearly connected to the matter at hand	Is there anything here that doesn't belong? Is there extraneous discussion?
	Deep: taking into account the complexities of the topic	Has the writer addressed the complexities of the topic?
	Broad: open to multiple relevant viewpoints	Has the writer examined all the relevant issues?
	Logical: free of contradictions and fallacies	Are there gaps in reasoning? Are there fallacies?
	Significant: focused on the most important info	Are the most important points considered? Is discussion absent that ought to be included? Does the writer address the prompt (if a prompt is given)?
	Fair: not merely self-serving or one-sided	Does the writer fairly present others' views? If the assignment calls for sources, has the writer acknowledged those sources clearly and fully and delineated between borrowed and original ideas?
	Correct: free from grammar, punctuation, spelling, and usage errors; guidelines followed	Are grammar, punctuation, spelling, usage correct? Appropriate to audience? Are guidelines followed?

Exemplary = All applicable standards met; writing is excellent/skilled.
Satisfactory = Most applicable standards met; writing is competent/effective.
Below Satisfactory = Some applicable standards met; writing is inconsistent/ineffective.
Unsatisfactory = Few/No applicable standards met; writing is unskilled.

■ Communication: Speaking Outcome

OUTCOME STATEMENT: SCC graduates should be able to speak in a manner that is clear, precise, coherent, perceptive, audience-aware, and correct (according to Standard Written English) in both small and large group settings.

RUBRIC: The following descriptions use the 100-point scale, but still conform to the 4-point rubric using the same performance descriptors as the others.

Exemplary (90–100 points)
■ The goal of the speech was clear. The speaker had high-quality and accurate information or material and used a variety of kinds of development with visual aids and/or vivid language to meet the audience's interests, knowledge, and attitudes. The introduction had an attention-getter; main points were easy to follow, coherent; the closure was solid. The language was appropriate, clear, vivid, and emphatic. Delivery was excellent!

Satisfactory (80–89 points)
■ The goal of the speech was basically clear. The information was good and a variety of development was used with visual aids to meet the audience's interests and knowledge. The introduction had an attention-getter; the main points were clear and coherent; the presentation had a closure. The language was basically clear, vivid, and emphatic. Delivery was pretty good, but could use more eye contact, enthusiasm, and originality.

Below Satisfactory (70–79 points)
■ The goal of the speech was discernible. Material was sufficient. The presentation's attention-getter was mediocre, but the main points were fairly easy to follow. A few more transitions might be used, but a solid closure was given. The language was basically appropriate, clear, but not as vivid or emphatic as it could be. Delivery was okay, but could use more eye contact, enthusiasm, and originality.

Unsatisfactory (0–69 points)
■ The goal of the speech was unclear. The information was mediocre at best. Visual aids and vivid language were poor or not used at all. The introduction was poor or weak; main points were difficult to follow. Few or no transitions were used. The closure was weak or absent. The language was unclear and poorly emphasized. Delivery was poor—didn't seem practiced—and little or no eye contact was made.

STANDARDS AND ASSESSMENT: In addressing a small or large group, assessment should consider content, organization, language, and delivery. The speaker's performance can be rated in small and/or large group situations on a scale from 0 to 5 (unsatisfactory to exemplary) for each item listed below.

1. Clear
   ■ Clearly implied or directly stated goal of the presentation
   ■ Clear and logical organization
   ■ Clear and varied development techniques (examples, facts, statistics, visuals, etc.)

2. Precise
   ■ Vivid language, examples, visual aids, etc.
   ■ High-quality/accurate information

3. Coherent
   - Smooth development (easy to follow)
   - Transitional devices from one main point to the next
   - Logical and signaled closure

4. Perceptive
   - Visual aids and/or vivid language for clarity
   - Anticipation of questions, concerns, objections
   - Appropriate length and content (key terms, buzz words, terminology)
   - Speech design (to appeal to a variety of listeners)

5. Audience-aware
   - Material adaptation to audience's knowledge, interests, attitudes
   - Appropriate language for audience
   - Appealing information
   - Adequate eye content
   - Comfortable delivery

6. Correct (Edited American English)
   - Proper grammar (avoidance of double negatives, slang, nonstandard language)
   - Clear, distinctive articulation and volume
   - Correct word usage and pronunciation

■ Speaking Worksheet

ID CODE: _____   SCORE: _____

Rate the speaker's performance in small and/or large group situations on a scale from 0 to 5 (unsatisfactory to exemplary) for each item. (**Note:** Deduct 5 points per nonapplicable item from each of the four grading scales at the bottom of the page.)

CLEAR

_____ 1. Clearly implied or directly stated goal of the presentation

_____ 2. Clear and logical organization

_____ 3. Clear and varied development techniques (examples, facts, statistics, visuals, etc.)

PRECISE

_____ 1. Vivid language, examples, visual aids, etc.

_____ 2. High-quality/accurate information

COHERENT

_____ 1. Smooth development (easy to follow)

_____ 2. Transitional devices from one main point to the next

_____ 3. Logical and signaled closure

PERCEPTIVE

_____ 1. Visual aids and/or vivid language for clarity

_____ 2. Anticipation of questions, concerns, objections

_____ 3. Appropriate length and content (key terms, buzz words, terminology)

_____ 4. Speech design (to appeal to a variety of listeners)

AUDIENCE-AWARE

_____ 1. Material adaptation to audience's knowledge, interests, attitudes

_____ 2. Appropriate language for audience

_____ 3. Appealing information

_____ 4. Adequate eye contact

_____ 5. Comfortable delivery

CORRECT (Edited American English)

_____ 1. Proper grammar (avoidance of double negatives, slang, nonstandard language)

_____ 2. Clear, distinctive articulation and volume

_____ 3. Correct word usage and pronunciation

_____ **TOTAL POINTS**

_____ Exemplary   _____ Satisfactory   _____ Below Satisfactory   _____ Unsatisfactory
(90–100 points)   (80–89 points)   (70–79 points)   (0–69 points)

■ Quantitative Literacy

SCC graduates should be able to apply college-level mathematical concepts and methods to understand, analyze, and communicate in quantitative terms.

Level	Understanding	Analysis	Communication
Exemplary 4	■ Demonstrates clear understanding of the problem ■ Understanding is deep and broad ■ Identifies the purpose and key questions involved in the problem ■ Identifies relevant information and underlying assumptions needed to solve the problem	■ Makes connections between relevant observations ■ Uses a logical strategy that leads directly to an accurate solution ■ Reasoning is logical, clear, and evident ■ Checks the solution to see if it is reasonable and accurate	■ A quantitative explanation is given that is clear, precise and accurate ■ Enough explanation is given so that it is easy to follow the student's thought processes ■ Precisely uses mathematical terms and notation
Satisfactory 3	■ Demonstrates some understanding of the problem ■ Identifies most of the purpose and key questions involved in the problem ■ Identifies most of the information and underlying assumptions needed to solve the problem	■ Makes some connections between relevant observations ■ Uses a strategy that leads to an accurate solution ■ Reasoning is mostly evident and logical; only partially clear ■ All mathematical operations are correct and complete	■ Explanation is quantitative and clear ■ Enough explanation is given so that it is easy to follow the student's thought processes ■ Correctly uses mathematical terms and notation
Below satisfactory 2	■ Demonstrates little understanding of the problem. Understanding is minimal ■ Identifies some of the purpose and key questions involved in the problem ■ Identifies some of the information and underlying assumptions needed to solve the problem	■ Makes few connections between relevant observations ■ Uses a strategy that is only partially successful. The strategy does not lead to an accurate solution ■ Reasoning is evident but faulty; reasoning is rarely logical and clear ■ Mathematical operations are partially correct but are incomplete	■ Explanation is given but is incomplete or unclear ■ Enough explanation is given so that it is easy to follow the student's thought processes ■ Uses some mathematical terms and notation correctly
Unsatisfactory 1	■ Does not understand the problem ■ No solution is given ■ Cannot identify the purpose and key questions involved in the problem ■ Cannot identify the information and underlying assumptions needed to solve the problem	■ No connections are made ■ No evidence of a logical strategy ■ No mathematical reasoning demonstrated ■ Many mathematical errors, solution is incorrect or no solution is given	■ No explanation is given or the explanation is irrelevant ■ The student's thought processes cannot be followed ■ Does not correctly use mathematical terms and notation

■ Quantitiative Literacy Worksheet

ID CODE: _____

Score	Criteria	Comments
4: Exemplary (Exceeds the Standard)	■ Evidence is present that the student fully understood the ideas in the assignment. The work illustrates a mastery of all concepts as well as interrelated ideas. ■ If calculations were involved in the assignment, they were performed accurately and completely. ■ Interpretation, reasoning, and analysis were present, clear, and explained in an in-depth manner showing relevant connections.	
3: Satisfactory (Meets the Standard)	■ Evidence is present that the student understood the ideas in the assignment. ■ If calculations were involved in the assignment, they were primarily performed accurately and completely. ■ Interpretation, reasoning, and analysis were present, but not necessarily explained in an in-depth manner that showed relevant connections.	
2: Below Satisfactory (Approaches the Standard)	■ Some evidence is present that the student understood most of the ideas in the assignment. ■ If calculations were involved in the assignment, most were performed accurately and completely. ■ Some interpretation and reasoning was present, but the work did not proficiently demonstrate an in-depth analysis.	
1: Unsatisfactory (Below the Standard)	■ Sufficient evidence is not present that the student understood key ideas in the assignment. ■ If calculations were involved in the assignment, most were performed inaccurately or incompletely. ■ Any interpretation or reasoning offered was inaccurate.	

Information Literacy

Students who graduate from Surry Community College should be able to recognize when information is needed and have the ability to locate, evaluate, and use effectively the needed information.					
Level	**Recognize when information is needed**	**Locate information**	**Evaluate information critically**	**Use information effectively**	**Acknowledge the use of information sources**
Exemplary 4	The student has clearly defined and focused the topic.	The student is able to identify and manage information using a wide variety of methods.	The student is able to summarize main ideas and restate concepts clearly.	All sources are valid, accurate, timely, and unbiased. Information is presented very effectively in a well organized manner that supports the purpose of the project.	Proper documentation style is used consistently throughout the project and citations for resources are extensive and complete.
Satisfactory 3	The student has defined the topic.	The student is able to identify and manage information using a variety of methods.	The student is able to summarize main ideas and restate concepts in a fairly clear manner.	Most sources used are valid, accurate, timely, and unbiased. Information is presented effectively in an organized manner that supports the purpose of the project.	Proper documentation style is used in most instances and there are a fair number of citations that are mostly complete.
Below satisfactory 2	The student has a topic but it lacks clarity and focus.	The student is able to identify and manage information using a minimum of methods.	The student is able to summarize main ideas and restate concepts with minimal difficulty.	Some sources used are valid, accurate, timely, and unbiased. Information is presented somewhat effectively in a fairly organized manner that supports the purpose of the project.	Proper documentation style is used in some instances and there are a minimum of citations that are fairly complete.
Unsatisfactory 1	The student has not defined the topic.	The student is unable to identify and manage information and/or use a limited number of methods.	The student is unable to summarize main ideas and restate concepts clearly.	Sources used are invalid, inaccurate, not timely, and biased. Information is not presented in an organized manner that supports the purpose of the project.	The student does not cite resources, permissions, or use proper documentation style.

Name: _____ Date: _____

Information Literacy Worksheet

ID CODE: _____ **SCORE** _____

Component	Comments	Score
Recognize when information is needed		
Locate information		
Evaluate information critically		
Use information effectively		
Acknowledge the use of information sources		

CHAPTER 4
Learning Style/ Instructional Style

Introduction

The population at any college is a diverse one. Look around you at the composition of the students in your class. They come from all ages, ethnic, national, social, cultural, and religious backgrounds. Each person is indeed a unique individual. Each student has his/her own strengths and weaknesses along with his/her unique learning style. Each instructor you will meet along the way will have a different teaching style. The people who will be guiding your educational experiences will also bring their personal attributes into the classroom. So what are you to do? How will you adapt to all of this diversity?

This chapter will focus on the differences in academic strengths, learning styles, and instructional styles. You will identify your strengths and learn how to compensate for your weaknesses. You will explore the many ways in which people receive information and determine the mode in which you learn best. You will learn how a preferred learning style affects your learning. As you read through and do the exercises, keep in mind that there are no right or wrong answers. The goal is to help you find your learning style and use it to your advantage. Lastly, you will examine the different teaching techniques used in your classes and develop strategies *to help you adapt your strengths, weaknesses, and learning styles to your instructor's teaching styles.* These strategies will help you to be successful in college.

What Is a Learning Style?

Before continuing, it is necessary to make clear just what is meant by learning style. Scholars have different opinions regarding what should or shouldn't be included in the definition. For our purposes, learning style is the characteristic and preferred way one takes in and interacts with information, and the way one responds to the learning environment. Think of your particular learning style as the way you prefer to learn new or difficult information, and the way you find it easiest and most comfortable to learn.

This chapter contains material adapted from *The Community College: A New Beginning*, third edition by Linda S. Aguilar, Sandra J. Hopper, and Therese M. Kuzlik. Copyright © 2001 by Kendall/Hunt Publishing Company. Adapted and reprinted with permission of the publisher. Further reproduction is prohibited.

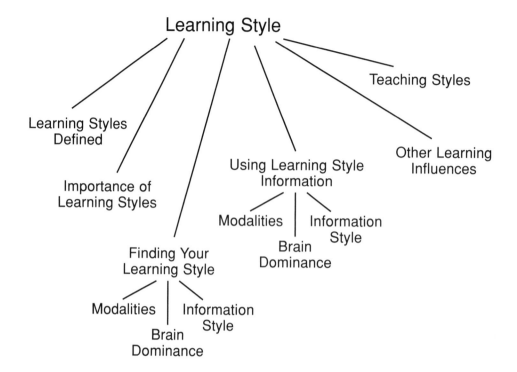

To illustrate, suppose that you are given a learning task. What is the first thing you would prefer to do to get the new information—read about it in a book; listen to someone talk about it; or do something with the information to prove that you know it? None of the ways is the right or best way, they are simply examples of different ways to learn. You may prefer one, or a combination of those listed. There is no best way to learn, just different ways. The goal for you is to find your preferred learning style.

Depending on which expert you ask, there are many different ways to consider learning styles and many ways to analyze them. This chapter will only touch on a few. If you feel that you would benefit from a more extensive diagnosis, you should get in touch with your campus counseling or testing center.

Your learning style may be more difficult to determine now than it would have been in elementary school. The reason is that as you get older and become a more mature learner, your learning style becomes more integrated. You have probably learned that you have to use many different ways to get information depending on the learning situation. When you answer the questions on the various learning style inventories given later in this chapter, keep in mind that you want to answer them thinking about your preferences. Answer them based on what you are most comfortable doing, and what's easiest for you. The more accurate the picture of your learning style, the more you can use it to help you.

■ The Three Basic Learning Modalities

Psychologists and educators have done a lot of research on learning styles and have tried to find out how students learn best. It's useful information, especially now that you're in college, paying tuition, and are serious about your education. One of the easiest theories to understand describes three main ways people take in and remember information. These are called *learning modalities*. The first is visual, the second is auditory, and the third is tactile or kinesthetic. Visual learners use their eyesight, or vision, as their preferred method of taking in information and learn best by reading or watching a demonstration. Auditory learners use their ears or sense of hearing the most. They prefer to learn by listening to a lecture, discussion, or audio tape. Kinesthetic/tactile learners are much better at getting information by using their sense of touch. They prefer to learn by doing or becoming physically involved with what they are studying. If they do have to read or listen, it helps if they can move around or do something with their hands.

These learning styles reflect preferences in the way we learn. Knowing that you are a visual learner doesn't mean that you don't understand what you hear. It means that given a choice, you would usually prefer to read or watch. Visual learners usually fare quite well in grade school, where teachers cater to this style. Go into any preschool through fifth grade classroom, and you will be bombarded with visual stimulation. Elementary school teachers all learn how to create effective bulletin board displays. They want to make sure that any kid who is not paying attention is still learning something while he/she stares at the walls, ceiling, windows, or even out the door into the hall. Since reading plays such an important role in education, visual learners who like to read seem to do well, even in high school. They will do well in college if they can take good notes. They should try to get everything important written into their notes to read and look at when studying for a test.

Auditory learners, on the other hand, may find college classes more to their liking because many instructors use the lecture/discussion method of teaching. In the lower grades auditory learners can get bored with too much seatwork and reading. However, they probably did fine in school since most teachers at that level explain everything in detail. As they get older, their auditory strengths are used even more as verbal reasoning skills are emphasized.

Tactile and kinesthetic styles vary slightly. Tactile learners like to use their hands, while kinesthetic learners use their whole body whenever possible. These two styles are so similar, though, that throughout this chapter we will use the terms synonymously. These learners are probably the least understood in schools. Although some teachers really try to bring in hands-on approaches to learning, others find it difficult to adapt their more audio/visual styles to a kinesthetic child. Because that child usually needs to be moving around while taking in the information, the typical classroom arrangement makes school more difficult. Not surprisingly, most of the developmental students in my college classes discover that they are kinesthetic/tactile learners. They never quite "got it" in grade school and high school because they were never given the opportunity to learn most subjects in their preferred style.

The Three Basic Learning Modalities Inventory Activity which you will complete later in this chapter is an inventory that will help you determine your learning style. It's great to know your strengths so you can use them to your best advantage. But since life is not always fair, and your instructors will not always teach in your preferred style, *you need to learn some strategies to compensate for the other styles that are less developed in you.*

■ Learning about Your Style

Purpose: What's the point? What are the benefits of knowing your learning style?

1. **Success in School**—Are you aware that everyone has a preferred learning style—just as teachers have a preferred teaching style? Have you noticed how you do very well in a given instructor's class, and other students might say that instructor "cannot teach" or vice versa? Have you ever thought you were just "dumb" because others seemed to grasp the subject matter more quickly than you? Just as you prefer a certain learning style, you may have instructors whose teaching

Visual learners learn best by:

Reading   Watching demonstrations   Seeing pictures

Strategies for visual learners include:

Printed materials	Movies	Blackboard demonstrations
Diagrams	Charts	Photos
Graphs	Handouts	Illustrations
Reading textbook before lecture	Taking notes to read after lecture	Overheads/transparencies

Auditory learners learn best by:

Listening   Conversation

Asking questions   Discussing

Strategies for auditory learners include:

Study groups	Study buddy	Audio tapes
Movies	Recitation	
Reading textbook following lecture		

Tactile/Kinesthetic learners learn best by:

Doing   Touching

Moving   Feeling

Strategies for tactile/kinesthetic learners include:

Hands-on learning	Experiments	Interactive learning
Teamwork	Role playing	Workshops
Performance models	Note taking (writing out what you see or hear)	Collecting samples

Becoming physically involved

Concentrating on how the reading and the listening will benefit you in experimentation.

style is opposite or does not "match" your learning style. The activities in this chapter will help you identify and understand the ways you learn best.

Differences between your learning style and your instructor's teaching styles can make learning new materials more difficult, *but knowing your learning style can help you develop strategies for success.*

2. **Success on the Job**—Any successful worker knows that learning, instead of stopping when you leave school, continues throughout your career and can keep you on the path of success. Your learning style is essentially your working style. If you know how to work, you will be able to look for an environment that suits you well. You will also be more able to adjust when you encounter situations that are difficult for you.

3. **Success in Relationships**—Outside class, you may tend to associate with people who have learning styles similar to your own or with people whose learning styles are different. Thinking about this may help you uncover some clues about compatibility between you and some of the significant people in your life, in both short-term and long-term relationships. Understanding more about learning styles can improve communication and reduce the likelihood of conflict.

"There are three ways of treating individual differences—you can consider the other person wrong and be indignant, you can consider yourself wrong and be depressed, or you can consider that the two of you are justifiably and interestingly different and be amused."

—Isabel Myers

No particular learning style is right or wrong.

■ Brain Dominance

Research on the two brain hemispheres began in the 1950s with Dr. Roger Sperry. Dr. Sperry found that the two hemispheres (or halves) of the brain processed information differently, and both were equally important to the whole person. The functions of the hemispheres had previously been found to be different—with speech being a left brain function and spatial (visual) capability being in the right. It was not known until Dr. Sperry's research that the processing of information was different for each of the halves. The left brain is linear and processes in a sequential manner, while the right brain uses a global process.

It seems that schools and their curriculums favor the left hemisphere. In other words, we are given a major dose of left brain learning in school, and the right brain is neglected. Most of us probably learned that success in school depended to a great degree on choosing the proper hemisphere to process information. We didn't consciously make this choice, but we could figure out what would be required of us, and we would do that to be successful. This may have caused many students problems if they were unable to use the left brain easily, or if they couldn't determine what to do to be successful.

Research findings indicate that the learning of most information is better when both the right and left hemispheres are used. If your results from the inventory indicate that you do not have a dominance in the right or the left hemisphere, and that you are integrated, you are achieving the best for learning. You can use both sides of your brain equally well. You can choose one over the other when the situation calls for it.

If you have a strong tendency or preference for either the right or the left hemisphere, you may find yourself having trouble in various learning situations. As with your modalities, integration is the key to becoming a better learner. Use the list of characteristics on the following page to find areas where you can develop or polish your weak areas. Also, use them to help you with difficult material—use your strong areas to compensate for your weak areas. The more integrated you become, the more you are free to choose different ways to process information, depending on what's best for a given situation.

Brain Dominance Characteristics

Left Hemisphere	Right Hemisphere
Objective	Use visualization
Rational	Intuitive
Sequential and systematic	Rely on images for thinking and remembering
Like right and wrong answers	Risk-takers
Structured	Need neat environment
Questioning	Long-term memory good
Need constant reinforcement	Short-term memory bad
Contract-liking people	Prefer subjective tests
Organized	Random learning and thinking
List makers	Short attention spans
Time conscious	Respond to demonstrated instructions
Follow directions closely	Need touching
Rely on language in thinking and remembering	Don't read directions
Good planners	Don't pay attention
Accomplish things quickly	Pilers
See cause and effect	More flexible
Prone to stress-related ills	More fun loving
Perfectionists	Accident prone
Control feelings	Need to have goals set for them
Do one task at a time	Multi-tasks needed
Need gentle risking situations	Creative
Analytic	Visual learners
Solve problems by looking at the parts	Solve problems by looking at the whole picture
Verbal	Like humor
Recognize names	Recognize faces
More serious	Like improvising
Dislike improvising	Think geometrically
Abstract thinkers	Dreamers
Focus on reality	Assuming
Work on improving the known	Like fantasy
Like non-fiction	Inventors
Learn for personal achievement	Intrinsically motivated
Extrinsically motivated	Learn for personal awareness
Prefer objective tests	Free with feelings

■ Student Environment

The environment around you is another factor that influences your learning. The time of day when people participate in an activity often will determine how well or how poorly they perform. Students who take courses or study at the times when they are most alert tend to do better. (Don't you wonder how many research studies it took to verify that amazing fact?!) Still, many people do not even consider this when they schedule their classes or plan their study time. Are you a morning person or a night person? Do you peak mid-morning or fizzle in the middle of the afternoon? If you can't keep your eyes open after 9:00 p.m., don't plan to study for your chemistry test after the rest of the family has gone to bed.

The surrounding environment will also have an effect on how you perform. Do you prefer a room that is loud vs. one that is quiet? Must you work on a neat desk, or does it matter whether or not it is cluttered? What about the lighting? Or the room temperature? What is it that makes you comfortable? It is very difficult to concentrate when you are uncomfortable. If the room is too cold, your mind may concentrate more on keeping warm than on your algebra problems. The Study Conditions Inventory will help you determine what kind of study environments provide the best "fit" for your needs. Find out for yourself and use the information to your best advantage.

■ Instructional Styles

Three types of instructional styles most often used by teachers are independent, student centered, and cooperative learning. The first is very formal and businesslike. The instructor delivers his/her class material primarily by lecturing, and the student has no input into the class lecture. The student is almost totally responsible for learning independently. S/he is expected to take notes, follow the syllabus, read the textbook, complete the assignments, and prepare for assorted quizzes and exams. This type of learning places the importance on the individual student's efforts and usually takes place in classes with large enrollments.

The second type of instructional style is less formal. Discussion is introduced into the classroom along with the lecture. The instructor attempts to involve the group into the learning process by asking probing questions that encourage students to think, answer questions and make comments. The lecture delivery is in a traditional format, but the instructor requires class participation by calling on students, if necessary.

The third type of instructional style makes a concerted effort to involve the students in group dynamics. Not only are lectures peppered with question and answer sessions, but students may be involved in lab work, demonstrations, presentations, and/or group problem-solving exercises. In some cases the teacher does not lecture at all, and the students are totally responsible for discovering the information on their own. The instructor serves as a facilitator and resource person. In cooperative learning the students work as teams and may even do their exams together.

You should try to find out about the teacher's instructional style before you sign up for a class. Your best bet is to talk to other students. Find out as much as you can about the person with whom you will be spending the next term. The instructor's personality will also influence his/her teaching methods. Try to select someone whose teaching style is compatible with your learning style. In order to do this, however, you must be prepared to register early so that you can get into the classes you want. Course sections taught by popular teachers fill up very quickly.

When it is impossible for you to find an instructor with a compatible teaching style, make an honest effort to learn. Sit in the front of the classroom to be certain that you do not miss anything. Not only should you listen to what your instructor is saying, but you need to watch for facial expressions and body language. Note where emphasis is placed during a discussion or lecture, pay close attention to board work and/or overhead transparencies used in class, and be aware of the material that will be covered in class. You can always do this by reading your textbook before each class.

Study for the class in your best learning style mode. Rewrite or tape your notes. Read your notes or textbook out loud. Do whatever it takes to learn. Talk with the instructor if you have problems; ask questions when you do not understand. Seek out available tutorial services to provide that extra edge.

■ What Can You Do?

It is important to recognize that all people do not learn in the same way and that there is no single right way to learn. These styles are merely a reflection of your personality and your particular preferences. Just as you prefer to use your right hand or left hand to do certain tasks, your mind prefers to use certain methods for taking in and processing information, coming to conclusions, and functioning on a daily basis. All of us use more than one style. However, you can become more proficient in the other, less preferred learning styles by practicing and using them more often. Try to adapt your style to the conditions under which you must learn.

Once you have determined whether your primary learning style is visual, auditory, or kinesthetic/tactile, use it to your best advantage. Find the strategies that work for you. Get to know yourself and your preferred study modes. Become aware of your best time of day for learning, and try to study under optimal conditions with regard to room temperature, lighting, noise level, furniture, etc. Finally, make every attempt to take classes with teachers whose instructional styles will motivate you and make it easier to comprehend the material.

■ Activity: Three Basic Learning Modalities Inventory

Please choose one response for each of the items on the inventory. Even if more than one state-ment is true for you, choose only the one that is most true, or that is true more often for you than the others.

1. If I have to learn something new, I would prefer:

   a. to read about it.
   b. to have someone explain it to me.
   c. to try it.

2. The strategy that helps me learn a new spelling or vocabulary word is:

   a. put it on a flash card and look at it often.
   b. spell or say it out loud several times.
   c. write it over and over until I remember it.

3. If I need directions to a new place, I would prefer:

   a. to follow a good map, preferably with landmarks drawn on it.
   b. to have someone tell me exactly how to get there.
   c. to have someone take me there.

4. I do well in classes where:

   a. the teacher uses visual aids and writes important things on the board or overhead.
   b. the teacher lectures on the important things to know.
   c. there is some kind of hands-on activity like an experiment or lab where I can learn by doing.

5. If I had to put something together, I would:

   a. read the manual or watch the instructional video first.
   b. ask someone to tell me how to do it.
   c. take out all the pieces and start trying to put it together. I read the instructions/ask for help only as a last resort if I can't figure it out.

6. I remember best the things I:

   a. see.
   b. hear.
   c. do.

7. I would rather:

   a. read a story myself.
   b. listen to someone else read a story.
   c. act out the story in a play.

8. In a casual setting when I'm listening to an interesting speaker:

   a. I visualize the people, places and events being described.
   b. I listen to the speaker's tone of voice to derive meaning.
   c. I need to have some kind of physical movement such as rocking, tapping, etc., to help me concentrate.

9. If I need to remember a phone number:

    a. I look it up, then picture the number in my mind.
    b. I repeat it to myself several times.
    c. I write it down, or remember it by where the numbers are on the phone key pad.

10. When teaching other people things:

    a. I would rather use a picture, diagram, chart, etc. to show them what to do.
    b. I would rather tell them how to do it.
    c. I would rather demonstrate how to do something than tell how to do it.

11. At a party:

    a. I like to watch people.
    b. I like to listen to others talk.
    c. I initiate conversations.

12. When I shop for groceries:

    a. I take a list.
    b. I talk to myself to remember what I need to buy.
    c. I walk through the store and remember what I need as I go.

13. In order to relax in my leisure time:

    a. I watch TV or read.
    b. I listen to music.
    c. I am involved in crafts or do-it-yourself projects.

14. In math class, I would prefer to:

    a. read and follow the example from the book.
    b. have the teacher explain how to do the problem.
    c. have the teacher show me how to do the problem, then have me work one on my own.

15. When I watch TV:

    a. I look at the screen and pay attention.
    b. I can be doing something else in the room as long as I can listen.
    c. I have to be eating or using my hands for crafts, or other hobbies.

16. When I need to spell a difficult word:

    a. I picture the word in my mind and mentally spell it.
    b. I spell it aloud.
    c. I must write it out.

17. I like to learn something new by:

    a. watching a person demonstrate how to do it.
    b. listening to lecturers, speakers, or tapes.
    c. getting involved by doing it myself.

18. In a group project I would rather.

    a. research other written material to gain knowledge about the project.
    b. talk to others about how to do the project.
    c. collect the information for the project.

19. I learn best when I:

    a. read the textbook.
    b. listen to the lecture.
    c. design a project.

20. When studying for tests, I do best when I:

    a. read my textbook and notes.
    b. listen to the tapes from class.
    c. explain the information to someone else.

21. To make best use of my class notes I:

    a. read them over.
    b. read them out loud or on to a tape so I can listen to them.
    c. organize the information using charts, diagrams, mind maps, etc.

Now, add up your scores to see which is your preferred learning style.

Total A's _____ Visual

Total B's _____ Auditory

Total C's _____ Tactile/Kinesthetic

■ Activity: Brain Dominance Checklist

Check the statements below which are most like you, or are like you most of the time.

1. ☐ I prefer to have things explained to me.
2. ☐ I prefer that someone shows me things.
3. ☐ I don't have a preference for verbal instructions or demonstrations.
4. ☐ I prefer classes where things are planned so I know exactly what to do.
5. ☐ I prefer classes which are open with opportunities for change as I go along.
6. ☐ I prefer both classes where things are planned and open to changes.
7. ☐ I prefer classes where I listen to "experts."
8. ☐ I prefer classes where I try things.
9. ☐ I prefer classes where I listen and also try things.
10. ☐ I prefer to take multiple choice tests.
11. ☐ I prefer essay tests.
12. ☐ I don't have a preference for essay tests or multiple choice tests.
13. ☐ I don't like to play hunches or guess.
14. ☐ I like to play hunches or guess.
15. ☐ I sometimes make guesses and play hunches.
16. ☐ I decide what I think by looking at the facts.
17. ☐ I decide what I think based on my experiences.
18. ☐ I decide what I think based on facts and my experiences.
19. ☐ I respond better to people when they appeal to my logical, intellectual side.
20. ☐ I respond better to people when they appeal to my emotional, feeling side.
21. ☐ I respond equally well to people when they appeal to my intellectual side or emotional side.
22. ☐ I prefer to solve problems by reading and listening to the experts.
23. ☐ I prefer to solve problems by imagining and seeing things.
24. ☐ I prefer to solve problems by listening to experts and imagining things.
25. ☐ I am primarily intellectual.
26. ☐ I am primarily intuitive.
27. ☐ I am equally intellectual and intuitive.
28. ☐ When I remember or think about things, I prefer to think in words.
29. ☐ When I remember or think about things, I prefer to think in pictures and images.
30. ☐ When I remember or think about things, I sometimes prefer words and sometimes prefer pictures.

31. ☐ I am very good at explaining things in words.

32. ☐ I am very good at explaining things with my hand movements and actions.

33. ☐ I am very good at explaining with words and hand movements.

34. ☐ I am almost never absentminded.

35. ☐ I am frequently absentminded.

36. ☐ I am occasionally absentminded.

37. ☐ I am very good at recalling verbal materials (names, dates).

38. ☐ I am very good at recalling visual material.

39. ☐ I am equally good at recalling verbal and visual material.

40. ☐ It is more exciting to improve something.

41. ☐ It is more exciting to invent something.

42. ☐ It is equally exciting to improve something or invent something.

43. ☐ I would rather read realistic stories.

44. ☐ I would rather read fantasy stories.

45. ☐ I don't have a preference for reading realistic or fantasy stories.

Score by marking the numbers below that you checked. Add up the total number of statements in each category. You will probably find that one area had more checks than the others. If so, you have a tendency for that area (left, right, or integrated) to be your stronger learning preference. If you are more integrated than left or right dominant, then you can use either side of your brain. A more detailed description of brain dominance is given later in the chapter.

LEFT BRAIN: 1   4   7   10   13   16   19   22   25   28   31   34   37   40   43   Total _____

RIGHT BRAIN: 2   5   8   11   14   17   20   23   26   29   32   35   38   41   44   Total _____

INTEGRATED: 3   6   9   12   15   18   21   24   27   30   33   36   39   42   45   Total _____

_____
Concepts & Ideas created by David Kolb, Paul Torrance, and Bernice McCarthy.

■ Activity: Study Conditions Inventory

Circle the letter that best describes you.

1. I prefer to take classes in the:
   a. morning.
   b. afternoon.
   c. evening.

2. I prefer to study in the:
   a. morning.
   b. afternoon.
   c. evening.

3. I learn best when I study with:
   a. soft background music.
   b. loud music.
   c. peace and quiet.

4. I like to study:
   a. at a desk.
   b. on the sofa or bed.
   c. in an easy chair.

5. I study best:
   a. in my room.
   b. at the library.
   c. at the kitchen or dining room table.
   d. in the living room.
   e. in the cafeteria.

6. I study best:
   a. alone.
   b. with a friend.
   c. with a study group.

7. If other people are around when I study they:
   a. annoy me.
   b. make it impossible to get anything done.
   c. do not bother me.
   d. help me.

8. I like to study in a room that is:
   a. hot.
   b. warm.
   c. cool.
   d. cold.

9. I get my best work done:
   a. when I rush to meet a deadline.
   b. when I have plenty of time to organize my work.
   c. in due time.

10. When I study I like to:
    a. eat my meal.
    b. drink coffee, tea, juice, or soda.
    c. snack on "junk" food.
    d. chew gum.

11. I like to study best:
    a. in a bright room with natural sun light.
    b. with a fluorescent lamp.
    c. with a desk light rather than an overhead light.
    d. with medium to bright overhead lighting.

12. I like to study with:
    a. the television set on.
    b. the radio on.
    c. no distracting noise.

13. When studying with a friend I prefer to:
    a. do so with the person present.
    b. use the telephone.
    c. it doesn't matter.

14. I prefer to study:
    a. indoors.
    b. outdoors when the weather permits.
    c. either indoors or outdoors.

15. I enjoy studying:
    a. early in the morning.
    b. during the day.
    c. in the evening.
    d. late at night.

Now that you have selected the study conditions that appear to best suit you, be sure that they are indeed the best ones for you. Try experimenting with different classes and study conditions. Students always tell me they can't study without loud music. But, actually, they have never tried a quiet approach. If you usually listen to loud music or have the television on while studying, be sure that a quiet room will not be better for you before you discard the idea. If you prefer to study alone, try working with a friend or group. You may find that you are more effective when learning with others.

■ Activity: Preferred Courses Inventory

List three or four of your favorite courses.

_____

_____

_____

What do these courses have in common?

_____

_____

_____

How was the class in each of these courses conducted?

_____

_____

_____

What kind of exams were given in these courses?

_____

_____

_____

Why did you like these courses?

_____

_____

_____

List three or four of your least favorite courses.

_____

_____

_____

Why did you not like these courses?

_____

_____

_____

How was the class in each of these courses conducted?

_____

_____

_____

What kind of exams were given in these courses?

_____

_____

_____

Do you see a pattern?

_____

_____

_____

What is it?

_____

_____

_____

Name: _____ Date: _____

◼ Activity: Index of Learning Styles

In this activity, you will complete the *Index of Learning Styles.* The Index of Learning Styles was created in 1991 by Richard M. Felder, a chemical engineering professor at North Carolina State University, and Barbara A. Soloman, then the coordinator of advising for the N.C. State First-Year College. The four learning style dimensions of the instrument were adapted from a model developed in 1987 by Dr. Felder and Linda K. Silverman, an educational psychologist then at the University of Denver. The instrument assesses preferences on four dimensions (active/reflective, sensing/intuitive, visual/verbal, and sequential/global) of a learning style model. Results provide an indication of an individual's learning preferences and an indication of the preference profile of a group of students (e.g. a class). A student's learning style profile provides an indication of possible strengths and possible tendencies that might cause difficulty in an academic environment. The profile does **not** reflect a student's ability to succeed in a particular subject or career.

Your instructor will direct you to use one of the following assessment methods and will lead a class discussion about what the profile results tell you as an individual learner and your class as a group of learners:

- ◼ Paper/pencil *"Index of Learning Styles"*
- ◼ Free Internet assessments—*http://www.ncsu.edu/felder-public/ILSpage.html* select the web-based version of the instrument, complete and submit it. A form showing your learning styles profile should be returned immediately. Print this form out and bring it to class.

An alternative to this index of learning styles could be another visit to the Career Center. The Career Center has alternate learning style investigations.

Richard M. Felder and Barbara A. Soloman, *Index of Learning Styles,* <http://www.ncsu.edu/felder-public/ILSpage.html>, accessed June 13, 2005.

■ Activity: Reflective Writing

Which of the learning styles described in this chapter seems to fit you best?

Why do you think so?

Analyze a course in which you are currently enrolled—or one in which you are doing well and enjoy. Why do you like this class? Why do you think you are doing well?

CHAPTER 5
Reading Critically and Note Taking

Reading *is the process of constructing meaning from written texts. It is a complex skill requiring the coordination of a number of interrelated sources of information*

Anderson, 1985

Reading *is the process of constructing meaning through the dynamic interaction among (1) the reader's existing knowledge; (2) the information suggested by the text being read; and (3) the context of the situation*

Wixson, Peters, Weber, Roeber, 1987

The Purpose of Reading

The Reader's Purpose

A reader must be able to translate the written words into meaningful language. Simply being able to recognize or "say" the printed words of text without constructing meaning is not reading. Constructing meaning from written text is impossible without being able to identify the words. Being able to arrive at the pronunciation of a printed word constitutes word identification; however if the reader is unable to attach meaning to the word, then he or she has not read the word since reading must end in meaning construction (Wambaugh, 1998). Skilled readers read for a purpose (goal or agenda).

Purposes of reading include:

1. **Sheer pleasure:** usually requires no specific skill level

2. **To figure out a simple idea:** which may require skimming a text

3. **To gain specific technical information:** skimming skills required

4. **To enter, understand, and appreciate a new view:** requires close reading skills in working through a challenging series of tasks that stretch our minds

5. **To learn a new subject:** requires close reading skills in internalizing and taking ownership of an organized system of meanings (Paul and Elder, 2003).

This chapter contains material adapted from *Practical Approaches for Building Study Skills and Vocabulary*, second edition, by Gary Funk et al, copyright © 1996 by Kendall/Hunt Publishing Company and from *The Community College: A New Beginning*, third edition by Linda S. Aguilar, Sandra J. Hopper, and Therese M. Kuzlik, copyright © 2001 by Kendall/Hunt Publishing Company. Adapted and reprinted with permission of the publisher. Further reproduction is prohibited.

The Author's Purpose

The reader must also be clear about the author's purpose in writing. Accurately translating words into intended meanings is an analytic, evaluative, and creative set of acts (Paul and Elder, 2003).

■ The Reflective Reader

The reflective mind is:

- purposeful—The reflective mind adjusts reading to specific goals.
- integrated—The reflective mind interrelates ideas in the text with ideas it already commands.
- critical—The reflective mind assesses what it reads for clarity, accuracy, precision, relevance, depth, breadth, logic, significance, and fairness.
- open to new ways of thinking—The reflective mind values new ideas and learns from what it reads.

The skilled reader/thinker:

- relates the core ideas within one discipline to the core ideas in other systems of knowledge.
- develops a reflective mind that seeks meaning.
- monitors what is being said from paragraph to paragraph.
- draws clear distinction between the thinking of the author and the reader's own thinking.

The skilled reader/thinker knows:

- **how** his or her mind operates
- **what** prejudices exist there
- **how** his or her thinking mirrors those around them
- **to what extent** his or her thinking has been influenced by the thinking of a culture
- **how** to evaluate his or her beliefs
- **whether** those beliefs can be upgraded

■ Thinking for Reading

Whenever we think, we think for a purpose within a point of view based on assumptions leading to implications and consequences. We use concepts, ideas, and theories to interpret data, facts, and experiences in order to answer questions, solve problems, and resolve issues.

Read to Develop a "Map" of Knowledge. Knowledge exists in "systems" of meanings, with interrelated primary ideas, secondary ideas, and peripheral ideas. The primary ideas are the core and are key to understanding all the other ideas. A skilled reader first takes ownership of the primary ideas. The sooner a reader/thinker begins to think in a system, the sooner the system becomes meaningful to the reader.

Map of Knowledge

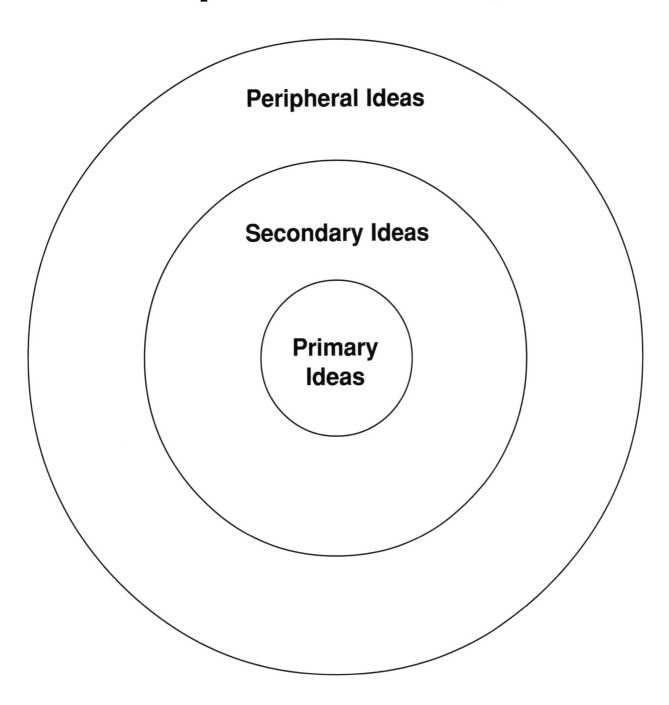

■ The Curriculum Impact of Reading

■ An examination of the literature concerning faculty expectations of the reading skills of freshmen and sophomore students and the kinds of reading tasks these faculty expect their students to be able to complete reveals a difference in expectations across disciplines. Angelo and Cross (1993) reported that faculty in quantitative disciplines gave a high priority to reading well in order to apply principles and generalizations to new problems and situations whereas faculty in qualitative disciplines gave high priority to reading well in order to think for oneself. Wambaugh (1998) conducted a similar study and reported:
  ■ 80% of instructors used textbooks for at least some of the required reading.
  ■ 100% of mathematics and science faculty reported textbooks constituted half or more of the reading for the course.
  ■ 65% of humanities and 88% of the social science faculty used a textbook for a majority of the required readings.
  ■ 33% of social science and humanities faculty required journal reading.
  ■ 52% of the humanities faculty required fiction and poetry reading.
  ■ 15% of all the faculty reported assigning magazines, newspapers, study guides, and other academic materials.
  ■ 73% of the faculty said that critical reading skills were essential for their students.
■ Mathematics and social science faculty said that the students should read with the purpose of familiarizing themselves with a topic so they can follow class lectures and fully participate in class discussions.
■ Science faculty said that their students should read with the purpose of acquiring knowledge of science facts, terms, concepts, and procedures in order to recall them later.
■ These results suggest that mathematics, science, and social science faculty believe that for their students the most important purpose of reading is to master a body of content and integrate this content knowledge with additional information discussed orally in class is central to success.
■ In contrast, humanities faculty said the most important purpose of reading in their courses is to teach students to exercise critical thinking, analytical thinking, and develop healthy skepticism.

■ Strategies Students Can Use to Read Critically

Strategy 1: Concept Maps for Textbook Reading

Graphic organizers provide an excellent tool to analyze and synthesize information. A concept map is a type of graphic organizer that can be used with textbook chapters that contain headings and subheadings. A concept map can be used before reading a chapter as a prereading strategy, and after reading the chapter as a postreading strategy.

Used as a prereading strategy, concept maps activate your background knowledge about the subject matter discussed in the chapter. As you write down the title of the chapter, the headings and the subheadings, you should begin to think about the content of the chapter. Once you have completed a concept map of the chapter with the chapter title, headings and subheadings, you can begin to read the chapter in order to understand the details from each of the sections.

Below is an example of a concept map that a student completed as a prereading activity for a textbook chapter entitled "Thesis, Main Ideas, Supporting Details, and Transitions." This concept map was created before the student read the chapter. The chapter title, headings and subheadings are identified in parentheses.

Concept Map Example 1

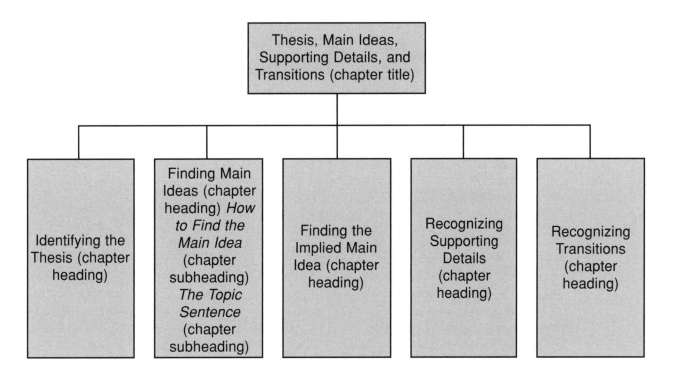

Notice that, in the example, this chapter contains five main headings. The second section of the chapter contains two subheadings. *Remember that each concept map you create will contain a different number of boxes depending on how many headings the chapter contains.* Once you have created the concept map with the headings and subheadings identified, you should read the chapter. As a postreading activity you should then add details from each section to your concept map. When you have completed this activity you have an excellent study tool to use later when you need to review the textbook information for a test. Below is the example of the same concept map including the details from each of the sections in the chapter.

Concept Map Example 2

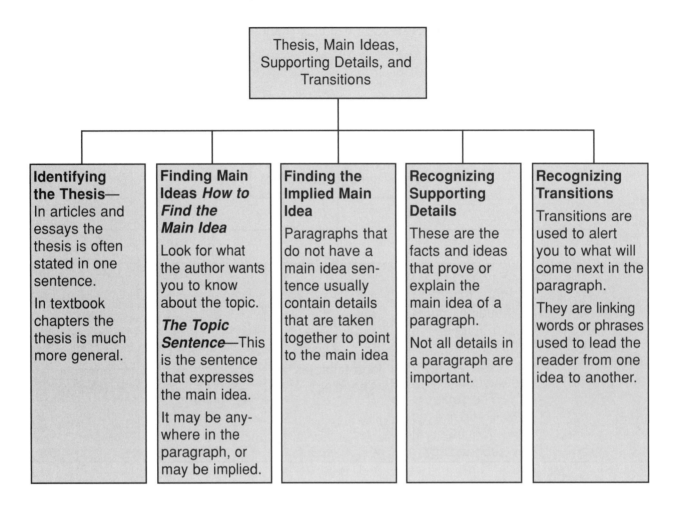

Strategy 2: Structural or Active Reading

Structural or active reading is a form of close reading applied to the overall structure of an extended text (usually a book). The reader focuses on what he/she can learn about the book from its title, preface, introduction, and table of contents. Structural reading has two main uses. First, it enables the reader to evaluate a book to determine whether he/she wants to spend the time to read it carefully. Second, it provides an overview to use as scaffolding in reading the text. If the reader can get a basic idea of what a book is driving at before he/she reads it in detail, the reader is much better able to make sense of the parts of it as he/she reads them paragraph by paragraph. Knowledge of a part helps the reader better understand the whole (which contains the parts).

To read structurally, the reader should ask himself or herself the following questions:

- What does the title tell me about this book?
- What is the main idea in the book? (You should be able to figure this out from skimming the introduction, preface, and first chapter.)
- What are the parts of the whole, and how does the book deal with those parts? (Again, this may be found in an overview in the introduction, preface, first chapter, and/or table of contents.)

■ In the light of my structural reading, what questions would I pursue during close reading?

Once the reader has the basic idea of the whole of a subject from the introductory chapter, the reader should be able to do some thinking within the system. Thus, with a basic idea of biology, he/she should be able to do some simple biological thinking. He/she should be able to ask some basic biological questions and identify some relevant biological information. This is crucial to success in reading the remainder of the textbook because if the reader does not have a clear concept of the whole, he/she will not be able to relate the parts (covered by the other chapters) to that whole.

The reading strategy should not be *whole, part, part, part, part, part . . .* but rather, *whole, part, whole, part, whole, part.* The reader should first ground him or herself in a basic (though introductory) idea of the whole and then relate each part (each subsequent chapter) to that whole. He/she should understand the whole through integrating the parts into it, use the whole as a tool of synthesis, and use knowledge of the parts as a tool of analysis.

...at You Read

...vrite in their books. In elementary school, students ...s because their books would be used by other stu-...ents own their books and are faced with the task of ...se reading requires a student to (a) interact with the ...bout meanings in the text, (b) write down ideas that ...(c) connect important ideas to ideas already under-

...o insert markings in books as they read. They should ...cts, assumptions, implications, points of view, doubts, ...e some ideas students might find useful in developing

...s and underline their definitions. Circle the foundational ...definitions the author gives to those ideas. Draw a line ...al ideas and the definitions in order to remember that they ...ional ideas explain most or many of the other ideas. Use a ...ng of a word is not clear.

...rks in the margins beside important conclusions. Use one ...an important conclusion, two for an even more important ...rucial one (!,!!,!!!).

...in the margin whenever there is a lack of understanding. ...uestion: "Do I understand what the author is saying?" If the ...te the question or put a question mark in the margin. Come ...s or question marks after reading further.

4. ... oblems or issues. Typically, each chapter in a book has an underlying key problem or issue. Identify the key problem or issue and mark it with some abbreviation (e.g., "iss" or "prob").

5. **Note important information, data, or evidence.** Circle information the author is using to support his or her conclusions and note it in the margin with an abbreviation (e.g., "info," "data," or "evid").

6. **Record in the margin the author's point of view.** Use an abbreviation (e.g., "pov").

7. **Record in the margin the author's most questionable assumptions.** Use an abbreviation (e.g., "assump").

8. **Record in the margin the most important implications of the thinking in the text.** Use an abbreviation (e.g., "implic").

9. **Formulate ideas of your own as they occur.** Write these ideas in the margin, on the extra pages at the back of the book, or at the end of the chapter. This helps the reader compare his or her thinking with that of the author's. The more the reader writes his or her own ideas, the clearer his or her own thinking becomes in relation to that of the author. Of course, the reader should be careful not to disagree with an author until the reader thoroughly understands the author.

10. **Diagram important concepts and how they are connected.** Formulate a sense of the whole. One good way to do this is by drawing diagrams that show interrelationships between concepts. Use the pages at the front or back of the book, or in a notebook if the drawings become elaborate and more space is needed.

Summary of Markings and Abbreviations

Circle around word or phrase	foundational or other important concept
def	an important definition
!, !!, !!!	important conclusion
?	reader doesn't understand something
prob or iss	a key problem or issue the author is addressing
info, data, or evid	key information, data, or evidence
pov	key point of view
assump	a questionable assumption is being made
implic	key thoughts or consequences
notes in margin or on extra pages	reader's thought being recorded
diagrams	drawing by the reader to show interrelationships between important ideas

Strategy 4: SEEI

Reading a sentence consists, first of all, of finding a way to **state** what the sentence says so we can think the thought the sentence expresses. Further ways to make the meaning of a sentence clear are: **elaborating** the sentence, finding an **example**, and **illustrating** its meaning.

- **State** the main point of the paragraph in one or two sentences
- **Elaborate** on what you have paraphrased (i.e., In other words . . .)
- Give **examples** of its meaning by tying it to concrete situations in the real world (i.e., For example . . .)
- Generate metaphors, analogies, pictures, diagram, and/or graphs of the basic thesis to connect it to other meanings (To **illustrate** . . .)

■ Taking Notes of Lectures

In this chapter, we discuss the important skill of listening. You spend about half of your college time doing this vital task, and yet it has been called the most used and least taught of communication skills. It has even been noted that, in respect to amount of words, we listen a book a day, speak a book a week, read a book a month, and write a book a year. Yet have you ever heard of a class called Listening 101? Somehow it is assumed that we need classes to improve our speaking, reading, and writing skills, but we all know how to listen and do not need improvement in this area.

We hope you realize by now that the skill of listening can be improved, but only by practice and hard work! You can't really listen half way—it's either on or off. Unless you mentally rehearse material you are trying to listen to, you can't retain the information in short-term memory for more than twenty seconds! Yet listening comprehension affects your college grades just as reading comprehension does! Evidently, something must be done to give us a back-up system, since we cannot count on our memories.

Some of you may not be convinced of this fact. You may feel that if you really set your mind to it, you WILL remember that lecture. An interesting study was done several years ago to see how well we really can remember when we are interested and pay attention. The members of the Cambridge Psychological Society (obviously, intelligent people!) had an enjoyable discussion one day that was secretly taped by the experimenters, and two weeks later they were asked to write down all the specific points of the discussion they could remember. These learned members—who spend their lives learning and remembering—could only remember 8% of the major points, and what is even more startling was that 42% of those points were wrong! Do you really think you could do much better? The simple truth is this: if you want to remember, you must write it down so that you can review it. In short, you must take notes!

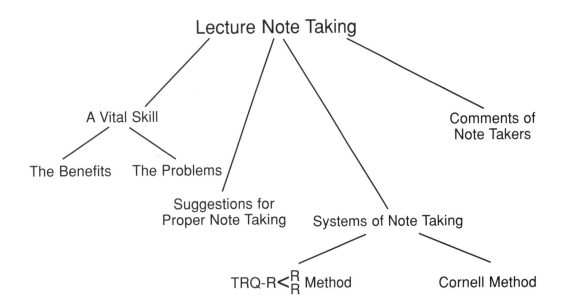

■ Why Is Note Taking So Vital in College?

It's really not vital to take notes, unless you want to remember what you are learning! It has been said that "we learn to listen in order to listen to learn." It is a proven fact that the normal student will forget 50% of what they have just heard within twenty minutes after a lecture. Unless you are terribly abnormal (and we doubt that!), you do not stand a chance of doing well on a test three weeks after a lecture unless you have some way to review that lecture—and there is no way to do that without notes. Material taken from lectures is usually a major portion of the material you will be tested over, and without notes you are almost guaranteed to go into the test situation only remembering a very small percentage of the material! You can always go back and review your textbook material, but your lecture notes are your ONLY lecture reference. They are vital to your college success! Add to these facts the sad but true thought that you will forget MORE and FASTER in lectures than in text reading or in writing, and you should begin to see the importance of note taking.

Another value of note taking is that it keeps you alert and listening during lectures. Note taking almost forces you to listen so that you can get the ideas to write down. Plus, as you learned when studying learning styles, the physical act of writing activates another one of your senses, thus helping you to retain a greater amount of what you are hearing. You will also tend to focus more on main ideas and begin to realize the relationship of sub-points to those main ideas as you try to take good notes. Even as you evaluate what is important to write, you are increasing your learning potential! Do we have you convinced yet? Well, let us give you one more huge benefit of lecture note taking. A proper note taking system will set up a way to review and make that review manageable, and that is at least half the test-battle won!

Don't plan on getting someone else's notes instead of taking your own. We can see those mind-wheels turning and planning to ask a very good note taker to let you borrow his notes. You are thinking, "A lot less trouble for me, and just as efficient in the long run!" Sorry, but that's not the way it works. As we have already mentioned, the act of writing and evaluating is important for the individual note taker, plus it is really difficult to make sense of most people's notes. They have a different style and use different symbols or abbreviations, and therefore, for the most part, someone else's notes—no matter how good they are for THEM—are not as effective for you. You must share the responsibility for communication, or it will not be as beneficial or effective for you. Sharing the responsibility for communication during lectures means taking a good set of your *own* notes.

If you leave a lecture totally unchanged, you have wasted your time and money. In order to get the most value out of any lecture, consider these three questions:

a. How important is the lecture *to you*? Does it directly influence your general education, your major, your career, or even your life in general? The more pertinent you can make the lecture to you, the more apt you are to listen attentively and retain the information.

b. How important is the lecture to *the lecturer?* Whether you think it's important to you or not, if it appears to be important to your professor you are apt to see that information again—probably on a test! How do you know if it is important to your professor? These are a few signs which may clue you in: time spent on a topic, repetition of topic, change in tone, pause in speech, change in posture (as in moving closer to the audience), writing on the board, or signal words, such as "Remember this," or "This is important to note." Mark these clues in your notes and make sure you MAKE these points important to you!

c. Does the lecture *duplicate* the textbook or *go beyond* it? If it's a duplication, a little of the pressure is off you because you have a second source with which to check information. But if the lecture goes beyond the textbook, it is doubly important that you conquer that information.

■ What Are Some Common Mistakes in Note Taking?

It has been said that most of us do one of two things when it comes to taking notes: we suddenly become a stenographer who feels that we must get everything down word-for-word, or we do the other thing—absolutely nothing! Both of these practices are incorrect and will lead to problems in learning. Another common problem involves worrying too much about grammar or spelling, and thus not getting enough information down on paper. A possible solution to this problem is to spell phonetically (or the way the word sounds) and correct it later that day. If you have no idea how to spell the word, leave a blank and write the first consonant. Then rely on the rest of the phrase or sentence to clue you in later that day as you look the word up and find out how to spell it. We have also seen problems with students who take notes, but do not take **enough** notes. They wait for the professor to write on the board before they write any information down, or they keep waiting to write the BIG idea only. Try to get as much information down as possible while still keeping up with the lecturer. You can always delete, but it is much more difficult to add on later.

Two final note taking mistakes are the failure to review notes and relying on tape-recorders. It defeats the purpose of note taking if you do not review the notes. Although it is beneficial just to write the information down, don't leave out the review step! As to whether to tape record lectures, our advice is that it is usually not a good idea. For one thing, if you rely on a machine you will probably not listen as actively. Secondly, if you find it difficult to listen to a live lecturer, how are you going to make yourself listen to an inanimate object? That is even more boring than the most boring of lectures! Finally, when will you find the time to listen to (and hopefully take notes from) the tape? You may soon find that you have a whole set of tapes to listen to and that is just one more thing to get you behind! If the lecturer speaks very quickly, you write very slowly, or the lecturer is difficult to understand due to an accent or other condition, it might be beneficial to tape record, as long as you follow these guidelines:

1. Take notes as if you did not have the tape recorder so you will promote active listening on your part.

2. Revise your notes with the tape THAT SAME DAY.

3. Only use 1 tape per subject so that you will be forced to stay caught up with your notes.

Take a minute to NOTE YOUR NOTE TAKING SKILLS by completing the checklist that follows. How do you measure up in this important skill? Your college grades—and more importantly, how much you learn from your college years—may depend on it!

Activity: Note Taking Skills Inventory 1

Note Taking Skills

PREPARING FOR CLASS	Yes	No

1. I check my course syllabus on a daily basis to make sure I'm aware of upcoming assignments. _____ _____

2. I read the textbook assignment before class so that the lecture material will seem familiar to me. _____ _____

3. I have a three-ring binder and loose leaf paper for classroom note taking. _____ _____

4. I have reviewed the table of contents of my textbook to have a general idea of how the information for this course is going to be organized. _____ _____

5. I have "tuned in" to my instructor's style and have a general idea of how s/he will deliver the material. _____ _____

PAYING ATTENTION IN CLASS

1. I am able to keep my attention on the subject matter even if the instructor wanders from the point or makes comments with which I don't agree. _____ _____

2. I am alert and actively listening during both lecture and discussion periods. _____ _____

3. I feel comfortable in asking questions if I don't understand the material presented in the lecture. _____ _____

4. I can identify introductory and concluding statements and can recognize transition words and phrases when the teacher is lecturing. _____ _____

5. As I listen, I can usually pick out the main ideas and supporting details without difficulty. _____ _____

NOTE TAKING TECHNIQUE

1. My notes are complete enough for me to understand them even when I look back over them many weeks later. _____ _____

2. I use my own words rather than trying to write down exactly what the teacher says. _____ _____

3. I make sure to copy down information put on the board and to include in my notes any examples the teacher used. _____ _____

4. I leave space to allow me to clarify my notes to add to them at a later point. _____ _____

5. I use a "personal shorthand" system of abbreviations and symbols which allows me to write down information more quickly. _____ _____

REVIEW AND USE OF NOTES   **Yes**   **No**

1. I review and edit my notes as soon as possible after class.   _____   _____

2. I use my notes to think of possible test questions to prepare   _____   _____
    for quizzes/tests.

3. I summarize the important ideas from each lecture on a daily basis.   _____   _____

4. I compare my notes with the text material I've read to make sure   _____   _____
    I fully understand the material.

5. In reviewing my notes, I can understand the connections between   _____   _____
    main ideas and supporting details and examples.

Look over your responses to the questions. In which sections did you have the most "Yes" responses? Which area needs the most improvement? Use the following sections on listening skills, preparing for note taking, recording information, note taking systems, and using your notes for test review to help you develop your note taking abilities.

Over 50% of what we hear is lost within the first hour. This makes it pretty clear that we can't depend on our memories for the material but need to have a written record for reference. Since college instruction is primarily lecture-oriented, good note taking skills are especially important.

■ Activity: Note Taking Skills Inventory 2

Note Your Note Taking Skills!

Put a check by each necessary skill of note taking that you currently practice. How do you rate?

BEFORE THE LECTURE, I

_____ 1. Read all textbook assignments.

_____ 2. Review yesterday's lecture notes.

_____ 3. Make sure I have all necessary supplies, including:

    a. an ink pen.
    b. my notebook for that class.
    c. the syllabus for that class.
    d. any special notebook set-up markings for my note taking system.
    e. any other special supplies needed for that particular class.

_____ 4. Arrive on time and attend each class, except in emergency situations.

DURING THE LECTURE, I

_____ 5. Label my notes with the date.

_____ 6. Use some type of outline form to see the visual organization of main and sub-points.

_____ 7. Make sure I have a heading for each topic as well as a heading for the entire lecture.

_____ 8. Try hard to get interested in the subject and stay mentally alert.

_____ 9. Ignore distractions.

_____10. Listen for clues that indicate important points and mark these in my notes.

_____11. Write legibly.

_____12. Get down as much information as possible, using my own words.

_____13. Use my own style of abbreviations and telegraphic writing.

_____14. Copy all information written on the board.

_____15. Ask questions if I do not understand.

AFTER THE LECTURE, I

_____16. Take a minute to write down a summary of the lecture.

_____17. Revise my notes that same day, adding, deleting, or clarifying information.

_____18. Review my notes by:

    a. making up questions over the notes.
    b. reciting the answers aloud.

_____19. Continue to review my notes weekly.

Your next preparation step is to **think about your instructor's lecture style.** You learned about instructor's teaching styles in the Learning Styles Chapter. Use the checklist in the following activity to "tune in" to your instructor's style. If s/he starts out with a recap of the previous lecture or closes by mentioning the next topic to be covered, pay attention! After several sessions, you'll be able to see how closely the lecture follows the text. If the lecture material is primarily new or supplemental material, your classroom notes will become even more important.

Name: _____ Date: _____

■ Activity: Evaluating Lecture Styles

Evaluating Lecture Styles

DIRECTIONS: Use the statements listed below to evaluate the lecture style of one of your instructors for this semester.

COURSE NAME	Yes	No
1. My instructor begins by giving a quick "recap" of the last class session.	____	____
2. My instructor clearly introduces each new topic.	____	____
3. Lecture pace is comfortable—neither too slow nor too fast.	____	____
4. Instructor's voice level and pronunciation are satisfactory— I can clearly understand what is being said.	____	____
5. My instructor keeps "on target" and generally doesn't wander too far off the topic.	____	____
6. Lecture material includes illustrations and examples which help me to understand the material.	____	____
7. Vocabulary level used is in my comfort zone. I don't feel overwhelmed with terms I don't understand.	____	____
8. My instructor encourages classroom discussion and is open to questions.	____	____
9. My instructor frequently uses the board or overhead projector to provide me with visual input.	____	____
10. The last few minutes of class are used to summarize main ideas covered and/or to clarify new assignments.	____	____

DISCUSSION: If your checklist reveals several checks in the "No" column, it is critical that you use the note taking strategies discussed in this chapter to get the most you can from the lecture and classroom discussion.

What's the Best Way to Take Lecture Notes?

The first item that is needed in order to take good notes is a well-organized notebook. It is best to have a separate notebook for each subject, preferably one with pockets or a three-ring binder so that you can add handouts to the proper place in your notes. At the very minimum, you need a separate section in the notebook for each subject. It has been stated that you can tell how a woman keeps house by the way she keeps her purse organized. We're not sure how accurate that is, but it is fairly safe to say that a well-organized notebook helps to promote well-organized thinking, and should also promote the possibility for a higher GPA! If your notebook is similar to the organization of a flea market, perhaps there is a reason for that confusion in your brain!

Now that you are armed with the proper notebook, consider the following suggestions as you begin to take notes and fill up that notebook:

1. **Assume a Position of Alertness.** This statement involves two suggestions: watch WHERE you sit, and watch HOW you sit. If you want to give yourself every advantage, SIT FRONT AND CENTER. Students who sit closer to the lecturer get higher grades—it's just that simple. No one seems to know for sure why this is true. Could it be because there are less distractions, or could it be that better students naturally navigate closer to the front? For whatever reason, it will be to your advantage to DO IT!. Besides watching where you sit, make sure you also watch your posture. For the most part, an alert body helps to promote an alert mind, and outward manifestations of interest may even create genuine internal interest, so watch how you sit. Slump in your seat, and your mind may slump with you! As you sit alertly, INTEND TO REMEMBER what you will be hearing. Pretend you are going to have a pop quiz after the lecture. It **will** make a difference in how carefully you listen!

2. **Be Prepared!** Have all your SUPPLIES together. You will need your trusty notebook, of course, and a pen with which to take notes. But you also need to prepare by making sure you have kept up with your TEXTBOOK READING, and also by REVIEWING YOUR PAST LECTURE NOTES before class. These two suggestions will make a large difference on how easily you can follow the lecturer. Keep your class SYLLABUS handy and refer to it often. It is a contract between the professor and yourself, and you are both obligated by what it says. Make sure *you* know what it says! Part of class preparation starts before the beginning of the semester by trying to SCHEDULE your classes in an organized fashion. Consider your own biological clock as you decide when the best time would be to take each class. If it is at 12:00 p.m., you may have difficulty concentrating due to hunger. So, as much as you can, prepare adequately before you start the class by considering all possibilities. Finally, prepare by ASSUMING YOUR RESPONSIBILITY. You will decide how much you get out of the lecture largely by this one act. If you are a responsible, self-motivated student, you will FIND reasons to listen and take notes. If you do not assume this responsibility, you will be a more passive listener who expects the instructor to GIVE you reasons to listen by motivating you and capturing your interest. Don't count on this happening. It's nice when it does, but the responsibility has to be yours—as is the education you gain or lose.

3. **Attend Class and Be Punctual.** You can skip class physically (as many do), or you can realize from the very start how much you are paying for each class period, and that it's your loss if you skip. Unfortunately, the habit of skipping is an easy one to get into and a hard one to stop. Don't start it. Be there, and be there on time! You need to also be aware of the fact that you can skip mentally even if you do not skip physically. If you do not listen actively or if you do not take notes, you might as well have skipped the class.

4. **Keep Your Eyes on the Instructor.** It does take PRACTICE to listen, watch, and write, but your skill will improve with practice. It is important to WATCH THE PROFESSOR FOR THOSE VISUAL CLUES mentioned earlier, and to NOTE THOSE as you take notes. Mark things with which you tend to disagree. For some reason we tend to remember best the things we agree with and ignore the rest. Try to listen with your mind, not your feelings. Is the lecture boring? You have some control over that, believe it or not, by your attitude and by your facial expressions. You can ENCOURAGE THE LECTURER by nodding your head, smiling, and looking alive and interested, and the lecture may improve. If you want it to get even more boring, try looking bored or even putting your head down on your desk. You can spice up the lecture by making your face look interested! Try it! VISUALIZE AND CATEGORIZE as you listen. See it as well as hear it and write it, and you will be planting it more firmly in your mind. Since the mind can only retain about seven "chunks" of information at a time, try to think in main ideas. These main topics will be easier to organize in your notes AND in your mind. Lastly, NEVER HESITATE TO ASK a professor to explain a point if you've read your assignment and been listening to the lectures. You're probably not the only one who has that question!

5. **Take Notes Aggressively!** Do not wait for something important to be said. It will be too late to get it down if you put your pen down and wait. You never know the importance of the statement until it is past, so keep your pen in hand, and use it! Perhaps the most crucial component of this suggestion is your attitude. The proper attitude has been called the most important requirement for good note taking. Realize that the lecture is supposed to save you time and effort, and that the teacher is a partner in your future success for your chosen career. This will make it a little easier to share the responsibility of the communication and cooperate in active listening. Take advantage of your professor's knowledge and time. It will add to yours—and we're speaking both of knowledge and time! Don't just write down what you think will be on the test. You are trying to learn all you can learn, remember?

6. **Write in Telegraphic Style.** Even though it is important to get down all the information you can in the time you have, it is beneficial to leave out words that are not crucial to the meaning of the message—like you would if you were paying for each word in a telegram. Invent your own symbols and abbreviations to make your notes more meaningful. For example, put a star by material that the lecturer mentioned might be test material, or put a box around material that was written on the board. Abbreviate words such as without (w/o), because (b/c), or a name that is used repeatedly can just be the first initial with a blank after you have used it several times. Make sure you USE YOUR OWN WORDS. If you try to copy the professor's words down word-for-word, you may bypass your brain! Rephrase the main idea into your own words, and you will increase your learning power. All of the above take practice, but you will improve with each good set of notes that you take.

7. **Neatness Counts!** Don't waste valuable study time trying to decipher notes that can only be read by a mind-reader. BLOCK PRINTING is often more easily read than cursive, and can also be much faster to write, so consider printing your notes in manuscript. Be sure to LEAVE PLENTY OF WHITE SPACE. Use blanks for words or ideas missed and fill them in after class by asking your professor or a friend for clarification, or by looking it up in your text. Review your notes as soon as possible after class so you can do some fix-ups. Add to or correct whatever is needed. "White space" aids in this revision process. KEEP YOUR NOTES DATED AND NUMBERED to avoid confusion at a later time and to be able to tell where test coverage will start. Remember, if the problem of spelling slows you down,

use the first letter plus a blank space, or use phonetic spelling. Also, USE INK as you take your notes. It is less likely to smudge or fade, and you will not have as much difficulty reviewing your notes several weeks later—or even years later, as the case may be!

8. **Don't Doodle!** If you do doodle—or write letters, or sleep, or knit, or whatever, you are making a judgment call that what you are doing is more important than the lecture, and you may be right! But remember, you must also be willing to accept the consequences of your actions, and usually that's a high price to pay. If you get bored, try reviewing your notes, questioning them, or predicting what's going to be said next. All of these strategies are important comprehension tools, and may help to review your interest. Even if that doesn't happen, you are not wasting your time as you are with the doodling syndrome!

9. **Go for Main Ideas, Not Details.** Note taking is a process of selection, condensation, and compression, and this very process is a wonderful learning experience. If you do it correctly, the act of note taking is a valuable study tool. Try to think in terms of headings and subheadings, and USE SOME TYPE OF AN OUTLINE SYSTEM to show the overall organization of the lecture. Headings or labels are extremely important! If you are not sure what the topic is, leave a blank, get down the information, and come back to create a heading later. You need to see some visual organization in order to think in an organized fashion. The outline form itself is not important—that there is some organization for main points and subpoints is vital!

10. **Always Copy Examples and Board Work.** These will tend to be the items that make the most sense to you and will be more easily remembered. They may help to clarify the rest of the material.

11. **Listen Carefully to the Very End** of the lecture! Professors typically get behind in a lecture, and they may be cramming in two last pages of notes while you are busy gathering up all your junk! Or they may be reviewing some important test questions right at the last minute, so you must listen until the "bitter end." Some of the most important information may be squeezed into the last few seconds. Take a few minutes to get the full benefits, or you may live to regret it!

■ Is There a System to Make Note Taking Easier?

There are many good systems to help you organize your notes, and we will present two excellent ones here.

The TRQ-R$<^R_R$ System

This system was created by Dr. Charles Tegeler of Southwest Missouri State University, and is an acronym standing for Take notes, Revise, Question, and Review. It is probably not that much different from the system you are using now, but it could make an enormous difference in your grades. Why? Because of the difference in the two words RECALL and RECOGNITION. Most of us have learned to study lecture notes by simply reading over them several times (if we're lucky), and hoping that we will recognize the correct answer on the test. We never reach the point where we can pull up (recall) the information without the clues. TRQ-R$<^R_R$ builds in a set of questions so you are forced to recall, not just recognize, and that difference will change those C's and B's to A's!

So here is what you should do:

Step 1: *Take Notes*

After you have dated your notes and made a title for what the lecture is about, write down the information as clearly and quickly as you can. But one very important aspect of this system is that you only write on the right page of your notebook—leave the left page blank for Steps 2 and 3. Make sure you keep up with the professor. Don't get behind. Go on when he/she goes on, and fill in missed information after class. Try to keep eye contact with the lecturer, and get as much down in your words as possible. As soon as the class is over, take a minute or two to summarize what the lecture was about at the bottom of the last LEFT page. This summarizing will aid in your comprehension and retention.

Step 2: *Revise Notes*

Some time after the lecture—and it must be the day of the lecture or this step will not work properly—take a few minutes to fix your notes. Although many students try to recopy or type their notes, we feel that this is not an efficient use of your time or an effective way to study. You could better be using this time by studying your notes, and recopying or typing does not necessarily mean you are learning the information. Instead of recopying, use the left page you have left blank to REVISE your notes. If some sections of your notes are fine and need no revision, then make a checkmark on the left page directly across from the notes and leave them alone. The checkmark will remind you that those original notes needed no revision. But for that section for which you now remember more information or need to clarify a point, add that information directly across from the old information. This section can also be used to REDUCE or condense information, or make up mnemonic memory strategies to aid with retention. When you study, you can then study back and forth as you follow your numbering or outline system.

Step 3: *Question Main Ideas (Analysis)*

This step is where you can apply the Elements of Reasoning discussed in the Critical Thinking chapter. Analyze your notes. Find the purpose of the lecture, identify key questions and information, note any inferences, assumptions, or conclusion there may be in your notes. In the margin of your left pages, come up with a good summarizing question for EACH main idea and sub-point of your notes. If you have used an outline form, this step will not be difficult. Good questions usually involve words such as describe, explain, how, or the 5 W's—who, what, when, where, why. Write the question directly across from the information that answers it, and as you study you can flip the right page over to cover the notes and revisions and see only the questions to make sure you are studying for recall, not recognition. If you do not know the answer, all you have to do is look directly across from your question to review the information in your notes. Make sure your question is a "reciting question," such as "What are the seven suggestions to improve listening skills?" or "Discuss the six major causes of the Civil War." It is helpful to clue yourself into how many answers you are trying to remember—if you remember six, was that good or were there twelve more you should have known? This question step is the most vital part of the system and is why this system will almost guarantee raising your grades, if you use it properly. The only way you will know if it works is to try this step!

Step 4: *Review Your Notes < Review what you know/Relearn what you have forgotten*

Your first review should happen as soon as you revise and question your notes—on the same day as the lecture. But since you have set up your notes for review, this is not a difficult process. Simply read your questions aloud (to involve more of your senses), and try to recall and recite the information. This review step consists of two parts—REVIEW-

ING WHAT YOU REMEMBER, and RELEARNING WHAT YOU HAVE FORGOTTEN. The first time you review your notes, unfortunately most of the review is in the second category—the relearning portion. But each time you review, and we would suggest you review each set of lecture notes once a week, more of the material should fall in the RE-MEMBERED category. You're not ready for a test until it is ALL in that category! Although it seems it would be impossible to review each set of notes weekly, each time you review you will remember more information for a longer period of time, so very soon you will be able to breeze through this set of notes. What a difference you will feel the night before the test if you have practiced weekly review!

■ The Cornell System of Note Taking

This system, devised by Dr. Walter Pauk of Cornell University, is another excellent way to organize your notes. You will need to make two-column note sheets for this system by drawing a vertical line 2 ½ inches from the left edge of your paper. End this line two inches above the bottom of the paper and draw a horizontal line across the paper there. In the narrow left column you will write questions about the notes which have been written in the wide column on the right. In the bottom two inch space you will summarize your notes. Now that your paper is set up, these are the steps you should follow in more detail:

1.   Record

In the wide column, get down as many of the facts of the lecture as you can. Remember to use the suggestions that were given earlier in the chapter, such as printing if it is more legible for you, using pen, and using telegraphic sentences. As soon as possible after class, "fix" any major errors in your notes, or add clarifications.

2.   Question (Analyze)

You now need to take a few minutes to reread your notes and make up questions based on the main ideas. Put these questions across from the main ideas in the narrow column on the left. Make sure they are broad, "reciting" questions.

3.   Recite

To recite means that you say the information in your own words AND aloud, without looking at your notes. It is such a valuable learning strategy! Not only are you using several of your senses, but you are working for recall again—not recognition. Studies have shown that students who recite remember 80% of the material. Those who only reread remember only 20% when tested two weeks later. You choose which will be the case for you. If you choose to remember 80% (or hopefully even more), cover up your notes, read the question, and recite your answer. Then take a minute to check your notes again, and recite any information that was left out or incorrect. Continue in this manner through the rest of your notes.

4.   Reflect

With "real" learning, you want to be able to do more than give back information verbatim, so this reflection stage is crucial. You now need to try to apply what you have learned to your own life. Make it pertinent and significant to you. Ask yourself how this new information "fits in" with what you already know. This added step will make you more enthusiastic and curious about what you learn, and will mean that you will retain the knowledge longer than you possibly could if you omit this important reflection step.

Critical Thinking

Two skills that are crucial to good note taking are summarizing—being aware of the main ideas, and paraphrasing—being able to state those ideas in your own words. Take a minute to look back over a set of past lecture notes. Try your skill at summarizing each page, and then go one step further and summarize the whole lecture at the end of the last page. Look back over the lecture notes. Did you record the information in your own words, or in the words of your professor? Paraphrasing the information will require understanding of it, and summarizing will then be an easy step with which to follow-up.

5. Review

Of course, no system could work without the necessary step of reviewing. We suggest you review your lecture notes before class, and also plan a time during the week to review all past lecture notes for each subject. Thanks to the organization of the system, the review step is set up for you. Now you just need to read the questions—aloud, recite the information, double-check the answer, and continue through your questions. Each review will prove you are remembering more information for a longer period of time.

6. Recapitulate

This term simply means that you summarize each page of notes at the end of the lecture. This summarizing step requires a higher level of thinking, and will help you to gain a deeper understanding of the material. Dr. Pauk also suggests that you go one step further for optimum learning and summarize the entire lecture on the last note page for that lecture. To be able to summarize will mean that you really got the "meat" of the lecture. It is also a fast and easy way to review just before a test is handed to you.

Steps 2, 4, and 6 in the Cornell System provides the note taker the opportunity to apply their critical thinking skills to the information provided in class. The note taker should be able to analyze information to identify the eight Elements of Reasoning discussed in the Critical Thinking chapter.

THE CORNELL METHOD: SETTING UP THE PAPER

2 ½ " Margin
For questions

6" column for taking notes

2" space for a summary

Excerpted from Aguilar "Active Listening and Note Taking Skills."

THE CORNELL METHOD: SETTING UP THE PAPER

1/16/96
Hist. 104

	CAUSES OF THE GREAT DEPRESSION
	Loss of Control By Fed. Reserve Bd.
What impact did FRB policies have on the Economy?	*1. No bail out for first banks to close*
	2. Raised interest rates
	3. No bank regulation
	4. No bank insurance for depositors
	5. Banks made too many loans to brokers and speculators
	Market Speculation
How did the lack of mkt. controls contribute to the "crash"?	*1. No control – "anything goes" attitude*
	2. Investors borrowed to buy stocks and used them as collateral to buy more.
Describe "margin" buying.	*3. Business sector speculated instead of re-investing in their own companies.*
What was impact of the Hawley-Smoot Tariff?	*Hawley-Smoot Tariff – Kept imports out but then Europe couldn't buy goods from us.*

Summary: No one cause of the crash.
"Margin" buying, poor economy after Post-War Boom, poor FRB Policies were major influences.

■ Does a Note Taking System Really Make a Difference?

We feel that you will be pleasantly surprised at what a difference a system WILL make! But don't take our word for it. Prove it to yourself! You may choose to adapt one of the systems in a few ways that would better suit it to your own needs. But in the meantime, read these comments of students who—just like yourself—had to try it before they would believe it.

- ■ I've only had one test using TRQ-R and got a B+ up to an A. It worked well!
- ■ With TRQ-R I got a 10% raise (in my grade).
- ■ TRQ-R helped me raise my grades. I went from a D in Econ to an A!
- ■ In religion—F on first test, C on second, B on third.
- ■ In Communications I went from a D to a C. My overall grades have gone from D's and F's to B's and C's. My study skills have improved tremendously using time and study habits with TRQ-R.
- ■ My fourth Soc test was returned to me during class today. Unlike my first three test scores which averaged 79%, the grade I received on this test was 91%.
- ■ I've not been able to tell a difference in my tests because I made high percentages before, but I have noticed an advantage in a reduction of needed study time.
- ■ Using TRQ-R raised my test grades. On the first test, I made a high F (58%); on the second test I made a 74%.
- ■ My letter grades in my classes have gone from C– to B+.

And finally, just one more comment:

- ■ I didn't use (TRQ-R) but I wish I had—I definitely will next semester!

So, try a system to organize and revitalize your notes. You'll be glad you did! All you have to lose is lower grades and frustration. But think what you have to gain!

■ It's Worth It!

Since most of our learning will take place by the work of our ears and mind combined, the adding of our hands with the skill of note taking will help to ensure that the knowledge stands a better chance of sticking in our brain. Yes, it does take more time and effort to write it down, but the improved results show that it's worth that time and effort! Have you ever stopped to consider how much you are paying for each lecture? You have to take into consideration not only what you are spending for classes, books, gas, and rent, but also what you could be making if you were working full time instead of investing in college. If you find out—as most of our students did—that you are spending at least FIFTY DOLLARS per lecture, you may decide that note taking is the least you can do to get the most for your money. Spend your time, your energy, your study efforts, AND your money in the best way possible. Find an effective system of note taking that works for you, and use it!

■ Summary

This chapter has stressed the necessity of reading well and taking lecture notes. Too much will be forgotten, or not even understood or heard correctly in the first place, if a student does not write it down and comprehend. The benefits are numerous and worthwhile. They include keeping you alert during lecture and reading and involving added senses to your sense of hearing. Often students get bogged down in note taking and annotating because they focus on the wrong things—like details, grammar, spelling, or the exact words. The best way to take notes includes using your own words, getting as much of the information on paper as possible, using ink, headings, and an outline form, and also using a note taking system. This chapter has presented the reader with two excellent ones—the TRQ-R System and the Cornell System. Either of these systems will help to organize your notes and set them up for efficient review—and that is what mastering lectures is all about!

◼ Activity: Editing Your Notes

Select and photocopy a set of lecture notes from one of your classes for this semester (at least two pages). Using a different colored pen or marker, edit these notes using the techniques described in the chapter. Rewrite any illegible words, complete incomplete thoughts or ideas, fill in any blanks, clarify abbreviations used, check your text or a friend's notes to fill in any information you might have missed.

Next, review your notes and jot down either "key words" or questions in the margin to identify the main ideas and topics covered.

CHAPTER 6
Test Taking

■ Taking Tests: Making the Grade

It has been estimated that in your college career you will spend from 25–40% of your time preparing for or taking tests! Evidently, this is a crucial skill to master if you want to succeed in college! It is very probable that no one has tried to teach you how to master this test-taking skill, yet your grade point average is affected more by this ability than by any other single thing! Every student has felt at one time or another the butterflies, nausea, or extreme terror caused by the mention of the word "test." No one likes to think that their life could possibly be changed by their performance on a mental examination, but that is often the feeling that we give ourselves (or is given to us by our professors). Maybe it is time to put some thought into the basic strategies that could make test-taking less traumatic.

There are just two basic problems caused by the necessity of tests—test anxiety and test smartness. Test anxiety is probably familiar to all students. It's that fear of failure, the fear of going blank, or the fear of feeling out of control, and it can have a negative effect

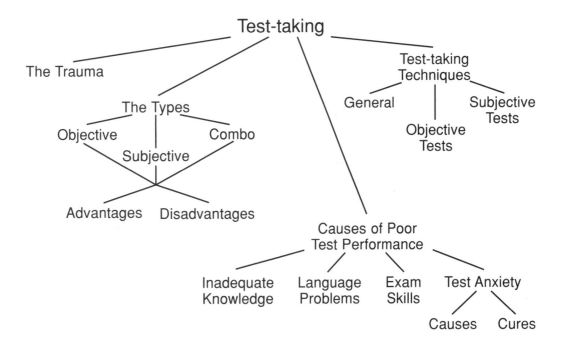

This chapter contains material adapted from *Practical Approaches for Building Study Skills and Vocabulary*, second edition, by Gary Funk et al. Copyright © 1996 by Kendall/Hunt Publishing Company. Adapted and reprinted with permission of the publisher. Further reproduction is prohibited.

on test scores. You actually may have learned the material, but forget it due to test anxiety. Test smartness is just as much a problem, but few students may realize it. The "A" is on the paper due to good test-taking skills, but the knowledge is quickly forgotten or never applied. Since most students could fall easily into one of these two problem areas, we may need to rethink our view of test-taking.

■ What Could Take the Trauma out of Test-Taking?

In the first place, we expect too much out of our memories! Due to the myth that cramming is effective, too many students believe that the best way to study for a test is to cram all the information possible into your mind the night before the test. That way all the information will be fresh! In no other area of life would we expect so much out of our abilities. Would you ever consider that you were physically fit for life because you had worked out at the gym last night? Or would you ever take a bath and feel that you had completed that task and would never have to do it again? Of course, these examples are obvious, but until we get in our minds the idea that information must be reviewed consistently to be remembered, test scores will consistently point out that we have not quite mastered the material. Many students make the mistake of trying to "view" the material the night before rather than "review." Information is retained by systematic, spaced over learning. There is no other effective means. Cramming MAY give you a passing grade, but it will not show much practical benefit as far as retaining the material—and isn't that why you are in college?

■ Okay, What Are the Rules for True Test Preparation?

Three basic rules—plus omitting the word cramming from your vocabulary—will make a great difference in your view of test-taking preparation (and the possible trauma it creates).

Rule 1: Start studying for each test the first day of class. Do not feel that you do not need to study biology today since you just had a test last Thursday. The way you study the material being learned this week will determine your test grade just as much as the way you study the night before the test.

Rule 2: Don't get behind on assignments! Finish each day's work on that day, if at all possible. Stay caught up on reading assignments and text-note taking, revising lecture notes, and extra assignments. Don't procrastinate or your grade will reflect it.

Rule 3: Incorporate the use of all three types of review—daily, weekly, and test-taking. EACH DAY spend a few minutes revising your lecture notes from that day and reviewing them. Read your text assignment, take notes, and review them. Do this for each class taken on that day. Sometime during the week, you need to go back and review all the PAST lecture and text notes from the current semester. Don't wait until test-time! Now is the time to start preparing. Think of what a difference you will feel if you have already reviewed each set of notes four or five times BEFORE you start to study for the test! Two or three nights before the actual test you can do an IN-DEPTH REVIEW of all the material, but it won't be cramming filled with panic and pressure. You will have built a solid foundation on which to study for the test.

■ What's the Difference between Recall and Recognition?

Along with these three test-taking preparation rules, you must also be aware of one more way that we need to change our view of test-taking. For many students, to study for a test means to be able to RECOGNIZE the material when it is presented on the test. That's why multiple choice test items seem to be easiest for most of us—we can recognize what we have studied. But if the test is a short answer, fill-in-the-blank, or essay test, our memories may fail us. There's nothing to recognize! We have not studied to the point of RECALL, and we cannot pull up the information from our memories. We stopped short of effective learning because we stopped reviewing when we felt we could recognize the material. To realize the difference between recall and recognition is the major step towards "de-traumatizing" test taking. You must learn the material to the point that you do not need clues to aid your memory, and studying with the use of *questions* and *recitation* is the way to conquer this crucial difference. Effective students do not just read over their notes—they make questions over the main ideas, cover up the material, and recite the questions and answers aloud. Extra work? Yes. Does it make a difference? You won't believe the difference!

■ What Are the Different Types of Tests?

There are really just three types of tests—objective, subjective, and a combination of the two.

    a. Objective tests include multiple choice, true-false, and matching items. These questions have only one right answer because the grader is looking for a specific letter or word. These items are all recognition items, because the choices are spelled out for you. You may choose true or false, or you may choose from a list of two or more possible answers.

    b. Subjective tests are also called essay tests. The question will call for a very broad answer, and the correct answer depends on the "subject" who is grading it. What one grader might call an acceptable and complete answer could be viewed as incomplete, or even completely wrong, to another grader.

    c. A combination of subjective and objective characteristics could involve sentence completion items (or fill-in-the-blank, as they are commonly called) or short answer items. These are more of a combination of objective and subjective traits because, even though one basic idea is being asked for, more than one specific word or concept could be the correct answer. Therefore, a little bit of subjectivity is being used.

■ What Are the Advantages of Each Type?

Objective tests are probably used more often than subjective tests for several reasons. An instructor can test over a lot of material in a very short amount of time with this approach. They are easy and fast to grade, and a student worker could help the instructor in the grading if time is a priority. Many instructors like to use these tests because they are less subjective and involve less decision-making when grading. No matter who grades the test, or when it is graded, the credit will be the same. So it may appear that this type of testing is a little more fair to all. But, as we all know, objective items can be worded in such a way that they may not appear "fair." Even so, ease in grading and equality in fairness are two definite advantages of objective tests. Also, since the student is not required to write long answers on objective tests, many instructors feel that these tests do not let a student's writing ability interfere with the test score. Poor writing ability does not hurt the grade; neither can a good writer cover up for lack of knowledge with outstanding writing ability. So in several ways the objective test may appear more fair.

On the other hand, subjective tests really do what a test is supposed to do—show what you really know. When you have to write out detailed answers on a topic, it quickly becomes obvious if you really LEARNED the material! Subjective tests force recall learning, and that's the best kind! Subjective tests are also much easier and faster for the professor to compose than objective tests.

■ What Are the Disadvantages?

Even though there are advantages to either of these two major types of tests, there are also disadvantages that make the choice hard for instructors to make. Objective tests may end up only testing "test-awareness," or the ability to recognize enough and bluff enough to make the grade. But the test has not accomplished its purpose—that of trying to show true knowledge learned. As mentioned previously, good objective items are fairly difficult and time consuming to write. Questions may end up being tricky or testing for details only.

Perhaps the main disadvantage of subjective tests is that they are very difficult to grade. This difficulty involves two aspects—time and fairness. It does take an enormous amount of time to grade essay tests. So if an instructor has several sections of one class, time factors make these tests a real trial to grade. This time and pressure factor may influence how fairly each test is graded. It may be all too true that one essay test could receive many different scores, based on the person who grades the test, the time of day it was graded, and even the order in which it was graded. Fatigue plays a role in fairness, time limits add to the problem, and personality factors of the grader complicate the matter. A student's writing ability may also influence the grader. Neat handwriting, correct spelling and grammar, a "way with words," and overall neatness of the paper may sway the judgment of the grader. Unfortunately, the opposite kind of paper may do the same thing—only in the opposite direction!

■ What Are the Causes of Poor Test Performance?

Even though the most obvious answer as to why students might not perform well on a test would be INADEQUATE KNOWLEDGE, this is certainly not the only answer. Part of the purpose of this chapter is to help you to analyze your typical test behavior and sort out the hindrances to your success. It is true that many students do not perform well on a test simply due to the fact that they did not study enough—or in the proper way. It is vital that you understand that it is not how MANY hours you study for a test that makes the difference. It is the QUALITY of those hours and the way they are DISTRIBUTED that spell out your success rate. Weekly reviews based on questions and recited answers over thorough lecture and text notes are the secrets to mastery. Intense cramming sessions the night before the test will not assure you that the information will be there when needed.

LANGUAGE-RELATED PROBLEMS can also affect your performance on tests. If you read the textbook but do not comprehend it, you will not perform to the best of your ability. If you have trouble understanding the test items, or knowing specifically what the question is asking for, your answer cannot be top-notch. Therefore, reading problems do influence many students' test grades.

Also, many students simply do not know how to take a test. Even though they may have taken hundreds in their lifetime, INEFFECTIVE EXAM-TAKING SKILLS may still be hindering their performance. Test-taking is a game one must learn to play—a skill that can be learned with practice. Certain rules must be learned and adhered to or the results will not please you. We will cover these "rules" in the next several sections.

Finally, TEST ANXIETY can cripple your test scores. You may have studied adequately, and you may feel you really do know the information, but if you panic during the test, your memory will not cooperate. Take a minute now to TEST YOUR TESTING SKILLS. Complete the inventory that follows to see if exam anxiety is a problem for you, or if you suffer from other "testing deficiencies."

■ Activity: Test Your Testing Skills

Answer yes or no to the following questions to check up on your ability to play the testing game.

Before a Test, I

	Yes	No

1. usually wait until a test is announced before reading text assignments or reviewing lecture notes. _____ _____

2. often think of tests as trials that can't be escaped and must be endured. _____ _____

3. often do not read my textbook because the instructor will cover it if it's important. _____ _____

4. feel that I have a good memory, so I do not usually take notes over lectures. _____ _____

5. sometimes have to memorize formulas, definitions, or rules that I simply do not understand. _____ _____

6. generally have trouble deciding what I really need to study. _____ _____

7. depend mainly on last-minute cramming to prepare for the test so that it will be fresh in my mind. _____ _____

During a Test, I

	Yes	No

8. am sometimes unable to finish answering all the test items within the allotted time. _____ _____

9. sometimes am forced to leave an item blank because I cannot decide on the correct answer. _____ _____

10. often find I cannot decide what the question is really asking for in an answer. _____ _____

11. frequently feel that I have not studied enough, or that I have not studied the correct information. _____ _____

12. start with the first item and answer each question in its correct order, regardless of difficulty. _____ _____

13. catch myself thinking about how much smarter other students are than myself. _____ _____

14. worry about what will happen if I flunk the test. _____ _____

15. get so nervous that I feel sick to my stomach and have trouble remembering what I studied. _____ _____

16. often think, "The more I study, the less I remember!" _____ _____

17. then realize I would much rather write two essays than take one test! _____ _____

After a Test, I

	Yes	No
18. almost always feel that I could have done better.	_____	_____
19. often find that I have made careless mistakes or left unintentional blank answers.	_____	_____
20. find that I should have changed an answer, but I did not because I felt my first answer is usually best.	_____	_____
21. try to forget about the test as soon as possible so that I can start fresh on new material.	_____	_____
22. only look over my mistakes, because the rest of the questions were correct and therefore do not need to be analyzed.	_____	_____

SCORING: Count up your yes responses. As in the game of golf, the lower your score, the better you play the game of test-taking. If you answered yes to three or more of questions 13–18, you have some problems with test anxiety also. What's a GOOD score for this test on test-taking? If you scored higher than a 7, practicing the suggestions from this chapter could completely change the way you feel about tests!

■ Critical Thinking and Questioning

Education is not limited to memorizing a lot of names, numbers, and definitions. Being educated means being able to find the best information and put it all together to create something of value. Educated people are expected to be decision makers, problem solvers, and innovators. They are expected to *think critically, to gather and evaluate evidence, weigh alternatives, and arrive at logical conclusions or valid opinions.* (Remember that machines can do the other stuff.)

One expert on thinking says that the difference between highly intelligent people and less intelligent people is more a matter of habit than of brain cells. He says that when we are not being intelligent, we practice "one-shot thinking": we look at something, decide either that we understand it or that we don't understand it, and move on. Intelligent people, on the other hand, examine ideas: they mentally take ideas apart, turn them around to see all the sides, and put them together in a way that makes sense. They find intelligent answers by asking intelligent questions.

We all go through this process of examining ideas and asking good questions when we are being our smartest. We all engage in one-shot thinking when we are being anything but smart.

When we want to know something about the Civil War or real estate law or domestic violence, we ask the basic *who?, what?,* and *where?* questions. When we really want to understand the Civil War or real estate law or domestic violence, we also ask the more thoughtful *how?, why?, like what?,* and *what if?* questions. These higher order questions require more thought because they ask for logical connections between ideas. They are also more productive than the more basic questions because they make it easier for us to remember, understand, and use the answers.

■ Activity: Critical Thinking

The following statements were taken from high school and college students' papers. Your job is to write a brief description of what is wrong with their thinking or their information. Apply the Elements of Reasoning and Intellectual Standards where appropriate.

1. The invention of the steamboat caused a system of rivers to spring up.

2. Socrates couldn't have died of an overdose of wedlock because wedlock is when someone is born when two people are not married.

3. Martin Luther was murdered at a motel because he made the Pope mad.

4. Sir Francis Drake circumvented the globe.

5. The Bible was written by Jesus in the Middle Ages, which is a place in Europe.

6. The speed limit on Highway 108 should be raised to 65 mph because the curves and hills and bridges along that stretch of road make good hiding places for carjackers. They wouldn't be able to steal a car going 65 like they would one going 55.

■ How Can You Become More Test-Wise?

We have already discussed the problem of test-smartness, but the goal is to be test-wise—to know how to play the game of taking tests successfully. Three main areas of test preparation need to be considered: physical, emotional, and intellectual preparation.

Be Physically Prepared!

You need to be in top physical condition to do your very best in a test situation. We don't mean you need to be able to run a marathon, but on the other hand, don't handicap yourself by not being physically prepared. Although you would not do this purposefully, you are in effect handicapping yourself if you do not accomplish these physical tasks before a test:

a. *Attend class*—each and every one. The worst class to skip is the one before the test. Never skip class in order to study more. Important reviews may take place right before the test session, so don't miss them!

b. *Ask questions*—These questions may include the type of test (objective or subjective), length of exam, time allowed, material covered, possible points and percentage of total grade, examples of test questions, and if any aids are allowed, such as pocket dictionary, calculator, etc. These answers may influence the way that you will study.

c. *Eat properly*—Don't skip breakfast, and try to include some protein in the meal before your test. Give yourself "brain fuel!"

d. *Sleep properly*—Don't skip study time to sleep, and don't skip sleep time to study. Schedule each for its proper time. Don't plan all night studying sessions. Sleeping seems to "cement" learning, or help your memory to consolidate what you have studied. If you do not get an adequate amount of sleep, your spontaneity and originality may be hurt, and your level of anxiety may be heightened. Also, the worst time to "party hardy" is the night before the test! You need a clear head and quick thinking ability to do your best on the test, and drinking will not help you in either of those areas!

e. *Study in a simulated test-taking atmosphere*—Try to make your study sessions like the real thing! Set time limits, sit at a desk, don't allow interruptions, and don't peek! Anxiety may be increased in a testing situation simply because it is so different than what you are used to.

f. *Use a multi-sensory approach to studying*—Remember to use your eyes to see, but also your voice to recite, your ears to listen, and your hands to write the information you need to learn. The more ways you put the information in your mind, the better chance you have of it sticking!

Be Emotionally Prepared!

Now that you've mastered the physical aspects of test-preparation, consider these emotional aspects:

a. *Think positively!*—Push for success, not just to avoid failure. Too many of us think as the little boy who reluctantly told his father, *"Dad, I'm afraid I flunked that math exam." "Son, that's negative thinking!" admonished his father. "Think positive!" "Then, Dad, I'm positive I flunked that test!" the son replied.* Don't dwell on the past or even what the future will bring. Think only on the OPPORTUNITY of this one test. A test is not a trial, but a chance to show what you know, and learn what you've missed. Use it to its full advantage!

b. *Visualize a good grade*—Although this is similar to the suggestion above, it is so helpful that we want to include it separately. See an A+ paper in your mind. Tell yourself, "It will be just like me to ace this test!" Instead of putting yourself or your ability down, pump yourself up! These "coping statements" will make a big difference in your attitude and confidence!

c. *Tie main ideas in with your life*—Try to apply the big ideas of what you have studied to your own situation. The more applicable you can make the information, the more apt you are to remember and benefit from it.

d. *Avoid pre-test hall chatter*—Have you ever noticed the typical statements of students before they go in to take a test? You hear things such as, "I didn't study at all for this test! Did you?" or "I hope to goodness I don't flunk this thing!" You don't need this type of talk! Whether you have studied enough or not, don't erode what you do have!

e. *Remember that some anxiety is helpful*—Although you can suffer from too much test anxiety, a little bit of nervousness will keep you alert and on top of things. Accept this as natural and helpful!

Be Intellectually Prepared!

Intellectual preparation for testing is the ONLY area that many students feel has to be dealt with, but as we have discussed, physical and emotional preparation are essential also. However, this area of being intellectually ready for the test is obviously crucial. Consider these vital components of being intellectually prepared:

a. *Review lecture and text notes weekly*—This vital weekly review has already been emphasized, but it cannot be stressed too much. This one step will make an enormous difference in how ready you *feel* for a test—and how prepared you REALLY are! Also remember to study handouts, past assignments, previous tests, and make use of study guides if they are provided. As much as possible, try to make your study notes manageable with mnemonic systems, questions, highlighted vocabulary, etc.

b. *Always study as for essay tests*—Many students tend to worry more about essay tests than objective tests. They feel that essay tests are harder, and in some respects they are because recall is necessary—not just recognition. Therefore, you should study for ALL tests as if they were essay, whether they are or not. Think in terms of main ideas, and recite questions and answers aloud. Force learning by recall, and all tests—whether essay or objective—will be easier and more beneficial.

c. *Get old tests and talk to "old" students*—If your instructor has old tests in his/her files, ask to see them or have a copy of them. Your library may even keep a "test bank" of past tests for you to look through. Former students of your current class are excellent resources. Ask them questions about what they remember of the tests, and see if they possibly still have old tests. Is this cheating? No! You are studying the instructor's format of testing, and you are also studying in the best possible way—with questions and answers.

d. *Anticipate test questions*—Some ways to do this have already been mentioned in the previous paragraph, but also think about some other clues for your instructor's possible test questions. Information that was written on the board is usually a good resource. The teacher may have even told you during lecture that certain information was important, or asked you to particularly note that section. You should have emphasized this in your notes in some way (such as a star, or a box). Information that is mentioned in both text and lecture would be good test questions. Don't forget vocabulary words that are often in italics or boldface print! They make excellent matching questions. Review questions at the beginning or the end of the chapter are also an easy way for your teacher to get a question. Don't omit any of these clues to help you to anticipate test questions.

e. *Understand question words*—This suggestion is especially crucial for success with essay tests. To be asked to diagram a concept is not the same as to explain it. To summarize does not mean to criticize. You cannot get full credit for an answer if you do not answer the question!

■ What Causes Test Anxiety?

In the TEST YOUR TESTING SKILLS worksheet, you may have been able to see if test anxiety is a problem for you. Many things can cause this problem, but you can help yourself by deciding to eliminate the following characteristics if they describe you during testing.

Test anxiety may strike if you:

- focus on yourself rather than the task at hand.
- associate a test score with your self-worth.
- allow negative self images.
- compare your performance with others around you.
- continually rethink an answer.
- allow panicky self-talk.
- begin to feel out of control.

You must stay in control and take care of your job one step at a time. Recognizing what causes test anxiety is the first step toward solving the problem.

■ What's the Cure for Test Anxiety?

The real cure for panicking during a test is over-preparation BEFORE the test! Better planning will replace panic with confidence. Then when you get into the testing situation, do not focus on yourself OR on what others are doing. Focus only on the task in front of you. If that scares you, focus on some other object for a minute, such as your shoe! Regroup your thoughts and talk positively and confidently to yourself. Remind yourself that you are competent and in control. Then start to work on the test. Only think of that one task. Don't allow negative thoughts to enter into your thinking. Plan to arrive a little earlier on test day so you won't be rushed. Then you could do some relaxation techniques to help you to relax. Always start with the easier questions on the test to build your confidence, and keep encouraging yourself with positive self-talk. Perhaps the best strategy is simply to realize that test anxiety is a learned set of responses that are only detrimental to your performance and that can be changed. Focus on changing them!

◼ How Can You Improve Test Scores?

There are many strategies that will help to improve your test scores—regardless of the type of test or the content. Take the WHAT'S YOUR TESTING IQ? Inventory that follows to see how many strategies you already know that are essential for test-wiseness—whether you know the information needed for the test or not. Some of the questions are serious, some are trivial, and some are downright silly, but they all illustrate test-taking strategies that every college student must master. The answers will be given to you also, and we will give you suggestions for test-taking in general and for each type of test specifically. You need to practice these suggestions for EVERY test, including pop quizzes, unit tests, and comprehensive finals. Learn to play the game!

What Are Some General Test-Taking Suggestions?

1. Avoid rushing. Get to the test early. Think calmly and act calmly.

2. Pick a good spot to sit and recite notes calmly. The best spot is usually your normal seat, because you will feel more comfortable there. But the best spot is also usually away from distractions and close to the front. That's why it's important to pick the right spot the FIRST day of class and stick with it. It is a good idea to study up to the last minute, as long as you can do so calmly.

3. Get rid of undue anxiety by relaxation techniques, positive self-talk, and focusing only on the task at hand.

4. Wait for oral instructions. Do NOT begin the test as soon as you receive it. After you put your name on the paper, WAIT. You may miss vital information or clues if you do not listen to instructions.

5. Jot down memory clues before you begin. If there are dates, names, or mnemonic strategies you are afraid you may forget, jot these down on the back of the test. This may relieve some stress immediately!

6. Skim the entire exam, reading directions carefully. This is a crucial step that is often overlooked. As you quickly look over the test, look for:

   a. point allotment—All questions are not created equal, and you should spend the most time on items worth the most points.

   b. type of questions—Which will take more time for you? What order would be best to answer the questions?

   c. clues—Often, test questions may have clues farther on in the test, or perhaps you may even find the answer!

   Although reading the directions is not a difficult step, it is one to which you should learn to give strong emphasis!

7. Ask specific questions if needed. Notice that you wait until the instructor has had time to explain, AND until you have had time to skim the test! Many questions can be answered by these two steps. If you still have questions, ask pointed, specific questions.

8. Do the easy ones first. This suggestion will make a big difference in your confidence level. It will also help you with the time problem, because you will make sure you complete the ones you know quickly, and you will have the rest of the time to concentrate on the harder ones.

9. Skip the harder ones, mark them so you will remember to come back to them, and return to them after you complete the easy ones and have warmed-up. A little mark beside the more difficult ones will also make sure you note these as you get your test returned after grading. Of course, you will notice it if you miss it! But if you get it correct, you may not remember the correct answer two weeks later unless you take special note of it.

10. Do all tests four times. Most of us hate the thought of doing a test once, but you need to go through four steps to do your best. First, skim the test as stated. Then do the easier ones while you mark and skip the harder ones. Return to do the harder ones, and finally, look over the entire test to check that you have answered all questions.

11. Change your answer if needed. Although this policy has been hotly debated, recent research seems to point out that when an answer is changed, more often than not it is changed from a wrong answer to a right one. But you also need to analyze your pattern. What usually happens for you? If the answer was clearly just a guess, perhaps your first guess IS your best answer. But, if after second thought you feel the need to change the answer, do so!

12. Budget your time. Do this before you start by considering the point value of the question. Also, make sure you allow enough time to complete the whole test with time to double-check.

13. Never leave blanks! A guess is better than a miss; so don't guarantee an error by leaving a blank. You may luck out. Usually a middle answer in multiple choice questions or true answers in true-false questions are more apt to be correct.

14. Write answers clearly. Do not try to fool the instructor by making your T also resemble an F in true-false items. Don't try to make the "a" also pass for a "c" in multiple-choice items. All you probably succeed in doing is aggravating the grader who may check the item wrong with a flourish.

15. Make the test serve you after it's over. You have paid for it, so get your money's worth. Don't purposely try to put it out of your mind. Talk about strategies with other students. Look up the ones you weren't certain about. (You will remember the answer much longer than any other question if you do!) When you get the test back, check errors and also guesses that turned out to be correct. If you have marked the difficult ones, this will be easier. Analyze why you missed the question. Learn for the next test—and there's ALWAYS a next one! Make the doing of the test in itself beneficial.

Okay, now that we've gone through helpful strategies for test-taking in general, let's see about your TEST-TAKING IQ!

■ Are There Any Specific Clues about Taking Objective Tests?

If you want to "show all you know," there are specific suggestions you should follow for each type of objective test. Remember to put into practice the general suggestions that have been given for all tests, and then study the specific suggestions that follow. Look back at your WHAT'S YOUR TESTING IQ? answers to see how these strategies work. We have included the reasons for the answers after each item.

Sentence Completion or Fill-in-the-Blank Questions

Fill-in-the-blank and sentence-completion statements require you to supply missing information. Read the questions carefully and decide on your answer. Look for key words to help you determine the correct answer. If you have studied the vocabulary, these questions should not be difficult.

Look for clues. The verb form of the question will tell you whether the answer is singular or plural. The number of blanks may tell you how many words make up the answer. If "an" rather than "a" precedes the blank space, your answer will begin with a vowel or an "h" instead of a consonant. If you are not sure how to interpret a question/problem, ASK!

How would you fill in the following blanks?

1. In October, _____, the stock market "crashed" to begin the Great Depression.

2. An _____ person can be trusted.

3. The U.S. entered World War II in 1941 after _____ planes attacked American Naval ships at _____ _____.

In the first item, you are asked to complete the date by adding the year (1929). The missing word in the second item is an adjective that begins with a vowel or a vowel sound. A logical choice would be the word honest. The third item asks for an adjective that describes planes (Japanese) and then a noun that names the location of the naval ships (Pearl Harbor).

Multiple-Choice Questions

Many students and instructors prefer multiple-choice tests because they provide specific answers to each question. It is easier for the instructor to grade this type of test because students can put their answers on scantron sheets, and tests may be corrected electronically, or, the instructor may have an answer key that makes for speedier scoring. Many students prefer these kinds of tests because they have a chance of guessing correctly when they do not know the answer. However, if the instructor deducts points for wrong answers, it may not be advantageous to guess.

Multiple-choice questions consist of two parts. The **stem** is the statement, question or part that needs to be completed. Then, there are typically four or five **possible answers or choices**. One option will be correct; the others will be distracters.

■   Watch for key words. Underline them so they stand out and help you focus on the major points. As you read the question, try to answer it without looking at the options. Then read the choices to see if any match the answer you gave. Do not make a choice without reading all the responses! Eliminate the obvious distracters to improve your chances of choosing the correct answer.

■ Be on the lookout for statements with absolute words or extreme modifiers. They are almost always incorrect because they do not allow for an exception. Very few things in life are absolute.

Ex. Elderly patients experiencing dementia

a. are always diagnosed with Alzheimer's disease.
b. only lose their verbal skills.
c. are never able to reside in their own homes.
d. sometimes exhibit aggressive behaviors.

The only answer that does not contain an absolute word is "d."

■ Along with absolute words, be aware of statements such as "all but one" or except for one." This means the majority of the options are correct.

Ex. All but one of the following Americans landed safely on the moon.

a. Neil Armstrong
b. Edwin Aldrin, Jr.
c. Jackie Robinson
d. Michael Collins

In this case, the correct answer is "c." Jackie Robinson was a famous baseball player, but he never landed on the moon.

■ Be attentive to double negatives that can make a statement true rather than false.

Ex. In some states it is not illegal to

a. transport heroin
b. manufacture LSD
c. use marijuana
d. sell cocaine

The answer is "c." Not illegal means it is legal. Some states allow the use of marijuana for medical reasons.

■ If you can choose only one response, choose the one that provides the most complete answer.

Ex. During the Civil War, major Union victories were won at

a. Shiloh
b. Gettysburg & Vicksburg
c. Bull Run
d. Gettysburg, Vicksburg, and Shiloh

The correct answer is "d." Although "a," and "b," are true, "d" is more complete.

■ When two options are the same, you will know that neither is correct.

Ex. A polar bear can run up to

a. 1.5 miles per hour
b. 5 miles per hour
c. 15 miles per hour
d. 1 1/2 miles per hour

The correct answer will be selected between "b" and "c." "a" and "d" are the same.

Absolute Words

All
Everyone
None
Always
Only
No
Invariable
Never
No one
Every

■ When alternatives seem equally correct, select the one that is longest and contains the most information.

Ex. Down's Syndrome in infants is most often caused by

a. *Heredity*
b. *Smoking*
c. *Genetic and environmental factors*
d. *Alcohol*

■ When statements contain digits, the answer usually is not the extreme, but rather a middle number.

Ex. A pound is equal to

a. *1.6 oz.*
b. *6 oz.*
c. *16 oz.*
d. *66 oz.*

"A" and "d" are definitely out of the ballpark. The answer is "c." An exception to this rule occurs when the real answer is actually lower or higher than most people would expect.

■ When responses are similar, one is likely to be correct. When the choices are opposites, one of them is always wrong. The other is often, but not always, correct.

Ex. The Caribbean Islands are located in

a. *The Pacific Ocean*
b. *The Atlantic Ocean*
c. *The Mediterranean Sea*
d. *The Panama Canal*

In the above example, the Caribbean Islands are located in the Atlantic Ocean.

■ The correct answer should agree with the stem in number, gender, and person. It will also match grammatically.

■ Carefully read those test items that use two or three combined options as a possible response. Sometimes this is the correct answer. If you know for sure that more than one of the choices are correct, it is likely that "all of the above" are true. Be cautious, however, when you see "all of the above" or "none of the above." These could be trick questions, or the examiner may have used it only because s/he couldn't think of another choice.

■ Unless there is a penalty for wrong answers, if you cannot figure out the answer—GUESS. If you have studied, choose the answer that sounds right. If you guess randomly, choose "b" or "c." The odds are higher that the answer is one of the middle choices. *Go over your test when you are finished to make sure you have answered all of the questions.*

True/False Tests

**Common
Qualifiers**

*Many
Seldom
Almost
Sometimes
Frequently
Can
Most
Usually
Rarely
Ordinarily
Occasionally
Few
Some
Likely
Often
Possibly
Generally
Might*

These are one of the most common types of examination questions. When answering, be careful not to overanalyze the questions. Do not be consumed with the fear that these are trick questions. Assume that the instructor is asking straightforward questions. Here are some things to watch for when answering true/false questions.

■ For a statement to be true, every part of it must be true. If any word or phrase is false, the statement is false.

Ex. Columbus tried to find a western route to the Orient in 1492 when he set sail with three ships, the Nina, the Pinta, and the Santa Clara.

The name of Columbus' third ship was the Santa Maria, not the Santa Clara.

■ Statements that have reasons in them are often false. Words such as "because," "therefore," "consequently," "the cause of," or "as a result of" are all words used to indicate reasons.

Ex. Obesity results from overeating.

This is a false statement because everyone who overeats is not obese. Likewise, obesity can be the result of a medical problem.

■ Statements that contain qualifiers leave open the chance for more "true" answers.

Ex. An instructor's personal preference generally determines which type of tests s/he gives.

This statement is true. Preferences often, but not always, influence tests.

■ Some of the same rules that apply to multiple choice tests will also apply to true/false exams. Remember what we said about absolutes.

Ex. All candy contains sugar.

With so many substitutes today, sugarless candy is readily available. However, be careful, because some absolute statements can be true.

Ex. Communication is always a two-way process.

■ Watch out for negative statements. Your mind is more likely to "read over" negative words, causing you to miss them. If you are allowed to write on your test paper, underline negative words as you read to draw attention to them. In the English language, a double negative makes the statement positive. This is one of those grammar rules that you may ignore in conversations with your friends, but ignoring it on a test will cost you valuable points

Ex. Different cultures must not be studied in an unbiased fashion.

This statement is false. An easy way to avoid the double negative trap is to cross out both of the negatives and read the sentence without them. The above example would then read: *Different cultures must be studied in a biased fashion.* Reading the sentence this way makes it clear that this is a false statement.

■ Once again, if you do not know the answer—GUESS.
Do not leave unanswered questions on a test. If you've followed the above strategies and still don't know which answer to guess, mark the answer true. It is generally easier for instructors to write true statements when making up a test, as they usually want to accentuate the positive.

Matching Tests

> **Negative Words and Prefixes**
>
> *Not*
> *Un*
> *In*
> *Dis*
> *Cannot*
> *Il*
> *Ir*
> *Im*
> *Mis*

Here are a few pointers for being able to logically match items on the test.

- Check to see if there are an exact number of matches. Also, check to see if any of the matches may be used more than once.
- Look for a pattern. Start with either column—whichever is easiest—and continue to work with that column.
- Read through the list of choices. Select the ones you know, and use them first to match with words in the other column.
- Use clues from other parts of the test.
- Apply all grammar rules—"a," "an," "subject/verb agreement," "singular/plurals," etc.

The key is to look for direction words and be sure to answer the questions accordingly. At the end of this chapter, there is a list of direction words with examples. By understanding what the instructor is asking, you can write a more effective response. Decide whether the question calls for fact, opinion, or both. Sometimes the instructor just wants facts; at other times the instructor wants you to form an intelligent opinion about a topic.

Here are some additional tips for answering essay questions.

- Jot down key words to help formulate your thoughts. A brief outline can help you ensure that your answer flows smoothly.
- Use the terminology from the course in developing your answer.
- Provide evidence to support your ideas. Be concise and to the point. Unnecessary repetition can lower your score.
- Some questions have multiple parts, so you need to address each part of the question, even if you only use one sentence to do so.
- Never leave ANY question unanswered unless there is a penalty for wrong answers. This could cost points that severely impact your grade.
- If you use dates, be certain they are correct. If you are unsure whether the year is 1876 or 1886, say "toward the end of the 19th century."
- Leave spaces between questions so you can make corrections or provide further explanations when you review later.
- Use the principles of writing from your English class. Be sure your answer has an introduction, body, and conclusion. You may use the question itself to introduce your response. Things to watch for include: correct spelling, subject/verb agreement, correct use of pronouns, logic, run-on sentences, sentence fragments, correct phrases, transitional words, etc.
- **Proof read all your work.**
- If you feel you are running out of time, outline the main points of your answer. The instructor will be able to see that you have some knowledge about the topic, and you may receive partial credit for your answer.

■ Direction Words

When writing an essay or short answer, your response should answer the question. Failure to follow the directions can drastically lower your grade. It is important that you understand the meaning of these common direction words so you can state your answer correctly.

Direction Words

Direction	Definition
Analyze	To break or separate the whole into its parts. To determine the nature, function, qualities, characteristics, relationships, and effects of the parts to the whole. In English, you may do this with a sentence; in science, with a substance; in math, with an equation. *Ex. Analyze the properties of water.*
Argue or Defend	To give reasons for or against something. A discussion or debate that supports or refutes a position. In preparing an argument, you try to defend a point or persuade others to a cause. *Ex. Argue whether or not courtroom proceedings should be televised.*
Comment	To present a pro or con opinion or viewpoint on a subject. *Ex. Comment on the choice of Beijing as a Winter Olympics site.*
Compare	To identify similarities and differences on a given topic. *Ex. Compare "Buddhism" with "Hinduism."*
Contrast	To stress the differences or dissimilarities among things; to show how things are "unlike" one another. *Ex. Contrast "assertive" and "aggressive" communication styles.*
Critique or Evaluate	To express your own views or the views of an "expert." You need to include positive and negative points/opinions. *Ex. Critique The Raven by Edgar Allan Poe.*
Define or Identify	To provide a clear and concise meaning, a comprehensive description, or the identifying characteristics. Do not use the term to define itself. *Ex. Define the term Existentialism. / Identify the major stressors for college students.*
Describe, Discuss, Explain, or State	Give a detailed account or picture, frequently in narrative form, to make something understandable. Include positive and negative points or cause and effect relationships for clarification. *Ex. Describe a balanced lifestyle. / Explain personality development from a Psychodynamic perspective.*
Diagram or Illustrate	To use a sketch, chart, graph, outline, labels, or examples to explain and clarify a point. *Ex. Diagram the anatomy of a heart. / Illustrate the human body's nervous system.*
Justify	Demonstrate or prove what is right, just, or valid by providing reasons or evidence for a decision or act. *Ex. Justify the use of pesticides in twenty-first century orchards.*
Label	To classify, designate, identify, and attach a name to some specific group or theory. *Ex Label the primary classes in the animal kingdom.*
List or enumerate	To provide an itemized list or to make points one by one in order. *Ex. List the qualities of a good public speaker. / Enumerate the steps involved in good decision-making.*
Narrate	To provide an accounting of something or to tell a series of events in story form. *Ex. Narrate the events that led to the economic blockade of Cuba.*
Outline	To summarize the main points or provide an organized listing of the main topics. *Ex. Outline the main events that led to the Civil Rights Movement.*
Paraphrase	To express an idea in your own words. *Ex. Paraphrase John Gardner's Theory of Multiple Intelligences.*
Prove	To present factual evidence and give logical reasons to support something. Frequently used in the sciences (tests or experiments) to establish something as true or valid. *Ex. Prove that Uranium 235 degrades to lead. Include all 17 steps.*
Relate	To show how things are connected with each other, to give cause and effect, or to explore relationships and correlations. This is usually done in narrative form. *Ex. Relate the importance of values, interests, and personality on career choice.*
Review or Summarize	To discuss the main points in a clear and concise manner. You may be required to give a critical analysis, as in a review of a book or play. *Ex. Review the study systems discussed in class. Summarize effective listening techniques.*
Trace	To narrate the development or process of something in a historical fashion, showing the sequence of events through time. *Ex. Trace the events that led to the exploration of Mars in the latter half of the twentieth century.*

■ How about Suggestions for Subjective Tests?

Many students may give an unconscious shudder at the sound of the words "essay test." Why do we fear them so much? Maybe because we feel in these tests we really have to KNOW what we're being tested over! The word recall is the key word again. But another major problem with subjective tests is that HOW you answer is almost as important—if not more so—than WHAT you answer. Organization, relevancy, writing ability, and even neatness all enter in as a vital part of your grade. Students typically do two things wrong with essays: they write everything they can think of about the topic (whether it is relevant or not!), or they write only their feelings to fill up space, rather than the facts that were asked for in the question.

Short Answer Questions

1. Carefully read the question several times. Think before you write, and then start off by restating the key words of the question in your answer.

2. Watch for the key question words (describe, evaluate) to make sure you do what it says.

3. Make sure your answer is clear, accurate, precise, relevant, deep, broad, logical, meaningful, fair, and correct.

Essay Tests

Essay questions require total recall, and they also require organization, grammar skills, and creativity. Most students either hate or love essay exams. There is no room for guessing on this type of test. You have to know the material, so you must be well prepared. You have an excellent opportunity to show what you have learned. Organization, grammar, spelling, and punctuation are very important on essay tests.

The Lab Bowl System

Critical Thinking

It may be an error in judgment to assume that most students do not score their best on tests because they do not know the material. Look back at one of your past tests and analyze your errors. Were they due to lack of knowledge, or was it possibly lack of reading skills, lack of exam skills, or exam anxiety? Before you can correct your test-taking errors, you have to know what is causing them. Then you can decide what steps to take to correct them.

L—ook over the entire exam before you begin. Read the directions carefully, and underline the testing words (verbs) that are crucial to your answer. As you answer, it is a good idea to come back and check off each verb to make sure you have done what the question asked.

A—sk for point allotment if it is not given. Don't assume all of the questions have equal value, and don't spend the same amount of time on each question.

B—udget your time based on the point allotment. Make a tentative time schedule before you begin to make sure you allow enough time to finish the test, and to make sure you spend the most time on the questions that are worth the most points. (But you know the most information about the question that's only worth three points? That's the way it usually goes, but you had better come up with more information for that 30-pointer!)

B—egin with the easiest question. This is an important practice in all testing, but especially when you have to write essays! This will increase your confidence, get you warmed-up, and get a large portion of the test done quickly. If you start each answer on a separate page, the order that you answer will not matter. You can then put the answers in the correct order before you turn in the test. You also have a way to add more information to a question later in the test if you allow this space.

O—utline each question before you begin on a pre-essay page. This page will be a thinking page to help you get started. Your time schedule could be figured out here, along with the order that you will answer the questions. You might want to copy the testing words here to make sure you answer in the correct way. Make an outline of each answer before you start to write, and the writing will be much easier and faster. Label this page Pre-essay Page and you will really impress your professor! As you try to outline one question, you may remember something else you needed to add to another question, and you can jot that down on this thinking page. Don't spend TOO much time here. You still have to write, so include this thinking time in your time schedule.

W—atch those key testing words! As mentioned before, to diagram does not mean the same as to discuss. Be very aware that you do what you are supposed to do!

L—ook over the exam again before you turn it in to correct errors or omissions. Teachers sometimes seem to make snap judgments on your grade based on the way your paper looks, so make it look good!

How Can I Raise My B's to A's?

Because HOW you answer is just as crucial as WHAT you say in an essay, there are a few impressive things that you can do to make your test give a good impression, and hopefully add points to your score. Your instructor may not consciously give you more points, but there is a natural tendency! So consider these steps to add the "icing to the cake":

1. Write in essay form. This means use paragraphs, topic sentences, transition words between paragraphs, complete sentences, etc. Also, repeat part of the question (usually the testing word) in the first sentence of each portion of the essay.

2. Be accurate grammatically and with spelling. You may want to bring a pocket dictionary with you to the test. It will pay off!

3. Start each answer on a new page and number the answers correctly.

4. Neatness is vital! So:

   a. Write in pen.

   b. Write on one side of the paper only.

   c. Remember to leave margins—side, top, and bottom.

   d. Use unlined paper with a line guide underneath if you really want to impress!

   e. Put your name on each page and staple all pages together.

5. If you run out of time because you did not budget correctly, outline your answer. You may get partial credit.

■ Special Testing Situations

Open-Book Tests

Many students feel that these are the easiest tests to take, but do not be led astray. Open-book tests are probably more difficult. They may have to be completed in a certain amount of time. Not only must you study and know where to find the material quickly for your answers, you must also learn to think critically. Questions are never verbatim. Always practice making up and answering test questions that you think the instructor might choose.

Take-Home Tests

Every student's dream! But, once again, don't be misled. Take-home tests are usually more difficult and ask for lengthier answers. You will still need to study and know the material. The biggest danger is waiting too long before preparing for the test. You do not want to wait until it is in your hand before learning the material. Critical thinking is also an integral part of take-home tests.

Standardized Tests

Tests such as the ACT, SAT, COMPASS, and ASVAB are standardized tests. They are prepared by a testing service and administered under prescribed conditions. Although there are often different versions of the tests, the questions test the same content and require the same kinds of knowledge. Many times these tests are mandatory entrance or placement tests at colleges and universities, or they may be required for scholarships or enlisting in the military. There are several things to remember about standardized testing.

- *Prepare* sufficiently in *advance* for these tests.
- *Use study guides.* These resources are available in most libraries and bookstores. Preparatory classes may also be available in your area. These may be expensive; however, they will provide you with review and practice for the tests.
- Before taking the test, always *check to see if you will be penalized for guessing*. On the SAT test, a percentage is deducted for incorrect answers to discourage guessing.

Math Tests

Use all of the strategies that you use for other tests when taking math tests. Note the following special considerations:

- Break down complex problems, and work the steps one at a time.
- Show all your work in an organized fashion.
- Draw pictures or diagrams to help you visualize problems.
- Check your computations. Be sure you are using the right formulas, have the correct order of functions, and sined numbers are correct.
- Ask yourself if your answer makes common sense!

■ Test Results

What do you do when the tests are returned to you? This is a great opportunity to learn from your mistakes and to help you prepare for the next exam. Go over all the errors that you made. If the instructor wants the tests returned, jot down the kinds of mistakes you made in order to develop new and better strategies for the next test. Analyze the instructor's style of testing. Was the test objective or subjective? Were the questions taken directly from the book, from lecture notes, or from both? Was there a pattern in the answers that would help you guess in the future? What kind of mistakes did you make?

Never throw away a returned test until after the final exam. You may use these tests to review for that final and improve your grades. See if you need to further develop any of the following:

- More effective time management for studying and taking tests
- Better note taking techniques
- Reviewing throughout the semester
- Better study and test-taking strategies
- Reading and following directions accurately
- Providing more details for your answers
- Getting a full night's rest before the exam
- Eating a healthy breakfast the day of a test

■ Using Critical Thinking to Survive Final Exams

Introduction: News flash! Final exams are just around the corner! Don't panic. Put all the skills you have learned in your ACA course to work for you. First, if you have not done so already, put all your exams on your calendar. Take a close look at what will be required of you to meet the exam schedule. If any of your courses have exams scheduled at a time you are not normally in school, how will this affect you? Will you need to change a work schedule, get a baby sitter, or make special arrangements with your instructors? If so, don't wait until the last minute to do it. This will just add more stress to what could already be a stressful time. Do it now!

Put all your time management knowledge to work. Arrange a special study schedule for this week. And use the study skills you have learned this semester. Finally, when the test day arrives for each of your classes, use the test time to your greatest advantage, and bring into each test situation the confidence that accompanies preparation.

Purpose: The purpose of today's session is to review test taking strategies, especially those that require critical thinking, and to develop a positive mindset as you prepare for your final exams.

Final Exam Hints

1. Find out from each of your instructors if the exam is going to be comprehensive or if it will cover only the last unit of study. This will make a big difference in how you will need to study. If it is comprehensive, you can probably expect more general questions that require your making connections between various themes or topics you studied throughout the semester.

2. If you are told that the exam will be comprehensive, ask the instructor to provide the class with a few sample questions. This will give you ideas on how to study.

Be sure you know what the instructor wants you to do with questions that begin with words such as "analyze," "explain" "contrast," "evaluate," "synthesize," etc.

3. Remember that your instructors are under as much pressure as you are at this time of the semester. They have time constraints and deadlines to meet just as you do. For this reason many of them may give more objective questions that can be easily graded. It would be very helpful at this point for you to review the information on test-taking strategies.

4. Pretend it is your job to make out a final exam. What questions would you ask? Make our your own test and use the exercise as a thorough review.

■ Two Final Considerations!

What If You Have to Cram?

Even though we feel that it is vital to distribute your studying throughout the weeks, you may find yourself in a bind occasionally. It may be the day before the test and you have not started your preparation. Should you cram? Definitely! If you haven't been reviewing, your memory level is somewhere between 2%–20%—a definite F percentage! You are starting from scratch the night before the test. So there are two words that you must abide by: SELECTIVITY and RECITATION. If you try to study it all lightly, you will probably forget it all. Pick the main ideas and recite them until they are solidly in your mind. You will do a better job on the test knowing the main points well rather than trying to remember the details fuzzily!

Can You Guess Successfully on a Test?

Although some students seem to be better at this "skill" than others, we do not suggest you count on guessing. However, as we have stated before, never leave blanks! Check and double-check to make sure you have an answer for each question. There is no reason to throw a point away! Take a minute to fill in the blanks of our multiple choice test with random "guesses" to see if it **might** pay to guess.

■ Summary

We have explore the idea that most students have an incorrect view of test taking. Taking a test may be traumatic because we view it as a trial instead of a challenge for which to prepare and "show all we know." We have discussed objective and subjective tests, and a combination of the two. The advantages and disadvantages of each have been pointed out, along with possible causes why students might not perform well on tests. Many suggestions have been given to help the student become more "test-wise" in general test-taking situations and for each of the specific types of objective tests. Test anxiety has been analyzed along with the best possible cure—over-preparation. Finally, the dreaded essay tests have been discussed along with a systematic way to tackle taking them. Several worksheets have been given to help you analyze your testing behavior and your testing skills. Now it is up to you, the student, to put these discussions and suggestions into practice. If you want to show all you know, learn how to de-traumatize test taking, and master the evaluation process. Prove to yourself that you are the master of the test-taking game and that you can "make the grade!"

■ Activity: What's Your Testing IQ?

Answer these questions to the best of your ability. Use every test-taking strategy that you know.

A. True-False

Answer + for each true statement and – for each false statement. Each item is worth 1 point.

_____ 1. Smart students always study 2–3 hours each day for every class.

_____ 2. Frequently, students leave too much studying to do until finals week.

_____ 3. Some students study a lot, but no one studies as much as they should.

_____ 4. The way to learn the most efficiently is not to succumb to distractions.

_____ 5. Hunger leads to decreased concentration and increased apathy when studying.

_____ 6. According to the textbook, most students study at a 1-1 ratio of hours studied versus hours in class.

B. Multiple Choice

Write the letter of the correct choices for each item in the blank. 4 points each.

_____ 7. Test-taking can cause:
  a. hardening of the arteries.
  b. students to study harder.
  c. professors to have papers to grade.
  d. late night studying.
  e. all of the above
  f. answers b, c, & d
  g. answers b and d
  h. none of the above

_____ 8. Students go to class because
  a. it is necessary.
  b. information is being taught.
  c. it is the most fun way to spend the day.
  d. the law of xfghot recommends it.

_____ 9. Which statement(s) is(are) not correct?
  a. Students often study in the library.
  b. Students do not study enough.
  c. Most students should try to study more.
  d. Professors should never give essay tests.

_____ 10. Colleges often
  a. blow up.
  b. get torn down.
  c. try to educate students in the best possible manner with the least amount of expense.
  d. change their names.
  e. try to educate students in the worst possible manner with the greatest amount of expense.

_____ 11. The distance from Paris to New York is approximately
  a. 3000–4000 miles.
  b. 10–20 kilometers.

    c. 9000–10,000 miles.

    d. 500–1000 miles.

_____ 12. Mass hysteria can result when large numbers of people

    a. believe something that is not true.

    b. fear an invasion.

    c. share delusory perceptions.

    d. all of the above

C. Matching

Write the letter of the correct answer in the blank. 2 points each.

_____ 13. preview	a. a writing system
_____ 14. test-taking	b. to manipulate data
_____ 15. survey	c. used for evaluation
_____ 16. time schedules	d. getting an overview of a chapter
_____ 17. quixotic	e. used for efficient studying
	f. idealistic, but impractical
	g. determines the appropriateness of using a dictionary

D. Sentence Completion

Write the missing word in the blanks. 10 points each.

18. _____ is the process for becoming a citizen.

19. The largest animal in the world is a _____ .

20. _____ _____ _____ is the collective name of Superior, Huron, Erie, Ontario, and Michigan.

21. Lions are most likely to be found in _____ .

E. Short Answer

Answer concisely but completely. 1 point each.

22. Describe the best way to make a time schedule.

_____

_____

23. Evaluate the practice of previewing in studying a chapter.

_____

_____

F. Essay Question

24. Trace the history of your immediate family. Enumerate how many people are included, list their occupations and ages, and discuss their personalities. State if you care for them or not, and make a decision as to their honesty when considered as a group.

■ Answers for "What's Your Test-Taking IQ?" Worksheet

Before you started taking the test, you should have skimmed over the entire exam to see the type of questions and to budget your time according to point value. Notice that you could have missed ALL of the True-False questions and only have done the damage of missing three Matching questions. Missing all of the Matching questions would have been the same as missing ONE Sentence Completion question. Also notice that the Short Answer questions were only worth one point. Therefore, it was not worth your time or effort to spend a lot of time on these answers. Examine the point value carefully before you take a test, and spend more time on the most points! Below are the correct answers. If there was a "clue word" in the sentence, it is given also.

A. TRUE-FALSE

If you did not answer with a "+" or a "−", you missed all six questions. You must follow the directions to get the credit!

1. − (always, each, every)

2. + (Frequently)

3. − (no one)

4. + (not)

5. − (Hunger)

6. + (According to the textbook)

B. MULTIPLE CHOICE

Notice that the directions said you might have more than one answer (the word was CHOICES).

7. f

8. b

9. b, d

10. c

11. a (kilometers)

12. d

C. MATCHING

Note that the directions clued you in to the fact that you would only have one answer for each question, but it did not say that you could not use the same option more than once! If this had been a real test, you may have needed to clarify these points.

13. d

14. c

15. d

16. e

17. f

D. SENTENCE COMPLETION

18. Naturalization

19. whale (a)

20. The Great Lakes (3 blank spaces)

21. Africa

E. SHORT ANSWER

    22. Possible answer—Denote class time, work time, and other necessary time by the hour and plan the best times to study and take care of other responsibilities.

    23. Possible answer—Experts say previewing is crucial to effective studying of a chapter because it increases concentration and comprehension, and I would agree.

F. ESSAY

    24. (If you were REALLY bored enough to answer this monster of a question, you should have first shown some type of a chronological review of your family history. This would be followed by a numbered list of the job and age of each person in your immediate family, and a brief description of their personalities. You should have stated your feelings for each one, and finally stated an opinion as to whether your family could be considered honest or not. This question really involved seven questions—trace, enumerate, list jobs and ages, discuss, state, and decide—and would have best been answered in six or seven paragraphs with the key word repeated in the topic sentence of each.)

By the way, how many points was this awful essay question worth, or does it matter? Would it make any difference how long you spent on it if it was worth *10* points rather than *100* points? Of course it would—or should! You need to ask, if point values are not given, and then write accordingly. If the essay is worth 100 points and you don't have anything to say, you had better come up with something! If it is only worth 10 points, don't spend three pages answering the question. BUDGET TIME BY POINTS AND DIFFICULTY!

What is your testing IQ?

Points excluding the essay question add up to 82, so let's say the essay question was worth a meager 18 points to make it a nice, even 100 points. But let's also say that you got all 18 points on that essay! What is your test score? Add up your points and judge yourself on this scale, and then read ahead to find out how you might have done better, or, more importantly, how you may do better on the next REAL test!

95–100 points	A	Hey, you've got a good handle on this test-taking game!
90–94 points	B	Not bad!
85–89 points	C	Look forward to improving!
84 points or less	D	Have we got some great tips for you! Read on!

Activity 1: Test Taking Awareness Check

DIRECTIONS: Please place an "X" in the appropriate box.

	Yes	No
1. Tests are given to determine your intelligence.	☐	☐
2. Cramming is more likely to keep the test information fresh in our minds for the test.	☐	☐
3. Students who pass tests are the most intelligent.	☐	☐
4. Taking daily notes is a part of test preparation.	☐	☐
5. There are basically only two kinds of formats for testing.	☐	☐
6. Multiple choice tests usually consist of the stem and the distracters.	☐	☐
7. Absolute words and qualifiers in test questions usually will tell you the answer.	☐	☐
8. In an essay question when you are asked to do a contrast, you must explain the similarities and differences.	☐	☐
9. Test preparation begins on the first day of class.	☐	☐
10. One of the key reasons for test anxiety is that some students cram for exams.	☐	☐

Activity 2. How Do You Know When You Have Test Anxiety?

Anxiety triggers

Symptoms	Causes

Activity 3. Things I Do (or should do) to Get Rid of Test Anxiety

Anxiety reducers

CHAPTER 7
Time Management

Introduction

"Time is the one thing they're not making any more of . . ."

Radio commercial for LaSalle Bank

When you hear the phrase "time management," do you envision yourself enslaved to a desk calendar, wall calendar, pocket calendar, computer scheduler, or pocket watch? Do you see yourself hurrying to finish one task so you can start the next one "on schedule?" Do you daydream about mountains of "to do" lists piled high on your desk; or are you, in the mind's eye, rushing to catch a train, briefcase in hand? Effective time management does involve some physical schedule tools, simply because most of us find it easier to retrieve information from a piece of paper (or software) than from the filing system in our minds. However, arbitrary schedules and lists will not do a thing for you until you have come to grip with the two factors that keep time under control: Priorities and Commitment.

In this chapter you will look at strategies for turning your long- or short-term goals into priority statements. A question that will weave through the discussion is "What's the best possible use of my time RIGHT NOW?" You will be introduced to scheduling tools that will turn the abstract "goal" into simple steps toward "action." Contrary to those mental pictures of lists and clocks, you will learn how scheduling can actually bring you more free time and less guilt!

You will also consider the concept of commitment, ways to motivate yourself to stay with your scheduling plan, and hints for conquering disorganization, procrastination and distractions. You will also learn hints from time management "experts"—useful ways to get control of your most difficult time-related challenges.

This chapter contains material adapted from *The Community College: A New Beginning*, third edition by Linda S. Aguilar, Sandra J. Hopper, and Therese M. Kuzlik, copyright © 2001 by Kendall/Hunt Publishing Company and *Keys to Excellence*, 4th edition by Carol Cooper et al, copyright © 1997 by Kendall/Hunt Publishing Company. Adapted and reprinted with permission of the publisher. Further reproduction is prohibited.

■ Activity: Pretest Test-Taking Skills

PURPOSE: To help you find areas to improve as you handle the responsibility of scheduling your own time as a college student.

A. How much time per week do you believe you devote to the following activities?

Activity	# Hours Per Week
1. Attending class	_____
2. Studying/reading/doing homework	_____
3. Working at a job	_____
4. Watching TV	_____
5. Sleeping	_____
6. Personal care (bathing, hair, etc.)	_____
7. Hobbies	_____
8. Shopping	_____
9. Eating	_____
10. Being with friends	_____
11. On the phone	_____
12. Other _____	_____

TOTAL HRS. = _____

B. Have any of the following happened to you since you started college?

	Yes	No
1. Overslept and missed/late to class	_____	_____
2. Forgot to do an assignment	_____	_____
3. Chose to go out with friends and didn't complete an assignment	_____	_____
4. Asked an instructor for a deadline extension	_____	_____
5. Got your work schedule mixed up	_____	_____
6. Missed or was late to class due to transportation problem	_____	_____
7. Skipped class for no particular reason	_____	_____

■ New Outlook on Time

You have probably already noticed that the way you use your time in college is much different from the way you used it in high school. In college, you are expected to be much more responsible for your own time scheduling. For example:

1. In college, many courses do not meet every day. You must keep track of class meeting times yourself.

2. College instructors take attendance. If you miss class, you may have a vague awareness that your grades will suffer, but attendance is up to you.

3. Usually "homework" is not turned in on a class-by-class basis, but assignments are more long-term. They require more sophisticated scheduling to be completed on time. The same is true for studying for tests—preparation is a more long-term project.

4. College work is demanding. You need to plan to study two hours outside of class for every hour in class. So if you're carrying 15 credit hours, your total time commitment is 45 hours—the equivalent of a full time job.

5. You are most likely the only person keeping tabs on your assignments; and your family and friends are likely to come up with tempting activities to distract you from your studies.

So, as you can see, going to college is very much about committing large blocks of time to this endeavor. Those whose lives include multiple commitments (job, children, athletics) find the time pressure even more intense. You need to have a clear picture of why you're devoting so much time to this college thing—what is it exactly you're hoping to accomplish?

■ Goal-Setting

Manage your time. Plan your life. *In case you have not caught on yet, you are talking about managing yourself. You are talking about getting rid of habits that tend to interfere with what you need to do.* You need to set goals and priorities around your commitment to obtain a college education and a profession. Managing your time will help you successfully achieve these commitments. If you are having problems on the job, evaluate the situation, set goals and give yourself a specified period of time to complete them.

Time management calls for planning. You cannot plan without making decisions about what you want to do and where you want to go. *Effective time management requires you to be a decision-maker.* When you make the decisions about what you want and where you want to go, you have established GOALS. *Goals are important because they allow you to put your values into action. Goals are no more than your aims in life and they give you purpose and direction in which to focus your energies.*

To develop a goal is the first step in time management. *The next step is to write your goal down in explicit and concrete terms. Until it is written, it is just an idea. A goal should have the following characteristics:*

REACHABLE—Set it up in small increments so you don't bite off more than you can chew at one time. If you do, you will only become frustrated. Set only moderate goals you know you can reach.

Long-Term Goal
I want to get my associate in arts degree in business in _____ (year).

Short-Term Goal
I want to pass English and Social Environment with a grade of "C" or above this semester.

Daily To-Do List
August 31, _____ (year).

Rank
Ordering

4 Visit with Mark and Gary
__ See "Star Trek" movie
3 Practice essay writing
__ Watch television
1 Go to work 8:00 a.m. to 12:00 noon
2 Study chapters 1 and 2 of Social Environment

REALISTIC—*Know your limitations and capabilities. Don't ask more of yourself than you know you are capable of doing.* Set a realistic time-frame to achieve it.

MEASURABLE—*State your goal in such a way that you as well as others will know when it has been achieved.* Be very specific and concrete about what you want to do.

For each goal, always write out a step-by-step plan as to what you are going to do to achieve it. Be concrete and specific. Each goal should always have a time-frame. Some people would put-off and put-off and never carry out the plan.

Goals are described as short-term and long-term. Long-term goals usually take a while to accomplish while short-term goals help you achieve the long-term goal. They are activities you carry out on a daily, weekly, or monthly schedule.

Now that you have your goal, you must develop a "TO-DO LIST" which may be daily, weekly, or monthly. Then PRIORITIZE. As a student, you should develop a "daily to-do list." Look at an example of how goals and priorities can be utilized.

According to the example above, the number one priority on August 31, ____ is to go to work. The second priority is to study, and the third is to practice essay writing. This is good prioritizing since this student's short-term goal is to pass English and social environment.

Remember, you must set your goals and then begin to organize your time by using "to-do" lists which you prioritize. Most students tend to function better if they divide their goal-setting into three levels:

DAILY—WEEKLY—SEMESTER

Goal-setting should be established at the beginning of each term. This includes analysis of information on course selection, what grades you want to receive in each course, how you plan to go about it, and the evaluation of your first class sessions. Put all of this information together before setting time schedules. Remember, a goal is no good unless it is explicit and concrete. For example, to say you want to do well would be too general and vague. "I plan to make an 'A' in Psychology" is better.

After you've taken a look at some of your goals and their relationship to your college education, you will see that time management is directly related to your goals. Now, examine the obvious priorities that are suggested by the goals that are part of your life. When you break down your goals, long-term to short-term, step by step, you become aware of activities that fall into the following three categories:

1. **Urgent**—Things that have forced themselves to the top of your pile by virtue of an impending deadline. Examples: finish an assignment due tomorrow, take out the garbage if tomorrow is collection day, go to work, attend class.

2. **Responsibilities**—Things that lead up to the completion of tasks which may or may not have a deadline; hopefully before they reach the level of "Urgent." Examples: prepare meals, call Mom, take the car in for service, make an appointment for advising, go to the library to research a paper.

3. **Relaxation**—Recreational activities which require "free time," that is, free of the pressure of being either a "Responsibility" or an "Urgency." Examples: clean your room, watch TV, shop for a prom dress, read a book. You will notice that even some of these can become "Urgent" in your life if they are attached to a time-frame event (the prom dress can be urgent if the prom is next week).

An awareness of these categories can help you answer the very important question, "What is the best possible use of my time RIGHT NOW?" You need to know how many "urgent" tasks you have in front of you, and how much time you must devote to "responsibilities" to keep them under control. You also begin to learn that you can't enjoy "relaxation" activities when deadlines are looming in the other areas. For instance, have you ever given in to the temptation to go to the movies with a friend, only to "remember" when you got home that you had a math test the next morning? To make matters worse, you missed two classes when you took off on that impromptu ski trip three weeks ago, and you never got around to asking anyone for the notes. Now it's midnight—no, 1:00 a.m.—and calling someone in your class for math notes feels a bit risky. This scenario is the result of several factors: trusting your memory to keep track of "responsibilities" and "urgent" deadlines, not having a focus on your goals so you don't know what the priorities are, and making a decision on the spur of the moment to let "recreational" desires come before your goals. Hey . . . don't beat yourself up about it; it's human nature! But let's get it under control.

■ How to Translate Your Goals into an Action Plan

The Action Plan is a chart which lists the steps you must take to reach your goal. It defines not only the action you must take, but also forces you to assign a deadline date to accomplish each step, describes the possible costs, and identifies the resources and people who may help you. Here's an example based on one of the short-term goals from the previous activity. Remember the short-term goals are steps in themselves, leading to the realization of one of your long-term goals—in this case, earning your degree.

The Goal: Complete four courses next semester with a final GPA of at least 3.0 at a cost of 180 hours study time.

Action Plan Chart

Steps	Date	Cost	Resources
1. Choose 4 appropriate courses	11/15	1 Hour	Counselor/Advisor
2. Purchase and survey textbooks	1/5	2 Hours	Bookstore
3. Make semester calendar	1/15	1 Hour	Calendar
4. Make weekly schedule	1/15	1 Hour	Schedule pad
5. Find study partners	1/28	2 Hours	Classmates
6. Cut back work hours at finals	5/5	less $$	Boss

Now it's your turn. The activity on the next page guides you in designing your own Action Plan Chart.

Reasons to Get a College Education

1. Statistics show the salary of the average college graduate is 33–50% higher than that of the average high school grad. This is true for both men and women.

2. Women college graduates are better able to support themselves, if need be, and have more opportunity to choose their own hours during the child-raising years.

3. Studies consistently show that each decade there has been an increase in the percentage of jobs that require some training beyond high school. This trend is expected to continue.

4. In recent years, America has seen a layoff crisis (downsizing, early retirement). It is easier to be flexible, mobile, and re-train for other occupations if you have a college education behind you. If you are trained to do just one job, as in the case of many high school grads, you'll find it tougher to be re-employed.

5. College graduates enjoy more prestige and respect in the community.

Where do you see yourself in 10 years?

Hold in your mind a picture of yourself: (your job, your lifestyle, the house you live in, the clothes you wear) in 10 years if you continue your education and finish your degree. Now, get a mental picture of yourself having dropped out and having no degree. Which picture is prettier?

■ Activity: Action Plan Chart

Choose a goal and use the chart below, and fill in as many steps as possible. Use as many details as you can.

Action Plan Chart

Goal Statement: _____

_____

Steps	Date	Cost	Resources

■ Scheduling Tools

Example: Chelsea's Scheduling Tools

Chelsea has stated a short-term goal as follows: "To complete the current semester with a GPA of 3.5 or above, limiting study time to 30 hours per week." (She has stated her "cost" as a limit rather than a dollar or time amount, which is perfectly ok). Her Action Plan for this goal includes the following steps:

Steps	Date	Cost	Resources
1. Find Chem study partner	1/22	2 hours	Classmates
2. Review for Spanish midterm	3/15	3 hours	Class notes and language lab
3. Complete research paper	4/20	?	Library, materials

Chelsea has identified three steps to accomplish her short-term goal of finishing this semester with a 3.5 GPA. She has set a deadline for the accomplishment of each of these steps. First, she notes those dates on her large wall calendar.

JANUARY

S	M	T	W	T	F	S
	1	2	3	4	5 Purchase and Survey Textbooks	6
7	8 Classes Begin	9	10	11	12	13
14	15 Make Weekly and Semester Schedule	16	17	18	19	20
21	22 Chem Study Partner	23	24	25	26	27
28	29	30	31			

APRIL

S	M	T	W	T	F	S
				1	2	3
4 Finish Reading for Research Paper	5	6	7 Research Paper Outline	8	9	10
11	12 Research Paper Rough Draft	13	14	15 Edit and Proofread Rough Draft	16	17
18	19	20 Complete Research Paper	21	22	23	24
25	26	27	28	29	30	

Next, she analyzes the activities necessary to meet those deadlines, and estimates the amount of time needed for each activity. For instance, if she plans to have her paper written by April 20th, she knows she needs to have the research done by April 4th. If she puts that notation on her calendar, she can see how many days she has to go to the library and do research.

	Sunday	Monday	Tuesday	Wednesday	Thursday	Friday	Saturday
6:00-7:00	Sleep						Sleep
7:00-8:00							
8:00-9:00	Church	Eng.		Eng.		Eng.	Flower Arranging
9:00-10:00		Hist.	Math	Hist.	Math	Hist.	class
10:00-11:00		Psyc.		Psyc.		Psyc.	Study
11:00-12:00	Lunch						
12:00-1:00			Chem		Chem		
1:00-2:00		Work		Work		Work	
2:00-3:00							
3:00-4:00			Study		Study		
4:00-5:00							
5:00-6:00							
6:00-7:00	Dinner		Dinner		Dinner		Dinner
7:00-8:00		Dinner	Ballet	Dinner	Ballet	Dinner	
8:00-9:00		Study		Study		Study	
9:00-10:00							
10:00-12:00							
11:00-12:00							
12:00-1:00							

Like most of us, Chelsea has a class schedule and also a job. So she'll probably need a second tool to keep tabs on those ongoing commitments. A weekly schedule can be kept in a small date book, or she might choose to include it on the wall calendar. Chelsea marks off the hours she's already committed to work and classes, and other standing appointments (ballet lessons, flower arranging class). The weekly schedule helps Chelsea keep in touch with the number of hours that are hers to devote to relaxation activities (everybody's favorite!). For example, suppose it's the evening of April 2nd. Chelsea knows she needs about six more pages of research notes to do a great job on her paper. It takes about an hour per page to get the notes. That cute guy in her history class, Newt Socks, calls and asks if she'd like to go to a showing of "JFK" at the local theater. Chelsea can look at her wall calendar and weekly schedule to see if she'll have enough time to finish the research notes by April 4th if she skips the library tonight. By asking that question again, "What's the best possible use of my time RIGHT NOW?" Chelsea knows, because she has a weekly schedule and has written down her Action Plan deadlines, that she has about 16 hours of "unscheduled" time before the April 4th deadline. Six of those hours she must devote to the responsibility of finishing the research. The movie will take about 4 or 5 hours, give-or-take for espresso afterwards, which leaves about 5 hours for other responsibilities or unexpected urgent tasks (cleaning the cat box, "surprise" homework assignments, or whatever). Chelsea decides she can go on the date.

The point we're trying to make here is that using scheduling tools doesn't enslave you to an hour-by-hour schedule, cross-off-lists, or any other freedom-reducing stressors. Instead, the tools buy you freedom by showing you exactly how many hours you can safely devote to activities you WANT to do without throwing the rest of your life into trauma.

■ Semester Calendar

Let's try setting up a system from scratch.

First you must break down and buy (or make) a calendar. If you use a computer every day, you can get software that will help schedule your time and even ring alarms to remind you of appointments. However, the best tool is probably a large wall calendar with room to write several messages for each day. Hang it where you'll see it all the time (next to the refrigerator? next to the mirror?). No, more likely you'll want it where you use it most—hanging on the wall or corkboard next to your desk.

Let's say your Action Plan goal is "Be able to earn a 3.0 average this term, without cutting back on work hours." So your first step will be to mark in the deadline date for accomplishing the entire goal: the date of final exams. If final exams are the week of December 13–17, all your preparations must be complete by then. Just write in big letters "FINALS" across those dates.

SEPTEMBER

S	M	T	W	T	F	S
			1	2	3	4
5	6	7 Chem Study Group	8	9 Music Listening	10	11
12	13	14 Chem Study Group	15	16 Music Listening	17	18
19	20	21 Chem Study Group	22	23 Music Listening	24	25
26	27	28 Chem Study Group	29	30 Music Listening		

OCTOBER

S	M	T	W	T	F	S
					1	2
3	4	5 Chem Study Group	6	7 Music Listening	8	9
10	11 1/2 Music Book Read	12 Chem Study Group	13	14 Music Listening	15	16
17	18	Per. Paper due 19 Chem Study Group	20	21 Music Listening	22	23
24/31	25	26 Chem Study Group	27	28 Music Listening	29	30 Research done 10 hrs. ⟶

NOVEMBER						
S	M	T	W	T	F	S
	1 1/2 Music Book Read	2 Chem Study Group	3	4 Music Listening	5	6
7	8	9 Chem Study Group	10	11 Music Listening	12	13
14	15	16 Chem Study Group	17	18 Music Listening	19	20
21	22	23 Chem Study Group	24 Rough draft due	25 Holiday Break ←	26 →	27
28	29	30 Chem Study Group				

DECEMBER						
S	M	T	W	T	F	S
			1	2 Music Listening	3	4
5	6	7 Chem Study Group	8 Research Paper due	9 Music Listening	10	11
12	13	14 ←	15 F I N A L S	16	17 →	18
19	20	21	22	23	24	25
26	27	28	29	30	31	

Next, you need to look at each of your classes to determine what's necessary to be prepared for each final. These are the steps defined in the Action Plan, complete with the deadline dates for accomplishing them.

GOAL STATEMENT: Be able to earn a 3.0 GPA this semester, without cutting back on my work hours.

English Class			
Steps	**Date**	**Cost**	**Resources**
1. Expository writing paper due	Sept. 30	4 hours	Follow text examples
2. Persuasive writing paper due	Oct. 19	4 hours	Follow text examples
3. Research for paper completed	Oct. 30	10 hours	Library
4. Rough draft completed	Nov. 24	6 hours	Textbook and style guide
5. Final draft completed	Dec. 4	6 hours	Style guide

Chemistry Class			
Steps	**Date**	**Cost**	**Resources**
1. Find chemistry study group	Sept. 7	2 hrs./week	Classmates
2. Finish all 8 chemistry labs	Nov. 19	16 hours	Lab and books
3. Break up chemistry study time	Weekly	2 hrs./week	Schedule time

Music Class			
Steps	**Date**	**Cost**	**Resources**
1. Read half of music book	Oct. 11	30 hours	Textbook
2. Read second half of book	Nov. 1	30 hours	Textbook
3. Break up music listening time	Weekly	2 hrs./week	Schedule tool
4. Get quizzed on music pieces	Nov. 12	3 hours	Tapes and friend Bob

In our practice example, you have three classes: English Composition, Chemistry, and Music History. Setting up goal steps for English Comp is easy—the teacher does it for you. There are three papers due before finals, and if you do well on the papers, you'll be prepared for the essay final. The due dates of the papers are as follows:

Expository Writing, Sept. 30
Persuasive Writing, Oct. 19
Research Writing, Dec. 8

Write these dates and any others not marked on the calendar. Now, working backwards, how many hours of work will it take from the time you've completed your rough draft until you have the final draft of your research paper ready (you're estimating—nobody really expects you to KNOW this exactly!)? Say, six hours?

Rule of Thumb #1

Never schedule yourself to work more than 4 hours in any one day on the same assignment! 3 hours is a better, reasonable "chunk" of time to schedule.

Rule of Thumb #2

Always give yourself an extra day.

If you use rule of thumb #1, you know you should divide those six hours into two "chunks" of three hours each, on each of two days. Rule of thumb #2 admonishes you to remember you're human (what if you get the flu?) and add in an extra day to meet your deadline. So, in this practice example, your "rough draft" deadline is two weeks before the paper is due. Remember you want to have the paper done by (at least) the night before it's due (you do want to sleep, don't you?). That's November 24th, then, as the deadline for the rough draft. Put it on the calendar. Now, to keep your sanity, write in the number of hours you estimated it would take to complete the next step (6 hours). Continue using the practice example to fill in the calendars, analyzing the time requirements for each step. Remember to jot a note at each deadline to remind yourself how many hours of work you've estimated it will take to meet the next deadline. This is the key to knowing exactly how much free time (relaxation time) you have. Complete the Scheduling Activity on the next page using your Goal Statements from the previous two activities.

■ Activity: Scheduling

Complete the blank calendars using your own goal statement and action plan steps from the previous Action Plan Chart Activity.

S	**M**	**T**	**W**	**T**	**F**	**S**

S	M	T	W	T	F	S

■ Weekly Schedule

When you were in high school, chances are your weekly schedule was so much the same week after week that you could keep it in your head. For college students, things are very different. To start with, your classes don't meet at the same hour every day, five days a week. Chemistry is Monday, Wednesday and Friday, from 9:00 a.m. to 11:50 a.m. Rhetoric is Tuesday and Thursday, 8:00–9:15 a.m. You registered late (it wasn't on your calendar!), so you got stuck with an evening section of Music History, Monday from 7:00–10:00 p.m. Now add to that: Chemistry study group, Tuesday evening at 7:30–9:00 p.m., and Drama Club, Friday afternoon at 4:00 p.m. (remember there will be rehearsals every night starting in October while you're rehearsing "Jesus Christ, Superstar"). Next week you have a dentist appointment on Thursday at noon. And . . . don't forget your job at Burger Biggie: this week they've given you 20 hours (supposedly scheduled around your classes), but next week it'll be 32 hours. How do you **remember** all of this?

Your day-to-day scheduling tool is a weekly schedule. If your life is not as complicated as the example above, you might get by with doing this right on your wall calendar. But most students find it better to have something small enough to carry around so additions and changes can be marked in as they occur. The format that works best looks like the following:

6:00–7:00							
7:00–8:00							
8:00–9:00							
9:00–10:00							
10:00–11:00							
11:00–12:00							
12:00–1:00							
1:00–2:00							
2:00–3:00							
3:00–4:00							
4:00–5:00							
5:00–6:00							
6:00–7:00							
7:00–8:00							
8:00–9:00							
9:00–10:00							
10:00–11:00							
11:00–12:00							
12:00–1:00							

You can buy calendars like this in office supply or book stores, or you can make your own and copy it for each week. First enter all your "fixed" commitments: classes, standing appointments, meetings. Then enter the items, like work schedule, which change each week. Next look at your wall calendar, and schedule in a "tentative" commitment for the number of hours you'll need to work on your goal-related projects. For example, your wall calendar tells you your research paper will be done on December 8th, and it will take you six hours to complete the final draft, which needs to be finished December 7th.

You can then schedule 3-hour blocks of time on December 3rd and 4th for writing the paper. Plan to commit to writing during those 3-hour blocks, and don't be swayed to do another activity unless it meets these two tests: 1) it is directly related to another of your stated, written long- or short-term goals, and 2) you can clearly see that you have other blocks of time available before the deadline to "make up" this commitment. Think of this as "trading" blocks of time—that is, you are not giving up or throwing away the time you were going to use for writing that paper, you are instead moving it to another spot where you had a block of time that was previously unscheduled "free time."

The weekly schedule is not designed to plan every minute of your week, but rather to show you where you do have "free time" available. No one expects you to pass up the once-in-a-lifetime opportunity to play flag football with your brother and his best friend, just count the cost and remember the concept of "trading" blocks of time.

	NOV. 28 Sunday	NOV. 29 Monday	NOV. 30 Tuesday	DEC. 1 Wednesday	DEC. 2 Thursday	DEC. 3 Friday	DEC. 4 Saturday
6:00–7:00							
7:00–8:00							
8:00–9:00	Church		Rhetoric		Rhetoric		Work
9:00–10:00		Chem.	↓	Chem.	↓	Chem.	
10:00–11:00							
11:00–12:00	↓	↓		↓		↓	
12:00–1:00	Work				Dentist		↓
1:00–2:00					↓		
2:00–3:00						Write Final Draft	
3:00–4:00							
4:00–5:00	↓			Work	Work	Drama Club	Write Final Draft
5:00–6:00						↓	
6:00–7:00							
7:00–8:00		Music History	Chem. Group	↓	↓		Could "trade" this block of time if something came up.
8:00–9:00		↓	↓	↓	↓		
9:00–10:00		↓					
10:00–11:00							
11:00–12:00							
12:00–1:00							

Name: _____ Date: _____

■ Activity: Weekly Schedule

DIRECTIONS: Using your current schedule and your semester calendar, make up a weekly schedule for next week.

6:00–7:00							
7:00–8:00							
8:00–9:00							
9:00–10:00							
10:00–11:00							
11:00–12:00							
12:00–1:00							
1:00–2:00							
2:00–3:00							

3:00–4:00						
4:00–5:00						
5:00–6:00						
6:00–7:00						
7:00–8:00						
8:00–9:00						
9:00–10:00						
10:00–11:00						
11:00–12:00						
12:00–1:00						
1:00–2:00						
2:00–3:00						

■ To-Do List

We promised you at the start of this chapter that you wouldn't have to deal with "cross-off lists." However, you should know that many people swear by this kind of list, usually labeled a "to-do" list, because it does one important thing: it provides for a concrete, visible reward for having accomplished a task. Many people find it very motivating to see the results of their work, to physically mark that item off the list. Many time-management experts recommend a to-do list or some version of the same idea, as you can see from "Tips From the Experts." Try using the to-do list as a tool for a few days, and see if you find it a motivator or a pain in the neck. Only you can make that decision!

■ Living with Time Management

COMMITMENT = DREAMS COME TRUE

The dictionary defines time as "a continuum in which events succeed one another from past to present to future." Thus, the basic element of time is an event. Getting time under control is a matter of controlling the events in your life.

Producing the scheduling tools is only the first step in managing your time. The tools won't do you a bit of good unless you make the commitment to use them faithfully; to actually act upon what you've written down! So here's a pep talk to help you make and keep that commitment: remember your calendars are tools to keep track of where your time should be going. No one is going to police you to see if you stick to your schedule. You have to be ready to learn to manage your time on your own. If you follow your system for a while, and see the changes it makes in your grades, your health, your stamina, and your level of stress, that will be enough reward to keep you going. Meanwhile, you have to face up to the concept of commitment. Once you've established your goals and priorities, tell yourself firmly that you are committed to following your system, even if the rewards are not immediately visible. Taking a few moments to close your eyes and visualize yourself having attained your long-term goal helps keep the commitment fresh.

Being able to make a commitment is a sign of maturity, and this time management system is a relatively painless way to prove to yourself that you're ready for bigger challenges. Good luck!

Advice from the Experts

Here are some helpful tips from a few of the thousands of books that have been written about time management:

1. *Pam Young and Peggy Jones,* The Side-tracked Home Executive: *Break down big tasks into small ones (things that take less than ten minutes). Use small blocks of time to do these tasks. Write the tasks on index cards, and when you accomplish one, move its card to the back of the box to get a feeling of accomplishment.*

2. *Alan Lakein,* How to Get Control of Your Time and Your Life: *Start with your major goal in life, the one you think of as your "MISSION IN LIFE." We all have one, even if we haven't defined it in words. Make lists of tasks to be done, then prioritize each task A, B, or C. Do the A's first, the B's as you can, and forget about the C's.*

3. *Stephanie Culp,* How to Get Organized When You Don't Have the Time: *Have a designated place for every item you own. Get control of paper by handling every paper that comes to you only once—decide then and there what to do with it, and do it.*

4. *James T. McCoy,* The Management of Time: *Divide all the tasks on your "to-do" list into "Have to" and "Should do." The dividing line is the following question: "Will my work, co-workers, or my family suffer in any significant way if I fail to do this today?" If the answer is "No," it's a "Should do," and can safely be left until tomorrow—or next week.*

5. *William Oncken, Jr.,* Managing Management Time: *The best part of this book is the appendix called "Collected Sayings of Ben Franklin's Grandfather." One example: "Our Maker gave us TIME to keep everything from happening at once."*

6. *Dave Ellis,* Becoming a Master Student:
   A. *Be aware of your best, most productive time of day.*
   B. *Avoid marathon study sessions.*
   C. *Learn to say NO.*
   D. *Accept less than perfection when perfection is not required.*
   E. *Try, when you are getting ready to quit for the day, to do "just one more thing."*

7. *Tim Walter and Al Siebert,* Student Success: How to Succeed in College and Still Have Time for Your Friends: *You may have heard it said, "If you want something done, ask a busy person." It does seem that the busiest, most involved students accomplish the most and get the best grades. That's because the busier you are, the more you MUST rely on scheduling tools, and those tools really do work.*

8. *Benjamin Franklin: "Dost thou love life, then do not squander time, for that's the stuff life is made of."*

■ The Spoilers: Procrastination and Distraction

Dealing with Procrastination

Everybody procrastinates at one time or another. Why? Two reasons: *inertia* and *avoidance*. *Inertia* is probably the easiest type of procrastination to overcome. You remember from science class that inertia simply means "a body once in motion tends to remain in motion, and a body stationary tends to remain stationary." So, if *your* body is tending to remain stationary (for instance, in front of the TV or under the covers), you can use a few simple tricks to get your body into the "in motion" category. Once again, begin by asking yourself the age-old question, "What is the best possible use of my time RIGHT NOW?"

Special Time Management Situations

Some students have more challenges than average, because of their lifestyles or circumstances. Here are some brief tips to help meet those extra time-management challenges:

1. Part-time students with full-time jobs:

You need to pay particular attention to the concept of dividing your time into blocks or chunks, and be certain to schedule in time for unexpected emergencies at work or at home. Your health and rest are of utmost importance; be especially careful of overextending yourself so that you are unable to get enough sleep. You probably need to decide which is your top priority—school or work—and if necessary, adjust the time frame of your goal to take fewer classes at a time. If you take more than one class at a time, ask your advisor to help you choose classes that are "balanced," for example don't take Chemistry and Calculus in the same semester.

2. Moms (or Dads) going to school and raising kids and running a home:

There's probably no one else in the world who needs time management skills more than you do. You need time for household chores, shopping, cooking, getting the kids to school and activities on time, helping with kids' homework, listening to problems and drying tears, doing your own studying, getting to class . . . the list goes on and on. Say, do you get to have a life, too? There is so much stress in this situation, sometimes you will be tempted to think it isn't worth it. Two hints for you: First, get a very firm grip on your goals. Why are you seeking that degree? What improvements will it make in your life and the lives of your loved ones? If you can see this clearly, it will make all the difference when things look bleakest. Second, everybody has to have a schedule, not just you. The scheduling tools include activities of each family member, and you can then remind and encourage each other. Also, try to find a friend at school who is in the same situation. That support can be crucial for both of you.

3. Students with health problems:

Once again, your health must be your top priority, even if it means slowing down the achievement of your goals by taking fewer classes at once. Whether you have a chronic illness or a disability, you need to schedule in time for rest, physical therapy, proper nutrition, visits to the doctor, etc. before you schedule your class and study time. Be realistic about what you can handle. If you become ill during

the semester, don't just stop going to class. See your instructor and try to work out time to catch up, or ask for an Incomplete grade which you can finish the following semester.

4. Multiple commitments:

Athletes, musicians, etc. If part of your reason for attending college is the opportunity it affords you to play your sport or perform using your talents, you need to consider your activity and your education as equally important. If eligibility is an issue, naturally you are going to want to keep your grades up. Your best bet is to rely on the "buddy system" with a teammate or friend who is in the same situation. Hold each other accountable for maintaining a wise study and practice schedule. Obviously, not enough can be said about picking out the right person for your "buddy." The guy who thinks it won't hurt to party on school nights is probably not the "buddy" to choose.

5. Overcommitment:

Full time school and work, too many activities, etc. What's your priority? We repeat, what's your priority? Get a firm vision of where you want to be in, say, five years. If you are working full time and going to school full time, your grades are going to suffer. You are going to be tired. You are not going to have time for relaxation or social activities. The same is true if you have committed yourself to too many activities. It's great to take advantage of the opportunities college has to offer for sports, music, theater, clubs, and new friends. But to handle your goal-related responsibilities, you just have to decide which of these activities you can't live without, and pass on the rest.

6. Personal problems:

When you are in college, the rest of your life doesn't just stop. You will fall prey to personal pitfalls of all kinds: emotional, relationship-related, or financial to name a few. If you find yourself overwhelmed by a personal problem while the semester is in progress, take advantage of your school's counselors. They are there to help, they've seen it all before, and most of them are easy to talk to and have lots of ideas to help you through. There is no better wisdom than knowing when you need help and asking for it. Don't even wait until it gets out of hand—go today!

Before your brain has a chance to tell you, "Sleeping is good," get a grip on your priorities. What's urgent? NAME IT! Look at your Action Plan, if it applies, or ask yourself what the very first step is in the direction of that goal or "urgency."

What does your scheduling tool tell you you're supposed to be doing right now? For example, you have a term paper in the works. You have to finish the research today if you're going to meet the deadline. But you stayed up late last night and at 9:00 a.m., your stationary body wants to stay that way. What's the first step? If you can tell yourself, "If I get up and get in the shower," you will usually find that's enough to get you "in motion."

But suppose the problem is really *avoidance?* What if that reluctance to get going on the research paper stems from the notion that a) you chose the wrong topic and there's not enough research to support it, or b) the subject is too difficult and you feel you may not be able to tackle the paper successfully, or c) . . . a myriad of other self-defeating thoughts. There are many reasons why we procrastinate based on the desire to avoid something unpleasant. For instance:

1. Fear of failure, or not doing as well as we'd like

2. Fear of not being able to handle success

3. Desire to avoid particular people, relationships or situations

4. Desire to avoid an unpleasant task, like doing dishes or figuring taxes

5. Feeling overwhelmed by the size or scope of a task

6. Perfectionism—"If I can't make it perfect, why even start?"

7. Fear of someone else's judgment of your work

Handling *avoidance* type procrastination is pretty much similar to your approach to the inertia type. You still want to break down your dreaded task into its parts or steps, then tackle the very first step without worrying about the others. But to really overcome avoidance you have to deal with the emotional issues and mental attitudes that are getting in your way. It's easy for someone else to tell you to "feel confident"; but only you can get to the bottom of this! In the next chart are some suggestions to help you.

■ Planning Your Time?

If you have not purchased your academic calendar planner for the year, you should rush right out and do it now. It should be large enough so you can write in your assignments. The ideal one would also have space for your daily "to-do" list. However, do not worry about that space since all you have to do is buy a pack of 3"x5" cards and on a nightly basis before going to bed, write out all the tasks you are planning for the next day. Don't forget to prioritize. Before writing in your planner, use these tips when planning your time.

Tip 1

Balance your time.

Balance your work, travel, sleep, domestic chores, class, study, personal, and recreational times. All work and no play truly do make Jack a dull boy. You will no doubt become frustrated if you spend too much time in some areas and your goals are not being met in other areas.

Tip 2

Plan for the semester.

Plan your school work for an entire semester based on the school's calendar. This refers to due dates for papers, hours for study time, dates for major exams, etc.

Tip 3

Set goals for each study session.

Always set a goal for each study session and be definite in your schedule about what you plan to study. Be definite about what you plan to do in each session.

Tip 4

Know how long your study session should be.

Study in short sessions. The idea is to avoid marathon sessions where you remember little of what you tried to learn. Plan to take at least a ten-minute break during every hour. During the break, try exercising or doing something else that will refresh your mind/body. This will help you maintain your concentration.

Tip 5

Study in the right place.

Select a quiet and not-too-comfortable place to study. It should allow you to concentrate on the task at hand. Make sure it has proper lighting, ventilation, and a comfortable temperature.

Tip 6

Let others in on your plans.

Let your friends and significant others know your study schedule so they will not disturb you. You are the person who must control someone else's use of your time. If you have children, plan activities for them while you study.

Tip 7

Plan to see your professor.

Make sure you understand your notes and/or assignment before trying to study. If you are not clear on what you have to study, make an appointment to visit your professor for clarification. Don't flounder. Record your appointment to see the professor if it is necessary in your appointment book.

Tip 8

Know how much time you should study for each class.

Plan two hours of study for every hour you are in class.

Tip 9

Prioritize subjects to study.

Study the subject you like least first since it will no doubt require more of your time and energy. Once you have completed this task, reward yourself by doing something you like.

Tip 10

Know when to review notes.

Review, study, and/or rewrite your lecture notes within 24 hours to help with memory and effective note taking. Forty-eight hours should be the maximum amount of time you allow to lapse before reviewing.

Tip 11

Know purpose of studying.

Study to pass tests. When reading and/or reviewing notes, always practice asking and answering questions. Study as though at the end of your study session, you will be required to pass a test.

Tip 12

Know how to begin reading text material.

Survey required chapters (material) before you begin to read.

Tip 13

Develop questions you should ask as you study.

Ask questions about what you must learn during the study period. Turn all headings into questions and then answer them.

Tip 14

Always read with a purpose.

Read the assigned chapters and/or material. Look for answers to questions posed in order to complete the assignment. Read with the purpose of finding the answers.

Tip 15

Memorize.

Go over the content which you want to remember. If necessary, orally recite and make notes to help you remember.

Tip 16

Review.

Review the material and ask questions.

Tip 17

Decide when you should study.

Determine your best time of day and schedule your study time then. In addition, a brief review before class and immediately after class is strongly suggested.

Tip 18

Use your time productively.

Don't waste time. If you are waiting, use that time for review. If you have recorded your notes and you are driving, listen to the tape. If you are riding with someone else, read your notes.

Procrastination Hints

1. Break the big tasks down into small steps. Schedule them, using your scheduling tools. Especially use your to-do list; it's motivating to see tasks checked off.

2. Find "step one" and start there without contemplating the rest of the project yet.

3. Set a time limit: "I'll work on step one (or two or ten) for 15 minutes." Sometimes you'll get involved and keep going.

4. Find a buddy to whom you'll agree to be accountable. Share your plan for tackling the project, and ask him to check up on you.

5. Suppose you missed something in class and the assignment doesn't make sense. You'll need to find a fellow student or ask the instructor for clarification. That, of course, would be your step one.

6. The trick is to train your mind that "When we sit here, it's time to study." Have all your materials ready, too, so you don't waste time looking for them.

7. Use positive self-talk. Remember Stuart Smalley on "Saturday Night Live"? "I'm good enough, I'm smart enough, and gosh darn it, people like me!" It was silly when "Stuart" did it, but actually the concept does work. Try to replace a negative thought with a positive one. Instead of, "I'll never get all this work done!", think, "I know I can at least read the chapter; I'll do that first."

8. It helps to hold out a carrot for yourself—something you will find really rewarding that you'll do for yourself after, say, reading three chapters or writing a rough draft.

■ Activity: Understanding Procrastination

1. List three situations in which you typically find yourself procrastinating, or, putting off what you need to do.

   a. _____

   b. _____

   c. _____

2. How do you feel about putting off what needs to be done in these situations (e.g., guilty, angry, depressed)? What thoughts come to mind when you think about these situations (e.g., "I tell myself I'll get started, but I never do")?

■ Overcoming Distractions: Sara's Demolished Study Plan

Sara had planned to study Saturday afternoon, and had made detailed plans for how she would use her time to finish assignments for math, physics, literature, and music history. She needed to be finished studying by 5:00 p.m. since she had a date Saturday evening. She planned to begin studying at 1:00, right after lunch.

Sara jumped into the car and ran down to Wendy's to get some chili for lunch. While there, she ran into her high school friend, Laura, whom she hadn't seen in a couple of months. They spent some time catching up—a lot of time, actually—and Sara didn't leave the restaurant until 1:30. On the way home she noticed she was nearly out of gas. She stopped at the gas station, and also checked out the mini-mart for some study-break snacks.

By the time Sara got home it was nearly 2:00. Sara had wanted to save some bucks while at community college, so she was still living at home. Sometimes her parents didn't realize that college studying was more time consuming than high school had been, and asked her to help out at home more often than Sara would like. Today, for instance, she arrived home and her mom asked her to please "keep an eye" on her little brother, age 10, so Mom could go shopping. Sara shoved a video into the VCR and told her brother to stay out of trouble while she studied.

Fifteen minutes into the literature reading assignment, the phone rang. It was the guy Sara was going out with that night, calling to ask if she'd rather see a movie or go to a dance club. They talked for a while, maybe twenty minutes, but after they hung up, Sara found it difficult to concentrate. She was really looking forward to the date.

After trying for a while to keep reading, Sara finally got up and went down to the kitchen for a soft drink. There she found the mess left after her brother had fixed himself a snack.

By the time Sara cleaned up the mess, got her drink, and got back to work, it was past 3:30. She decided to switch to working on math problems. About half an hour later, the doorbell rang. Sara grudgingly plodded downstairs, opened the door, and there stood her best friend Kim, jumping up and down, thrusting her hand under Sara's nose—she was wearing an engagement ring! Naturally, Sara had to hear every detail of the proposal, and the ring selection . . . and it was more than an hour later when Kim left.

Obviously, Sara faced a lot of external distractions which sabotaged her studying plans. We think of distractions as "things" (or people) that tend to pull us off course, but there are also internal distractions that may plague us. For example, Sara faced that type of distraction when she was unable to maintain her concentration after the call from her date. Look at this list of possible distractions and see how many are best avoided simply by adjusting personal habits or attitudes:

1. Physical: hunger, thirst, fatigue, illness

2. Mental: daydreaming, personal problems, worrying, stress, thinking about other activities, or someplace you'd rather be.

3. Environment: uncomfortable room/chair, wrong lighting, too hot or too cold, noise (phones, people, music, TV)

4. Other: negative attitude about assignments, course, or instructor; other people wanting your attention.

The chart below offers some suggestions to avoid being distracted. You also have to plan ways to handle distractions when they occur and get yourself back on target.

Suggestions for Avoiding Distractions

1. Close your door. Unplug your phone. Simply be unavailable.

2. Avoid the temptation to "finish one more errand," "make one more phone call," anything that takes up time you've already scheduled for studying.

3. Schedule your breaks and be specific about what you're going to do on your break. Just saying, "take a break" invites prolonged malingering.

4. Pile a whole bunch of junk on your bed so it's a real pain to try to get in it. Remember, we're trying to avoid temptation.

5. Identify people, places, and things that tend to tempt you and waste your time. Don't answer Carla's knock at your door. Don't go to the college cafeteria to study.

6. Get enough sleep. Eat right. Exercise.

■ Activity: Crisis Management

A. Crisis One: Emotional Shipwreck

You have been engaged to be married since the night you graduated from high school. You are now a second-semester sophomore in college, hoping to transfer to the state's best university school of business next fall. You are in the middle of the hardest courses you've ever taken. You have two midterms this week, as well as an oral presentation (complete with computer graphics), and you have a group presentation due next week which involves a detailed case study analysis.

Your heavy work load has taken its toll on your relationship with your fiancé. Last night your fiancé came over and dropped the bombshell: it's over; there's someone else. So sorry.

You don't feel much like studying, researching, or trying to pull it together to even go to class. But the timing couldn't be worse. If you don't do well on these tests and projects, your whole semester could go up in smoke. Business school is very competitive—they don't cut much slack for someone who did a crash-n-burn in the middle of sophomore year.

You must analyze your situation, determine your options, and make a plan.

1. Explain the problem in your own words.

2. Analyze how the situation affects your goals and priorities. Do you feel being married is a higher priority than a successful career?

3. Is there anything that might be done to save the situation, or is it necessary to re-group?

4. Assuming the relationship cannot be saved, what steps can you take to salvage the semester? Be specific. What is urgent?

5. What ideas do you have for keeping rein on your emotions during this crisis?

6. What is the very first step you must take?

B. Crisis Two: Sleep Deprivation

You are a full-time freshman at college, living at home. During the summer you worked at a factory, and they were so happy with your work they offered you a permanent full time job. The only shift available, however, was midnights. You figured that would be ok—you could take classes in the morning and still have time to sleep and study in the afternoon and evening.

But, you were in for a couple of surprises. First, you have a lot more homework than you expected. You are already falling behind, and it isn't even midterm yet. Second, after your work shift, your body wants sleep. You find yourself dozing off in class, especially later in the morning. It's been weeks since you stayed awake all the way through your 11:00 history lecture.

You have a new car, and you need your job to keep up with the payments. You'd also really like to get an apartment of your own. If you keep up this pace, however, you're going to flunk out of school. Of course, you'll always have your factory job . . . but is that really what you want?

How will you make the necessary choices? Is money your priority? What about your dreams of the future?

1. Explain why money/possessions/a place of your own are so important to a young adult. These issues cannot be minimized, but it helps to understand the personal and developmental factors which underlie them.

2. How can a young adult train himself to look beyond today's "immediate gratification" to see the need to set goals for the future?

3. What are your options in the situation above? The pros and cons of each?

4. Design a workable Action Plan for this situation. Define the very first step you'll need to take to get started on this plan.

C. Crisis Three: Dysfunctional Family

You are the single parent of three bright and active kids. For the past few years, you've been working as a teacher's aide at their elementary school. The hours have been ideal, but the pay is low, and you know at this rate you'll never dress these kids for high school, let alone save for college. You've decided to go back to school part-time to work on your nursing degree.

But, ever since you've been back in school (working days, taking two evening classes, and studying), you notice your family seems to be falling apart. The kids are fighting, they don't get their homework done, they have to be reminded six times to take a bath, they don't get up in the morning, they make messes they won't clean up, and they say things like, "Mom, you never have time to . . ." Frankly, you're exhausted and about to give up.

How can you figure out what's going on here; and what plans can you use to deal with it?

1. Think of some ways to explain in words why your going to school is important for everybody in the family.

2. Try setting up a semester calendar/weekly schedule for the family as a group. Color code: green for Johnny, red for Susie. What ideas can you think of to motivate everybody to stick to the schedule?

3. How can you, the student, get some "me-time" to reduce stress?

4. What ideas do you have for your family to communicate better and get the family time and attention they need?

■ How to Be a Student

Introduction

The typical college campus is a friendly place; but it is also a competitive environment. The education you receive there, and the attitudes you develop, will guide you for the rest of your life. Your grades will be especially important in landing your first job, or when applying to graduate school. To be a successful student requires certain skills; but, these are skills that can be *learned.*

The Basics of Being a Student

- Prioritize your life: Doing well in school should be your top priority.
- Study: There is no substitute.
- Always attend class.
- Do all of the homework and assigned reading.
- Develop self-discipline.
- Manage your time.

Self-Discipline Made Easy

Human beings are creatures of habit. Therefore, form a *habit* of doing what you reason you should do. Is it not foolish for your behavior to contradict your own reasoning? And what could be more harmonious than finding yourself *wanting* to do what you know you should?

Train yourself so there is an immediate reaction-mechanism within you: Your reason that you should do something, and thus you do it. Other people who seem to have less difficulty with self-discipline probably have simply had more *practice* at it, thereby *making* it less difficult; because, practice is what it takes.

Time Management

No matter how you slice it, there are only 24 hours in a day. Good time-management requires:

1. Not taking on more than you can handle.

2. Reasonably estimating the time required to perform each of the tasks at hand.

3. Actually *doing* what needs to be done.

Only you can do these things. A couple of thoughts, though, that may help spur you on:

- A minute now is as precious as a minute later. You can't put time back on the clock.
- If you're not ahead of schedule, then you're behind schedule. Because, if you try to remain right *on* schedule, then any mishap or misjudgment will cause you to fall behind—perhaps right at the deadline, when no recovery is possible.

Introspection

- Understand, and be honest with, yourself. All else follows from this.
- Be both athlete and coach: Keep one eye on what you are doing, and one eye on yourself.
- Take command of, and responsibility for, yourself.
- Face your insecurities head-on. Some common signs of insecurity: Asking a question to which you already know the answer; being artificially social with instructors or other students, when the real reason is to temporarily kill the pain.
- Form a positive self-image: Those students who are first entering college will probably have doubts about how well they will do. Try to do well immediately to instill an expectation of continuing to do well. Settle for nothing less. Nevertheless, try not to be restricted by your past performance and experiences, good or bad. Learn from the past, but don't be bound by it. Seek out your weaknesses and attack them. Be realistic about your limitations; but, don't let this lead to becoming satisfied with them.

Taking a Course

Each student's attitude is some mixture of the following:

- He/She wants to learn the material.
- He/She wants to get a good grade.
- He/She doesn't care.

Each instructor's attitude is some mixture of the following:

- He/She wants students to learn the material.
- He/She wants grading to be fair and reflect students' knowledge and abilities.
- He/She doesn't care.

In order to do well in a course, it is up to you (the student) to do two things:

1. Learn the material.

2. Learn the instructor.

As for the latter, pay attention in class to the instructor's patterns, to what he/she emphasizes, etc. Gather information about the instructor from other students. A good instructor, however, will present their course in such a way that it will be of little benefit for the student to try to learn him/her, thereby forcing their students to learn the material.

Homework

- Keep in mind that your work is being graded by a *human being*. Thus:
  - Write legibly, orderly, and coherently.
  - Supply any commentary necessary to make it clear what you are attempting to do.

Making the grader's job easier will more likely lead to you getting the benefit of doubt when it occurs.

- Don't think that getting the right answer to a homework problem implies that you have mastered the corresponding material. All you have done is solve *one* particular problem; that does not mean you have necessarily learned how to solve *all* such problems (such as the ones to appear on your exams). It's up to you to view the homework problems from this wider perspective.

■ If available, always look over the solutions provided by the instructor, even if you did well on the assignment. He/She may demonstrate methods (perhaps more efficient) or provide useful information that you hadn't thought of.

Exams

■ Preparation:
  ■ Roughly prioritize material as to its importance (primary, secondary, tertiary), and concentrate your studying on the most significant topics. Remember, the instructor only has a limited amount of time to test what you know and can do. Thus, keep in mind when preparing for an exam that the problems cannot be too complicated if they are to fit within the allotted time.
  ■ Study in ways that are suited to you.

    ❏ Study with a group or alone based upon which is *really* best for you.
    ❏ Do your most strenuous and important work during those times of the day that you work best.

  ■ Summarize or outline the course or text material in your own words. Writing a summary not only forces you to examine the subject matter in detail, but provides a compendium to review just prior to the exam.
  ■ Play it safe: Memorize somewhat more than what the instructor says is required. Bring a calculator even if it's not suggested, etc.
  ■ Study old exams if the instructor is known to give similar exams. But, don't be fooled into thinking that since you were able to work through an old exam, it means you understand all the course material in general, and can perform in a test situation.
  ■ Bring your own paper and a watch.
  ■ Fighting exam anxiety: Convince yourself that all you can do is all you can do; but, don't let that lead you to become complacent. Just be determined to be "on" for the duration of the exam. (Give yourself a pep-talk to this effect prior to each exam.)

■ Starting the exam:
  ■ Read the instructions thoroughly and carefully.
  ■ Skim over the entire exam prior to beginning work.
  ■ Don't necessarily do the problems in order. Instead, get those problems out of the way you feel confident you can do quickly and well. Observe how the problems are weighted, and direct your efforts to where you believe you can pick up points most easily. This does not necessarily mean attempting the most heavily weighted problem first; rather, it means first doing the problem for which you can accumulate points at the fastest *rate*. Indeed, there is a good chance that this is *not* the most heavily weighted problem, since many instructors dislike giving any one problem significantly greater or fewer points than the average, thereby under weighing the harder problems and overweighing the easier ones.
  ■ Before writing on any given problem, *think*. A small investment in time at the beginning can save time overall (for you might thereby choose a more efficient method of solving the problem).
  ■ Do *precisely* what is requested. In particular, don't waste time doing things that will not receive credit. For example, unless explicitly required, do not rewrite the exam problems on your paper.

- Pace yourself through the exam. Example: On a 50-minute exam worth 100 points, you should be accumulating 2 points per minute; thus, a 26-point problem should be completed in 13 minutes. Do this calculation at the start of the exam if the problem weights are given.
- If only for psychological reasons, most graders use nonlinear grading by which the early points of a problem are easier to get:

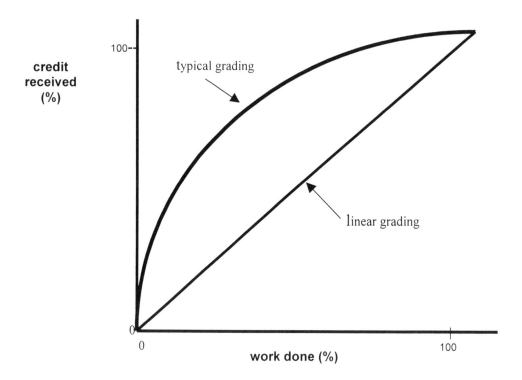

Therefore, always write something (meaningful) down for every problem, if only a little. At the other end, even with linear grading, there are diminishing returns in terms of points-per-effort in trying to squeeze every last point out of a given problem; if time is low, it may be better to move on.

- Communicate with the grader. In particular, if you are running out of time, state the steps you would perform if you were to continue the problem.
- Show your work and make clear your reasoning in order to have a chance to receive partial credit.
- As with homework, and even more importantly, neatness counts.
- In courses on subjective material (e.g., humanities), just *regurgitate* the material from class and the text(s). Supplying your own opinions may sound good in theory, but it has the risk of running counter to the opinions of the instructor or grader. Conversely, restatements of the class/text material are easy for the grader to recognize as something deserving credit. Remember: Unless the exam is multiple-choice, then a human being—who typically wants to grade the many exams in front of him/her as quickly and painlessly as possible—is doing the grading.
- Always check over your answers if you have time.

Further Suggestions

- Unify and simplify your knowledge: A textbook presents the subject in a particular form, as does an instructor. By their very natures, however, textbooks and lectures tend to present subjects sequentially. Take the extra step of understanding the material in *your* terms, which may involve recognizing relationships that could not be conveniently expressed in the order presented in the text(s) and lectures.

- Remember, almost every logically consistent topic is simple at its foundation. Try to recognize the simple underlying relationships in the subject at hand; these are often left unstated by instructors and textbooks.

- Try to learn *general* principles and methods. Learning by examples (putting the new in terms of the familiar) can only take you so far.

- Learn as many methods of problem-solving as you can. This is especially helpful for exams, when time is of the essence.

- Ask yourself questions. Why didn't the instructor or text(s) do this or that? Explore your own ideas. Try to understand the course material in *detail*.

- It is often said that the best way to learn something is to teach it. Do you know the subject matter well enough to explain it clearly and completely to someone else?

- Learn by observing others. Notice what works for them and consider incorporating those methods into yourself. Ask yourself "Why didn't *I* think of that?", and try to develop the related ability.

- Attempt to be methodical, neat, legible, deliberate, precise, knowledgeable, and reliable on the one hand, and creative, spontaneous, imaginative, smart, clever, articulate, and flexible on the other. The first mentality thrives on order, and inherently tries to do well what it already knows how to do; the second mentality thrives on disorder, and inherently tries to expand upon its abilities. Adopt the best of these two mentalities. Remember, every tool is a potential crutch. The first mentality may rely too heavily on already-mastered skills; but, the second mentality may fail to carefully apply those same skills.

- Think about the question, question everything, even the statements appearing here (*and*, yourself!). But, realize that it is equally foolish to be different, as it is to mindlessly conform to the norm.

- For maximum efficiency, have several projects going at once. Then, if you get tired, frustrated, or bored working on one item, you can easily move onto something else, thereby staying productive as well as giving pending problems a chance to work themselves out subconsciously.

- Anticipate. For example, you may need to ask the instructor about the present assignment, but he/she is only guaranteed to be available at certain times; therefore, you should look over the assignment early.

- Forget pulling "all-nighters." These merely amount to borrowing from tomorrow, at which time you will find yourself considerably less functional. All-nighters are really an indication of not having properly planned your activities.

- If possible, bring your textbook(s) to class.

- Take your lecture notes in pencil, since any modifications can then be made quickly and neatly.

Closing

Overall, there is one basic trait that distinguishes successful students from those that are not:

Successful students *forced* themselves to understand.

They do not merely go through the motions of attending class, reading the text(s), and doing the homework, expecting these actions to necessarily suffice. Rather, they are continually asking, "Do I *really* understand what's going on here?" They ask this question of themselves honestly, applying an internal barometer formed from experience to detect the slightest lack of understanding, be it ignorance or confusion. And, if the answer is "No," then the situation is viewed as unacceptable, and more effort is the response.

Summary

In this chapter, we've discussed why time management is such an important part of a successful college career. You've learned that the first step in managing time is to understand your goals or priorities. You have seen how to express your goals in measurable goal statements, and make an *Action Plan* to get started toward achieving those goals. We have shown you some handy tools to schedule your time and get a better idea of how much free time you have available to relax. The three major scheduling tools are the *Semester Calendar*, the *Weekly Schedule*, and the *To-Do List*. We've discussed the "spoilers": *procrastination* and *distraction*, and offered some suggestions to help conquer each of those problems. After completing this chapter, you should be better able to handle the challenges related to the wise use of your time as a college student.

Activity: Summary

1. What is the SECRET to time management?

   _____

   _____

2. Identify what you think are the three most important goals in your life and map out how you plan to go about achieving them.

   _____

   _____

   _____

3. Why is it so important to use a daily "to do" list?

   _____

   _____

4. Develop a plan of action showing how you would assist students to stop procrastinating. Be ready to share and discuss this plan with the class.

   _____

   _____

   _____

   _____

   _____

   _____

   _____

   _____

   _____

CHAPTER 8
Wellness

Wellness/Fitness

Each year over one million Americans die from cardiovascular disease, cancer and other chronic illnesses that are a result of unhealthy lifestyles. Eighty-four percent of these deaths are related to lifestyle decisions made on a daily basis. Active participation in a Wellness/Fitness program can positively affect the length and the quality of your life. This participation includes adopting healthy lifestyles that include a combination of cardiovascular endurance/aerobic exercise, strength training, sound nutritional habits, ideal body weight maintenance, avoidance of substance abuse, and knowledge of disease prevention, and using stress management techniques concerning assertiveness and anger. Adopting these positive lifestyle practices while in college will help make you responsible for your own health care. Developing intelligent and life-long wellness practices is what this chapter is about.

Nutrition

College students have many demands placed on them. Performance in school, athletics, work and leisure time activities can be affected by foods eaten or not eaten. Only YOU can control the amounts and types of food you consume. Just as a car won't run well with poor quality fuel, your body will eventually suffer if you deprive it of essential nutrients.

Nutritionally good food costs no more than nutritionally inadequate food and can sometimes actually cost less. Having a thorough knowledge of nutrition can enable you to choose foods which enhance your diet and give you the best food value for your dollar. Following the seven recommendations of the U.S. Department of Health and Human Services will help you improve your nutrition and can help prevent dietary problems.

1. **Eat a variety of foods.**

	Number of Daily Servings
Vegetables	3–5
Fruit	2–4
Grains (cereal, bread, pasta, rice)	6–11
Milk, Yogurt, Cheese	2–3

This chapter contains material adapted from *Keys to Excellence*, 4th edition by Carol Cooper et al. Copyright © 1997 by Kendall/Hunt Publishing Company. Adapted and reprinted with permission of the publisher. Further reproduction is prohibited.

Meat, Poultry, Fish, Dry Beans, Eggs, Nuts   2–3

2. **Maintain a healthy weight.**
   Evaluate your weight as it relates to your body fat percentage, blood pressure (leading value) and blood cholesterol level. It may be necessary to reduce your weight if any of these measurements is high. Consult your physician first for advice regarding a weight-loss program. You may be referred to a registered dietitian by your physician if you require a nutritional program.

3. **Choose a diet low in fat, saturated fat, and cholesterol.**
   Limit your fat intake to 25% to 30% of your total caloric intake. A maximum of 10% of total calories should come from saturated fats. Saturated fats are found in foods such as whole milk, butter, ice cream, meats, and hard cheeses which tend to raise the blood cholesterol level. Only foods from animal sources contain cholesterol; thus, consuming fewer high cholesterol foods such as eggs, shrimp, red meat, and organ meats can help lower/control the total cholesterol level. Approximately 15 percent of the total daily caloric intake should come from protein. Good sources are beans and peas, non-shell fish, skinless poultry, and lean meat. Practice broiling, baking, or boiling rather than frying food. Trim all the visible fat and skin from meat prior to cooking.

4. **Choose a diet with plenty of vegetables, fruits, and grain products.**
   Carbohydrates, primarily found in plants, are the body's most important source of energy. Simple sugars such as those found in fruits, candy, donuts, and jellies are quickly broken down and absorbed by the body. Complex carbohydrates (starches) such as whole grains, cereals, vegetables, and beans are more slowly broken down and thus provide a more stable form of energy over time. They also supply the body with other necessary nutrients such as vitamins, minerals, and fiber. This is why it is especially important to eat complex carbohydrates and a sufficient amount of protein such as orange juice, cereal and skim milk rather than a sugary donut for breakfast.

5. **Use sugars only in moderation.**
   An excessive intake of refined sugar can contribute to obesity, tooth decay, and hypoglycemia. Hypoglycemia occurs when rapid elevation of blood sugar is followed by a period of lower-than-normal level of blood sugar caused by the release of insulin into the bloodstream. This condition may make you feel lightheaded, weak, and/or dizzy. Many refined foods such as candy, baked goods, and soft drinks contain high amounts of "hidden" sugar. If the label on a food product lists sugar as one of the first or second major ingredients, avoid or cut down on that food. Be aware that sugar comes in many forms such as corn syrup, honey, molasses, dextrose, fructose, maltose, glucose, sucrose, lactose, and sorbitol. Often several of these forms of sugar are listed as ingredients on a single label.

6. **Use salt and sodium in moderation.**
   Most people consume much more salt (sodium chloride) than is needed by the body. Reduction of salt intake in a diet may help to lower high blood pressure. The body needs about 220 mg. (about 1/10 of a teaspoon) daily, but the average American eats 10 to 20 grams (2 to 4 teaspoons) per day. Processed foods in particular are high in salt content. Much of this salt is hidden in processed foods. Reduce the amount of salt used in cooking and at the table; cut down on foods containing visible salt such as chips, pretzels, and salted nuts; and reduce consumption of canned vegetables, frozen dinners, and other processed foods.

7. **If you drink alcoholic beverages, do so in moderation.**
   One alcoholic drink is equal to one beer, a five-ounce glass of wine, or 1 ounce of distilled spirits such as gin, rum, or vodka. Moderate drinking is defined as a maximum of two drinks per day for men and one drink per day for women. Pregnant

women or persons on any kind of medication should not drink alcohol.

The following information came from www.mypyramid.gov

Your food and physical activity choices each day affect your health—how you feel to-day, tomorrow, and in the future.

These tips and ideas are a starting point. You will find a wealth of suggestions here that can help you get started toward a healthy diet. Choose a change that you can make to-day, and move toward a healthier you.

■ Tips to Help You Eat Whole Grains

At meals

- To eat more whole grains, substitute a whole-grain product for a refined prod-uct—such as eating whole-wheat bread instead of white bread or brown rice instead of white rice. It's important to *substitute* the whole-grain product for the refined one, rather than *adding* the whole-grain product.
- For a change, try brown rice or whole-wheat pasta. Try brown rice stuffing in baked green peppers or tomatoes and whole-wheat macaroni in macaroni and cheese.
- Use whole grains in mixed dishes, such as barley in vegetable soup or stews and bulgur wheat in casserole or stir-fries.
- Create a whole grain pilaf with a mixture of barley, wild rice, brown rice, broth and spices. For a special touch, stir in toasted nuts or chopped dried fruit.
- Experiment by substituting whole wheat or oat flour for up to half of the flour in pancake, waffle, muffin or other flour-based recipes. They may need a bit more leavening.
- Use whole-grain bread or cracker crumbs in meatloaf.
- Try rolled oats or a crushed, unsweetened whole grain cereal as breading for baked chicken, fish, veal cutlets, or eggplant parmesan.
- Try an unsweetened, whole grain ready-to-eat cereal as croutons in salad or in place of crackers with soup.
- Freeze leftover cooked brown rice, bulgur, or barley. Heat and serve it later as a quick side dish.

As snacks

- Snack on ready-to-eat, whole grain cereals such as toasted oat cereal.
- Add whole-grain flour or oatmeal when making cookies or other baked treats.
- Try a whole-grain snack chip, such as baked tortilla chips.
- Popcorn, a whole grain, can be a healthy snack with little or no added salt and butter.

What to look for on the food label

- Choose foods that name one of the following whole-grain ingredients *first* on the label's ingredient list:

  "brown rice"   "whole oats"
  "bulgur"   "whole rye"
  "graham flour"   "whole wheat"

"oatmeal"   "wild rice"
"whole-grain corn"

■ Foods labeled with the words "multi-grain," "stone-ground," "100% wheat," "cracked wheat," "seven-grain," or "bran" are usually *not* whole-grain products.

■ Color is not an indication of a whole grain. Bread can be brown because of molasses or other added ingredients. Read the ingredient list to see if it is a whole grain.

■ Use the *Nutrition Facts label* (http://www.mypyramid.gov/related_links/index.html#nutritionfacts) and choose products with a higher % Daily Value (%DV) for fiber—the %DV for fiber is a good clue to the amount of whole grain in the product.

■ Read the food label's ingredient list. Look for terms that indicate added sugars (sucrose, high-fructose corn syrup, honey, and molasses) and oils (partially hydrogenated vegetable oils) that add extra calories. Choose foods with fewer added sugars, fats, or oils.

■ Most sodium in the food supply comes from packaged foods. Similar packaged foods can vary widely in sodium content, including breads. Use the *Nutrition Facts label* (http//www.mypyramid.gov/related_links/index.html#nutritionfacts) to choose foods with a lower % DV for sodium. Foods with less than 140 mg sodium per serving can be labeled as low sodium foods. Claims such as "low in sodium" or "very low in sodium" on the front of the food label can help you identify foods that contain less salt (or sodium).

■ Tips to Help You Eat Vegetables

In general

■ Buy fresh vegetables in season. They cost less and are likely to be at their peak flavor.

■ Stock up on frozen vegetables for quick and easy cooking in the microwave.

■ Buy vegetables that are easy to prepare. Pick up pre-washed bags of salad greens and add baby carrots or grape tomatoes for a salad in minutes. Buy packages of baby carrots or celery sticks for quick snacks.

■ Use a microwave to quickly "zap" vegetables. White or sweet potatoes can be baked quickly this way.

■ Vary your veggie choices to keep meals interesting.

■ Try crunchy vegetables, raw or lightly steamed.

For the best nutritional value

■ Select vegetables with more potassium often, such as sweet potatoes, white potatoes, white beans, tomato products (paste, sauce, and juice), beet greens, soybeans, lima beans, winter squash, spinach, lentils, kidney beans, and split peas.

■ Sauces or seasonings can add calories, fat, and sodium to vegetables. Use the *Nutrition Facts label* (http://www.mypyramid.gov/related_links/index.html#nutritionfacts) to compare the calories and % Daily Value for fat and sodium in plain and seasoned vegetables.

■ Prepare more foods from fresh ingredients to lower sodium intake. Most sodium in the food supply comes from packaged or processed foods.

■ Buy canned vegetables labeled "no salt added." If you want to add a little salt it will likely be less than the amount in the regular canned product.

At meals

- Plan some meals around a vegetable main dish, such as a vegetable stir-fry or soup. Then add other foods to complement it.
- Try a main dish salad for lunch. Go light on the salad dressing.
- Include a green salad with your dinner every night.
- Shred carrots or zucchini into meatloaf, casseroles, quick breads, and muffins.
- Include chopped vegetables in pasta sauce or lasagna.
- Order a veggie pizza with toppings like mushrooms, green peppers, and onions, and ask for extra veggies.
- Use pureed, cooked vegetables such as potatoes to thicken stews, soups and gravies. These add flavor, nutrients, and texture.
- Grill vegetable kabobs as part of a barbecue meal. Try tomatoes, mushrooms, green peppers, and onions.

Make vegetables more appealing

- Many vegetables taste great with a dip or dressing. Try a low-fat salad dressing with raw broccoli, red and green peppers, celery sticks or cauliflower.
- Add color to salads by adding baby carrots, shredded red cabbage, or spinach leaves. Include in-season vegetables for variety through the year.
- Include cooked dry beans or peas in flavorful mixed dishes, such as chili or minestrone soup.
- Decorate plates or serving dishes with vegetable slices.
- Keep a bowl of cut-up vegetables in a see-through container in the refrigerator. Carrot and celery sticks are traditional, but consider broccoli florettes, cucumber slices, or red or green pepper strips.

Keep it safe

- Wash vegetables before preparing or eating them. Under clean, running water, rub vegetables briskly with your hands to remove dirt and surface microorganisms. Dry after washing.
- Keep vegetables separate from raw meat, poultry and seafood while shopping, preparing, or storing.

Tips to Help You Eat Fruits

In general

- Keep a bowl of whole fruit on the table, counter, or in the refrigerator.
- Refrigerate cut-up fruit to store for later.
- Buy fresh fruits in season when they may be less expensive and at their peak flavor.
- Buy fruits that are dried, frozen, and canned (in water or juice) as well as fresh, so that you always have a supply on hand.
- Consider convenience when shopping. Buy pre-cut packages of fruit (such as melon or pineapple chunks) for a healthy snack in seconds. Choose packaged fruits that do not have added sugars.

For the best nutritional value

- Make most of your choices whole or cut-up fruit rather than juice, for the benefits dietary fiber provides.
- Select fruits with more potassium often, such as bananas, prunes and prune juice, dried peaches and apricots, cantaloupe, honeydew melon, and orange juice.
- When choosing canned fruits, select fruit canned in 100% fruit juice or water rather than syrup.
- Vary your fruit choices. Fruits differ in nutrient content.

At meals

- At breakfast, top your cereal with bananas or peaches; add blueberries to pancakes; drink 100% orange or grapefruit juice. Or, try a fruit mixed with low-fat or fat-free yogurt.
- At lunch, pack a tangerine, banana, or grapes to eat, or choose fruits from a salad bar. Individual containers of fruits like peaches or applesauce are easy and convenient.
- At dinner, add crushed pineapple to coleslaw, or include mandarin oranges or grapes in a tossed salad.
- Make a Waldorf salad, with apples, celery, walnuts, and dressing.
- Try meat dishes that incorporate fruit, such as chicken with apricots or mango chutney.
- Add fruit like pineapple or peaches to kabobs as part of a barbecue meal.
- For dessert, have baked apples, pears, or a fruit salad.

As snacks

- Cut-up fruit makes a great snack. Either cut them yourself, or buy pre-cut packages of fruit pieces like pineapples or melons. Or, try whole fresh berries or grapes.
- Dried fruits also make a great snack. They are easy to carry and store well. Because they are dried, 1/4 cup is equivalent to 1/2 cup of other fruits.
- Keep a package of dried fruit in your desk or bag. Some fruits that are available dried include apricots, apples, pineapple, bananas, cherries, figs, dates, cranberries, blueberries, prunes (dried plums), and raisins (dried grapes).
- As a snack, spread peanut butter on apple slices or top frozen yogurt with berries or slices of kiwi fruit.
- Frozen juice bars (100% juice) make healthy alternatives to high-fat snacks.

Make fruit more appealing

- Many fruits taste great with a dip or dressing. Try low-fat yogurt or pudding as a dip for fruits like strawberries or melons.
- Make a fruit smoothie by blending fat-free or low-fat milk or yogurt with fresh or frozen fruit. Try bananas, peaches, strawberries, or other berries.
- Try applesauce as a fat-free substitute for some of the oil when baking cakes.
- Try different textures of fruits. For example, apples are crunchy, bananas are smooth and creamy, and oranges are juicy.
- For fresh fruit salads, mix apples, bananas, or pears with acidic fruits like oranges, pineapple, or lemon juice to keep them from turning brown.

■ Tips for Making Wise Choices

- ■ Include milk as a beverage at meals. Choose fat-free or low-fat milk.
- ■ If you usually drink whole milk, switch gradually to fat-free milk, to lower saturated fat and calories. Try reduced fat (2%), then low-fat (1%), and finally fat-free (skim).
- ■ If you drink cappuccinos or lattes—ask for them with fat-free (skim) milk.
- ■ Add fat-free or low-fat milk instead of water to oatmeal and hot cereals.
- ■ Use fat-free or low-fat milk when making condensed cream soups (such as cream of tomato).
- ■ Have fat-free or low-fat yogurt as a snack.
- ■ Make a dip for fruits or vegetables from yogurt.
- ■ Make fruit-yogurt smoothies in the blender.
- ■ For dessert, make chocolate or butterscotch pudding with fat-free or low-fat milk.
- ■ Top cut-up fruit with flavored yogurt for a quick dessert.
- ■ Top casseroles, soups, stews, or vegetables with shredded low-fat cheese.
- ■ Top a baked potato with fat-free or low-fat yogurt.

Keep it safe to eat

- ■ Avoid raw (unpasteurized) milk or any products made from unpasteurized milk.
- ■ Chill (refrigerate) perishable food promptly and defrost foods properly. Refrigerate or freeze perishables, prepared food and leftovers as soon as possible. If food has been left at temperatures between 40° and 140° F for more than two hours, discard it, even though it may look and smell good.
- ■ Separate raw, cooked and ready-to-eat foods.

For those who choose not to consume milk products

- ■ If you avoid milk because of lactose intolerance, the most reliable way to get the health benefits of milk is to choose lactose-free alternatives within the milk group, such as cheese, yogurt, or lactose-free milk, or to consume the enzyme lactase before consuming milk products.
- ■ Calcium choices for those who do not consume milk products include
  - ■ Calcium fortified juices, cereals, breads, soy beverages, or rice beverages
  - ■ Canned fish (sardines, salmon with bones) soybeans and other soy products (soy-based beverages, soy yogurt, tempeh), some other dried beans, and some leafy greens (collard and turnip greens, kale, bok choy). The amount of calcium that can be absorbed from these foods varies. For more information about non-dairy calcium sources. (http://www.health.gov/ dietaryguidelines/dga2005/document/html/appendixB.htm#AppB4)

■ Tips to Help You Make Wise Choices from the Meat and Beans Group

Go lean with protein

- Start with a lean choice:
  - The leanest beef cuts include round steaks and roasts (round eye, top round, bottom round, round tip), top loin, top sirloin, and chuck shoulder and arm roasts.
  - The leanest pork choices include pork loin, tenderloin, center loin, and ham.
  - Choose extra lean ground beef. The label should say at least "90% lean." You may be able to find ground beef that is 93% or 95% lean.
  - Buy skinless chicken parts, or take off the skin before cooking.
  - Boneless skinless chicken breasts and turkey cutlets are the leanest poultry choices.
  - Choose lean turkey, roast beef, ham, or low-fat luncheon meats for sandwiches instead of luncheon meats with more fat, such as regular bologna or salami.
- Keep it lean:
  - Trim away all of the visible fat from meats and poultry before cooking.
  - Broil, grill, roast, poach, or boil meat, poultry, or fish instead of frying.
  - Drain off any fat that appears during cooking.
  - Skip or limit the breading on meat, poultry, or fish. Breading adds fat and calories. It will also cause the food to soak up more fat during frying.
  - Prepare dry beans and peas without added fats.
  - Choose and prepare foods without high fat sauces or gravies.

Vary your protein choices

- Choose fish more often for lunch or dinner. Look for fish rich in omega-3 fatty acids, such as salmon, trout, and herring. Some ideas are:
  - Salmon steak or filet
  - Salmon loaf
  - Grilled or baked trout
- Choose dry beans or peas as a main dish or part of a meal often. Some choices are:
  - Chili with kidney or pinto beans
  - Stir-fried tofu
  - Split pea, lentil, minestrone, or white bean soups
  - Baked beans
  - Black bean enchiladas
  - Garbanzo or kidney beans on a chef's salad
  - Rice and beans
  - Veggie burgers or garden burgers
  - Hummus (chickpeas) spread on pita bread
- Choose nuts as a snack, on salads, or in main dishes. Use nuts to replace meat or poultry, not in addition to these items:
  - Use pine nuts in pesto sauce for pasta.
  - Add slivered almonds to steamed vegetables.
  - Add toasted peanuts or cashews to a vegetable stir fry instead of meat.
  - Sprinkle a few nuts on top of low-fat ice cream or frozen yogurt.
  - Add walnuts or pecans to a green salad instead of cheese or meat.

What to look for on the food label

■ Check the *Nutrition Facts label* (http://www.mypyramid.gov/related links/ index.html#nutritionfacts) for the saturated fat, *trans* fat, cholesterol, and sodium content of packaged foods.

   ■ Processed meats such as hams, sausages, frankfurters, and luncheon or deli meats have added sodium. Check the ingredient and Nutrition Facts label to help limit sodium intake.

   ■ Fresh chicken, turkey, and pork that have been enhanced with a salt-containing solution also have added sodium. Check the product label for statements such as "self-basting" or "contains up to _____% of _____."

   ■ Lower fat versions of many processed meats are available. Look on the Nutrition Facts label to choose products with less fat and saturated fat.

Keep it safe to eat

■ Separate raw, cooked and ready-to-eat foods.

■ Do not wash or rinse meat or poultry.

■ Wash cutting boards, knives, utensils and counter tops in hot soapy water after preparing each food item and before going on to the next one.

■ Store raw meat, poultry and seafood on the bottom shelf of the refrigerator so juices don't drip onto other foods.

■ Cook foods to a safe temperature to kill microorganisms. Use a meat thermometer, which measures the internal temperature of cooked meat and poultry, to make sure that the meat is cooked all the way through.

■ Chill (refrigerate) perishable food promptly and defrost foods properly. Refrigerate or freeze perishables, prepared food and leftovers within two hours.

■ Plan ahead to defrost foods. Never defrost food on the kitchen counter at room temperature. Thaw food by placing it in the refrigerator, submerging air-tight packaged food in cold tap water, or defrosting on a plate in the microwave.

■ Avoid raw or partially cooked eggs or foods containing raw eggs and raw or undercooked meat and poultry.

■ Women who may become pregnant, pregnant women, nursing mothers, and young children should avoid some types of fish and eat types lower in mercury. See www.cfsan.fda.gov/~dms/admehg3.html or call 1-888-SAFEFOOD for more information.

■ Tips for Increasing Physical Activity

Make physical activity a regular part of the day

Choose activities that you enjoy and can do regularly. Fitting activity into a daily routine can be easy—such as taking a brisk 10 minute walk to and from the parking lot, bus stop, or subway station. Or, join an exercise class. Keep it interesting by trying something different on alternate days. What's important is to be active most days of the week and make it part of daily routine. For example, to reach a 30-minute goal for the day, walk the dog for 10 minutes before and after work, and add a 10 minute walk at lunchtime. Or, swim 3 times a week and take a yoga class on the other days. Make sure to do at least 10 minutes of the activity at a time, shorter bursts of activity will not have the same health benefits. To be ready anytime, keep some comfortable clothes and a pair of walking or running shoes in the car and at the office.

More ways to increase physical activity

At home

- Join a walking group in the neighborhood or at the local shopping mall. Recruit a partner for support and encouragement.
- Push the baby in a stroller.
- Get the whole family involved—enjoy an afternoon bike ride with your kids.
- Walk up and down the soccer or softball field sidelines while watching the kids play.
- Walk the dog—don't just watch the dog walk.
- Clean the house or wash the car.
- Walk, skate, or cycle more, and drive less.
- Do stretches, exercises, or pedal a stationary bike while watching television.
- Mow the lawn with a push mower.
- Plant and care for a vegetable or flower garden.
- Play with the kids—tumble in the leaves, build a snowman, splash in a puddle, or dance to favorite music.

At work

- Get off the bus or subway one stop early and walk or skate the rest of the way.
- Replace a coffee break with a brisk 10-minute walk. Ask a friend to go with you.
- Take part in an exercise program at work or a nearby gym.
- Join the office softball or bowling team.

At play

- Walk, jog, skate, or cycle.
- Swim or do water aerobics.
- Take a class in martial arts, dance, or yoga.
- Golf (pull cart or carry clubs).
- Canoe, row, or kayak.
- Play racket ball, tennis, or squash.
- Ski cross-country or downhill.
- Play basketball, softball, or soccer.
- Hand cycle or play wheelchair sports.
- Take a nature walk.
- Most important—have fun while being active!

Web links

http://www.mypyramid.gov

http://www.mypyramidtracker.gov/

http://www.cfsan.fda.gov/~dms/foodlab.html

http://www.nutrition.gov/

■ Fitness

Lack of exercise is one of the major risk factors for both cardiovascular disease and cancer. A good fitness program should include cardiovascular endurance/aerobic exercise, strength training and flexibility. Take advantage of the physical fitness, weight training, and activity classes to learn how to exercise properly and learn how other fitness and sports can help you to develop lifetime activity programs.

■ Cardiovascular Endurance/Aerobic Exercise

Cardiovascular endurance exercise is continuous, rhythmic exercise using the large muscle groups performed for 20 to 60 minutes, three to five times a week. Some examples of cardiovascular endurance exercise include: walking, jogging, running, biking, swimming, hiking, aerobics, and skating.

■ Resistance/Weight Training

Resistance/
strength
training

Resistance/strength training programs are designed to increase the strength, size, and endurance of fibers that make up muscles. Utilizing all the major muscle groups of the body, resistance weight trainees perform eight to 12 repetitions per set on 12 different exercise machines with proper form and with a full range of motion during workouts two or three times per week. A variety of different training methods can be developed. Combining aerobic and resistance weight training with a daily regimen of stretching movements is recommended for a total training program for college students. Aerobic exercise, resistance weight-training, and flexibility training are for almost everyone. Students with high blood pressure should participate in weight training only with the consent of their physician. Beginning or accomplished exercise enthusiasts can improve their flexibility, balance, strength, endurance, and respiratory/circulatory systems as well as maintain a lean body.

Staying strong and flexible is the key to staying active in later years. Basic everyday movements such as getting up from a chair require muscular strength. Strength is a benefit at any age and any level of fitness. The development of muscle mass is important in losing and maintaining weight. Lean body tissue (muscle) expends calories at a faster rate than fat tissue. Certain chronic problems such as lower back pain are often related to poor abdominal muscle strength and inflexible posture muscles (hamstrings). Getting stronger and maintaining flexibility can improve your performance in sport, exercise, and dance activities.

Other specific benefits of a regular systematic program of exercise include:

- Increased self-confidence and self-esteem
- More energy
- Improved circulation and lower blood pressure
- Reduced tension and assistance in stress management
- Lowered resting heart rate (aerobic training)
- Decreased total blood cholesterol (aerobic training)
- Maintenance of proper weight.

■ Stress

Stress—without it, life would be boring! Stress is the body's response to demands made upon it by physical or psychological stimuli. Positive stress, called eustress, results in better health and improved performance. Winning the lottery, receiving a promotion at work, or becoming engaged are examples of eustress. Distress, which occurs when responding to negative stressors such as a failing grade, loss of a job, death of a loved one, or a divorce can be accompanied by deterioration in health and poor performance.

Your body responds to eustress and distress in a similar manner. You may experience some of the following temporary effects of stress on your body:

- increase in heart rate
- rapid breathing and/or shortness of breath
- constipation or diarrhea
- lower back pain
- tiredness
- headaches and/or dizziness
- sleep problems
- irritability and/or moodiness
- inability to concentrate

If you are unable to deal with stress for a prolonged period of time, serious physical and mental problems such as stomach ulcers, heart disease, severe headaches, hypertension, depression, weight problems, and drug and/or alcohol abuse may develop. Research indicates that people who are very stressed seem more likely to catch the common cold.

Managing Stress

You must recognize that stress is a problem in your life before you can deal with it. Life is full of daily hassles such as misplacing your keys, getting stuck in traffic, waiting in lines, and experiencing other minor annoyances at school, work, and home. When you realize that these situations are not worth getting upset over, you will learn to put up with them and be proud of the fact that you have control over your emotions.

Sometimes stress is difficult or not possible to control. In those cases, you must learn to cope with the stress.

Managing Stress Techniques

- Participate in activities which are enjoyable for you. This is important to your well-being. Make time each day in your life for fun. Laughter is also a great stress reducer.
- Exercise can be a great stress-reducer. People who exercise regularly are able to handle stress better.
- Release emotions in a positive manner. Crying is a very healthy way to release emotions, as long as it is not excessive.
- Practice good time management techniques. Organize your time by keeping an appointment calendar indicating important dates, events, and assignments.
- Set reasonable goals for yourself. Challenging but realistic goals will help you stay on track. Goals which are too difficult will only add to your frustration and stress.

- Talk with someone such as a counselor, teacher, family member or friend whom you trust. Sharing your problems and concerns with another person helps, and he/she may offer another view of the problem. If you feel very distressed, overwhelmed, or depressed, possible sources of help are your doctor, school psychologist or counselor, and local health agencies.
- Practice techniques such as deep breathing, meditation, yoga, massage, imagery, or progressive muscle relaxation.

Remember that the way in which you react to the stressor, not the stressor itself, is the cause of many stress-related illnesses. Take the time to learn which stress-reduction techniques work best for you.

■ The Importance of Sleep

You will probably spend about one-third of your life sleeping. During sleep, the regeneration of body cells accelerates; thus, young people who are growing and older people who need more time to recuperate often require more sleep than others. Most college students find that six to eight hours of sleep per night is sufficient, but some require more or less.

Insomnia can be caused by many factors:

- stress brought about by physical, social, psychological or economic problems
- excessive fatigue
- excitement or anticipation of a trip or event
- intake of caffeine or other stimulants late in the day
- eating or drinking too much.

If you experience occasional problems in falling asleep, try any of the following:

- Sleep in a dark, quiet room.
- Go to bed at approximately the same time each night.
- Keep the room temperature comfortable.
- Sleep in a comfortable bed.
- Drink warm milk or eat a high carbohydrate dessert just before bedtime.
- Take a warm bath just before bedtime.
- Listen to relaxing music.
- Have a good day, free of stressful situations.

■ Communicable Diseases

Ways to decrease chances of contracting communicable diseases

College students should become informed about the many different kinds of communicable diseases that exist in the world. Attending college for the first time translates into more independence for the student and, consequently, less observation and monitoring by parental authority than in the past. Additionally, frequenting a new environment populated by a great number of human beings will generally increase the chances of contracting a communicable disease. Obtaining booster shots and various immunizations, following good personal hygiene practices, and maintaining high personal sanitation standards are ways to decrease the chances of contracting a communicable disease.

Virus

Communicable diseases are caused by microorganisms called germs. Fortunately, very few microorganisms are disease-producing in humans. Besides, germs must find a way to be transmitted and find entry into a human being to be pathogenic (disease-producing). Disease-producing germs come in various sizes from microscopic sizes to almost visible forms. Viruses are the smallest germs while Rickettsia are barely detectable under a microscope. Bacteria germs come in three micro shapes: rod, spherical, and spiral. Fungi germs include molds and yeasts, and other plantlike microorganisms. Protozoa are single-celled parasite germs while worms are larger, multi-celled animals.

Transmission of communicable diseases

Communicable diseases can be transmitted by several common ways: respiratory discharge, discharges from the intestinal tract, contaminated water or soil, contaminated food or milk, association with animals, insect bite, intimate contact, and sexual activity. Some communicable diseases can be prevented by artificial immunization (inoculations), but many more cannot be controlled by this means. Being alert to the danger signals of the onset of various diseases and seeking early medical treatment are prudent practices to follow. Avoiding the causes of such diseases is also an important practice.

Improved environmental sanitation conditions help to decrease the number of communicable disease cases. The development of antibiotic drugs and penicillin with its derivatives has improved the treatment of individuals who have symptoms or have been diagnosed as having a communicable disease.

Sexually Transmitted Diseases

Of all the infectious communicable diseases, sexually transmitted diseases (STDs) rank highest with students of college age. STDs are caused by sexual contact or intercourse when one person infects the other(s). The five most common STDs are chlamydia, gonorrhea, syphilis, genital herpes and Acquired Immune Deficiency Syndrome (AIDS). Three other STDs are hepatitis, genital warts, and trichomoniasis.

Chlamydia

Chlamydia is a bacteria-like microbe with some characteristics of a virus. It can be mistaken for gonorrhea. Chlamydia must be treated with tetracycline rather than penicillin.

Gonorrhea

Gonorrhea is caused by a bacterial infection. Painful urination and pus discharge from the penis in males, and possible minor urinary discomfort and/or vaginal discharge in females are the typical symptoms. Treatment of choice for gonorrhea is penicillin. Females often cannot detect gonorrhea in its early stages. It is common for gonorrhea and syphilis to be contracted together, so be aware!

Syphilis

Syphilis is a four-stage disease caused by spirochetes. In the initial stage, a lesion appears on the genitals while a genital rash is common in the second stage. The third stage is one of latency with no symptoms; however, syphilis remains highly contagious. The final stage is one of tissue destruction and possibly death. Treatment includes maintaining high levels of penicillin, erythromycin or tetracycline in the blood stream for a specified period of time until all spirochetes are dead.

Genital herpes

Genital herpes is caused by a virus which promotes sores near the infected genitals (type 1) or on the labial area (type 2). Herpes simplex virus type 1 or type 2 can be treated without drugs. However, herpes cannot be cured or completely eradicated unlike most other STDs.

AIDS

Acquired Immune Deficiency Syndrome (AIDS) caused by the Human Immunodeficiency Virus (HIV) can be transmitted during sexual contact, via body fluids, or by sharing needles. The HIV attacks white blood cells in the human blood, weakening the immune system and damaging one's ability to fight off other invading diseases. Currently, there is no vaccine to prevent AIDS; nor is there any proven AIDS cure. In the early stages of AIDS, there are no physical symptoms or signs that indicate a person has been infected.

With a weakened immune system, individuals are subject to infection by various other diseases or to damage to the nervous system and brain by the AIDS virus itself. Death will eventually occur.

Consider some of the situations which may cause a high number of STDs among college students. Do college students know much about STDs? Do parents, and society in general, overemphasize the moral implications of STD infections? To avoid embarrassment, do infected persons try self-medication or receive "quack" treatment? Has the effectiveness of antibiotic drugs used to treat STDs been overrated? Has greater sexual freedom and/or relaxed restrictions by parents contributed to the spread of STDs? Are college students who do not practice "safer sex" uninformed regarding the transmission of STDs?

Safer Sex

Control of certain human behaviors is essential to the prevention of the spread of STDs and AIDS. Abstinence from sexual intercourse and/or intravenous drug use are preferred behaviors. Faithful monogamous relationships and "safer sex" practices—use of latex condoms combined with the spermicidal chemical Nonoxynol-9 from the beginning to the end of sexual intercourse—are desirable behaviors. Oral sex should not be performed when either partner is considered at high risk. College students must understand and put into practice sexual behaviors which are prudent, conscientious, and healthful.

■ Substance Abuse

Influence of friends

Admission to and attendance in college is a new and exciting experience for students. New friendships and acquaintances are formed. Time is spent on campus, in the classroom, and at organized activities where students are faced with the many influences of campus life which can result in either positive or negative impacts. The use of drugs, steroids, alcohol, or tobacco is a dangerous practice for college students. Research indicates that the influence of friends is the most-cited reason for experimentation in substance use among college students.

Will power

The most important factor regarding substances is not the question of legality, but rather the effect a substance or combination of substances has on the mind, body, and life of a college student. The key to abstaining from the use of substances is to develop sufficient will power rather than to rely on imposed external forces. Will power can be developed just as one develops sound study habits. However, a genetic predisposition to substance abuse may overwhelm an individual's will power. In these instances, external safeguards may be helpful in substance abuse control for certain individuals.

Knowledge, emotional maturity, and will power are qualities which will help students avoid harmful substances whether the substances are considered to be prescription, illegal, addictive, synthetic, natural, dietary, or social.

Alcohol

College students should keep in mind that alcohol is the most abused of all the substances. Its low cost, legal status and easy availability make it popular among college students and, therefore, subject to abuse.

Steroids

Steroids are synthetic derivatives of the male hormone testosterone. In particular, male students take steroids to help produce large muscles. Steroid-takers are subject to aggressive behavior, high blood pressure, cardiovascular disease, cancer and a long litany of other side effects. The irony is that the intended larger muscle tissue that is produced is highly susceptible to injury by the steroid-taker.

Remember—your heart is a muscle too! Steroids are taken in series that are ingested and/ or injected. Steroid use is illegal and is a felony.

Drugs

Drugs can enter the body by injection, inhalation, ingestion, and topical application, or through the mucous membranes. Review the following list of classifications and examples of drugs to become familiar with and to avoid use of these substances.

■ Classification of Drugs

1. **Inhalants**
   Airplane glue
   Amyl nitrite (poppers)
   Nitrous Oxide
   Cleaning fluids
   Hair sprays
   Paints

2. **Barbiturates and Methaqualone**
   Sedatives
   Sleeping pills
   Depressants
   Quaaludes
   Phenobarbital
   Valium

3. **Amphetamines**
   Stimulants
   Uppers
   Speed
   Diet pills
   Dexedrine

4. **Narcotics**
   Opiates
   Morphine
   Codeine
   Methadone
   Heroin

5. **Hallucinogens**
   D-Lysergic Acid (LSD)
   Phencyclidine (PCP)
   Mescaline (Peyote Cactus)
   Psilocybin (Mushrooms)
   Marijuana (THC)

6. **Cocaine**
   Cocaine Hydrochloride

7. **Alcohol**
   Beer
   Wine
   Liquor
   Rubbing alcohol

8. **Tobacco (nicotine)**
   Smokeless tobacco
   Cigarettes
   Cigars
   Pipe tobacco

9. **Anabolic Steroids**
   Winstrol
   Deca-Dianabolin
   Depo-Testosterone

■ Activity: Health on the Internet

The instructor will assign one or both of the procedures described below. The student is to complete the required procedures by the instructor's due date.

Purpose:

- ■ to become enlightened to means of maintaining good health
- ■ to discover sources of information pertaining to health issues
- ■ to lightly research particular health problems
- ■ to become familiar with the use of the Internet

Time:

1 ½ hours

Procedure 1:

1. Choose three health topics of interest to you.

2. Visit three of the five Internet addresses listed below and research the three topics you chose.

3. Write a typed two-page double-spaced report on how you will use the information on the three health topics to benefit your own personal health.

Procedure 2:

1. Prepare a day-by-day menu plan for one week and a weekly exercise plan using information learned from three sites in the list below.

2. The exercise plan should give the type of exercise and length of time (hours/minutes) in exercise each day during the week.

3. Name the days you plan to participate. Back up your exercise plan and daily menu with information obtained from the Internet sites.

4. Type or hand-write the assignment.

5. List the sites used and the information used from each site.

Site Recommendations:

http://health.yahoo.com/health/women	(Yahoo! Health)
http://content.health.msn.com/living_better/emo	(MSH Health: Emotional Wellness)
www.msnbc.com/news/mentalhealth_front.asp	(MSNBC Mental Health Headlines)
www.msnbc.com/news/menshealth_front.asp	(MSNBC Men's Health Headlines)
www.4woman.org	(The National Women's Health Information Center)

Instructor: These sites will need to be reviewed prior to assigning the exercise in order to assure they are still intact.

_____

Mary Emily Cooke, Surry Community College.

■ Activity: Top Ten Leading Causes of Death

Instructions: Investigate and list the top ten leading causes of death in the United States as identified by the National Center for Health Statistics. Place them in the correct order with number one being the leading cause and number ten being the cause responsible for the least number of deaths. Please do not respond to Part B of this activity until instructed to do so.

Part A   Your list might include some of the following:

HOMICIDE	BRONCHITIS/EMPHYSEMA
PNEUMONIA/INFLUENZA	CANCER
INJURY	SUICIDE
AIDS	HEART DISEASE
DIABETES	STROKE

1. _____

2. _____

3. _____

4. _____

5. _____

6. _____

7. _____

8. _____

9. _____

10. _____

Part B

I believe that I control _____ % of my risk of premature death.

Source: Isothermal Community College, *ACA 115 Success and Study Skills.*

■ Activity: Assessing Your Health Risk

Instructions: This questionnaire was developed by the United States government for the purpose of assessing health behaviors and risks. The questionnaire has six sections. Complete one section at a time by checking the number of the response that most accurately describes your behavior. Add the numbers you have circled in the section and write your score on the line provided at the end of each section.

	Almost Always	Sometimes	Almost Never
1. CIGARETTE SMOKING			
a. I avoid smoking cigarettes	2	1	0
b. I smoke only low-tar and low nicotine cigarettes, or I smoke a pipe or cigars only. **If you never smoke anything, circle 2.**	2	1	0

Your Cigarette Smoking Score: _____

	Almost Always	Sometimes	Almost Never
2. ALCOHOL AND DRUGS			
a. I avoid drinking alcoholic beverages, or I drink no more than one or two a day.	4	1	0
b. I avoid using alcohol or other drugs (especially illegal drugs) as a way of handling stressful situations or my problems.	2	1	0
c. I am careful not to drink alcohol when I am taking certain medicines (for example, medicines for sleeping, pain, colds, and allergies).	2	1	0
d. I read and follow the label directions when I use prescribed and over-the-counter drugs.	2	1	0

Your Alcohol and Drugs Score: _____

Source: Isothermal Community College, *ACA 115 Success and Study Skills.*

	Almost Always	Sometimes	Almost Never
3. EATING HABITS			
a. I eat a variety of foods each day, such as fruits and vegetables, whole grain breads and cereals, lean meats, dairy products, dry peas and beans, and seeds.	4	1	0
b. I limit the amount of fat, especially saturated fat, and cholesterol I eat (including fats in meats, eggs, butter, cream, shortening, and organ meats such as liver).	2	1	0
c. I limit the amount of salt I eat by not adding salt at the table, avoiding salty snacks, and making sure my meals are cooked with only small amounts of salt.	2	1	0
d. I avoid eating too much sugar (especially) frequent snacks of stick candy or soft drinks).	2	1	0

Your Eating Habits Score: _____

	Almost Always	Sometimes	Almost Never
4. EXERCISE AND FITNESS			
a. I maintain a desirable weight, avoiding overweight and underweight.	3	1	0
b. I do vigorous exercise for 15–30 minutes at least three times a week (examples including running, swimming, and brisk walking).	3	1	0
c. I do exercises that enhance my muscle tone for 15–30 minutes at least three times a week (examples include yoga and calisthenics).	2	1	0
d. I use part of my leisure time participating in individual, family, or team activities that increase my level of fitness (such as gardening, bowling, golf, or baseball).	2	1	0

Your Exercise and Fitness Score: _____

	Almost Always	Sometimes	Almost Never
5. STRESS CONTROL			
a. I enjoy the school or other work I do.	2	1	0
b. I find it easy to relax and express my feelings freely.	2	1	0
c. I recognize early, and prepare for, events or situations likely to be stressful for me.	2	1	0
d. I have close friends, relatives, or others with whom I can talk about personal matters and call on for help when it is a needed.	2	1	0
e. I participate in group activities (such as church/synagogue or community organizations) or hobbies that I enjoy.	2	1	0

Your Stress Control Score: _____

	Almost Always	Sometimes	Almost Never
6. SAFETY			
a. I wear a seat belt while I am riding in a car.	2	1	0
b. I avoid driving while I am under the influence of alcohol or other drugs. I also avoid getting in a car with someone who is driving under the influence of alcohol or other drugs.	2	1	0
c. I obey traffic rules and the speed limit when I am driving and ask others to do so when I am a passenger in a car with them.	2	1	0
d. I am careful when I am using potentially harmful products or substances (such as household cleaners, poisons, and electrical devices).	2	1	0
e. I avoid smoking in bed.	2	1	0

Your Safety Score: _____

■ Your Health Risk Score

After you have totaled your score for each of the six sections, record each score in the table below in the appropriate column.

CIGARETTE SMOKING	ALCOHOL AND DRUGS	EATING HABITS	EXERCISE AND FITNESS	STRESS CONTROL	SAFETY

■ Interpreting Your Score

SCORES OF 9 OR 10 are excellent! *An exception is the cigarette smoking section for which a score of 3 or 4 is excellent. Review your responses to the items in this section to better interpret their meaning.* Your answers show you are aware of the importance of this area to your health. More important, you are putting your knowledge to work by practicing good health habits. Even so you may want to consider areas in which your health habits can be improved to enhance your level of wellness.

SCORES OF 6 TO 8 indicate that your health practices in this area are good but there is room for improvement. Look again at the items you answered with "sometimes" and "almost never". What changes can you make to improve your score?

SCORES OF 3 TO 5 mean your health is at risk. You should seek more information about the health risks you are facing.

SCORES OF 0 TO 2 mean you may be taking serious, unnecessary risks with your health. Maybe you are unaware of the risks and what to do about them. Consult with a health expert or your doctor to improve your health. *For the cigarette smoking section a score of 0 or 1 means you are taking unnecessary risks with your health.*

Name: _____ Date: _____

■ Activity: Health Behavior

INSTRUCTIONS: Across the top of the table below are listed a number of health behaviors. In the first column of the table a number of major health conditions and diseases are listed. Rate the effectiveness of each of the health behaviors as a prevention measure for each of the conditions or diseases listed using the following scale:

   3 - highly effective in preventing this health problem
   2 - moderately effective in preventing this health problem
   1 - somewhat effective in preventing this health problem
   0 - of no value in preventing this health problem

Behaviors / Conditions	No Tobacco	Low-fat Diet	High-fiber Diet	Avoid Alcohol	Avoid Salted, Pickled Foods	Diet High In Vegetables And Fruits	Exercise Weight Control
CANCER Lung							
CANCER Breast							
CANCER Colon							
CANCER Liver							
Heart Attack							
Stroke							
Adult Onset Diabetes							

■ Self-Management

Four Things to Remember:

1. People cannot read minds.

2. The goal is communication, not winning.

3. You can control only your own behavior.

4. You do not have to be assertive all the time. Once you learn to be assertive, you can *choose* not to be assertive.

The Assertiveness Bill of Rights:

1. You have the right to judge your behaviors, thoughts, and emotions, and to take the responsibility for their initiation and consequences upon yourself.

2. You have the right to offer no reasons or excuses for justifying your behavior.

3. You have the right to judge if you are responsible for finding solutions to other people's problems.

4. You have the right to change your mind.

5. You have the right to make mistakes and be responsible for them.

6. You have the right to say, "I don't know."

7. You have the right to be independent of the goodwill of others before coping with them.

8. You have the right to be illogical in making decisions.

9. You have the right to say, "I don't understand."

10. You have the right to say, "I don't care."

11. You have the right to say, "NO," without feeling guilty.

Source: Isothermal Community College *ACA 115 Success and Study Skills.*

■ Activity: Assertiveness

Here is an instrument to help you determine where you are now in Assertiveness. Assign a number to each item with 1 being never, 2 almost never, 3 once in a while, 4 almost always and 5 always.

_____ I believe my needs are as important as those of others and I am entitled to have my needs satisfied.

_____ When considering doing something I have never done, I feel confident I can learn to do it.

_____ I assume that most people are competent and trustworthy and do not have difficulty delegating tasks to others.

_____ When discussing my beliefs, I do so without labeling the opinions of others as "crazy," "stupid," "ridiculous," or "irrational."

_____ Meeting new people in social situations is something I do with ease and comfort.

_____ I tell others when their behavior creates a problem for me.

_____ When I make a mistake, I will acknowledge it.

_____ If I disagree with the majority opinion in a meeting, I can "stick to my guns" without feeling uncomfortable or being abrasive.

_____ I am comfortable speaking up in a group situation.

_____ When I express anger, I do so without blaming others for "making me mad."

_____ When I experience powerful feelings (anger, frustration, disappointment, etc.) I verbalize them easily.

_____ I confidently express my honest opinions to authority figures (such as my boss).

_____ I am comfortable when speaking to a large group of people.

_____ When someone asks me to do something I don't want to do, I say "no" without feeling guilty or anxious.

_____ I ask others to do things without feeling guilty or anxious.

_____ I understand and do not get angry when others tell me "no."

■ Activity: Anger Management

How do you handle anger? The purpose of this exercise is to help you convert anger from a negative response to a creative and powerful source of energy.

All of us have developed counter productive patterns for dealing with anger. These patterns will persist unless we actively change them. The best way to do this is to take action. Each time you take action, you implement the psychological interventions that help you to manage anger.

How To Know If You Have A Problem With Anger

Place a check beside the item(s) that are true for you.

_____ When you get angry, you don't get over it.

_____ You never get angry. You just don't have the emotion. There are times when you know you should be angry, but the emotion just doesn't seem to come.

_____ You feel frustrated, disappointed or irritable much of the time, but you just don't ever get angry.

_____ You are sarcastic or cynical about yourself, others or the world around you.

_____ You may be depressed frequently and for long periods of time.

_____ You are angry all the time. You may be verbally, emotionally or even physically abusive to others in personal and professional relationships.

_____ You feel powerless in your own life.

If any of these examples apply to you, then it's a safe bet that you have suppressed anger or even rage.

■ Activity: What Makes You Angry?

Everyone experiences anger—most of us experience it every day; sometimes several times a day. Below are some of the most common answers to the question, "What makes you angry?" Which ones are true for you? Are there some you'd like to add?

_____ Traffic		_____ Feeling trapped
_____ Prejudice		_____ Tailgaters
_____ Wasting my time		_____ Waiting
_____ Taxes		_____ My paycheck
_____ People who cheat me		_____ People not believing what I say
_____ Workers who are lazy		_____ People who won't listen
_____ People who cut in line		_____ My car breaks down
_____ Crime		_____ People who are always late
_____ Rude people		_____ Yelling
_____ Lies		_____ People who are critical

_____   _____

How do you respond when other people get angry with you?

What is your fantasy response of what you said or did in an angry situation?

What do you think you need to change about the ways in which you deal with anger?

■ Negative Effects of Anger

heart problems	fatigue
hypertension	arthritis
headaches	respiratory disorders (common cold, asthma)
stomach problems	
weakens the immune system	strokes
skin disorders	stuttering
backache	

- ■ Repressed anger can make a person more likely to have accidents.
- ■ In patients with severe heart disease, simply recalling anger produces a physical reaction similar to a heart attack.
- ■ If you don't want a heart attack to hit, think about how you express anger. A study found that people who always suppress anger, or always blow up, tend to have a higher risk than people who modulate their anger.
- ■ New studies show that it isn't Type A behavior in general that harms you, as used to be thought, but very specific acts of attitudes (cynical, aggressive, hostile, being under constant pressure at work, and having lack of control over work and workload).

■ Strategies for Dealing with Anger

It takes time, practice, and lots of effort to learn new ways to deal with anger.

Using Deep Breathing—Breathe slowly through your nose, deep full-bodied breaths, until your stomach pushes out nearly as far as it will go.

Talking to Someone You Trust

Using Positive Self-talk

Using Prayer and Meditation

Using Exercise

Screaming in Your Car

Using Deep Muscle Relaxation

Using reminder cards that tell you specific things to do in a situation when you are angry.

Writing to help organize and structure your thoughts. Heart felt confessional writing will put you in touch with your feelings.

Keeping an Anger Journal to record feelings of anger and the situations in which they occur. Include people involved, your thoughts related to your feelings, how you coped, and ideas on how you could have handled the situation better.

Learning more about anger. Knowledge is power!

Learning to recognize and label anger. Recognition paves the way toward accepting anger and dealing with it. Find out what your anger signs are. How does anger show in your body? In your thoughts/In your behaviors?

Evaluating your beliefs about anger. Do you think that anger should be suppressed, kept inside, or let loose as soon as it is experienced? You need to examine your beliefs closely in order to deal effectively with your anger.

Reminding yourself of the negative effects of dealing with anger in appropriate or irrational ways.

Identifying the potential benefits of handling anger in constructive ways.

CHAPTER 9
Transferring to a Four-Year College or University

Introduction

If you intend to transfer from Surry Community College to a four-year college or university, you need to start planning now. You want your transition to a four-year institution to be as trouble-free as possible so that you can progress toward your ultimate goal—a bachelor's degree—in a timely manner. You don't want to have to repeat courses upon transfer: you want to start working toward your major. This chapter provides the information you need to transition efficiently and effectively from the community college to a four-year institution. You should read this chapter before beginning your Strategic Plan for Transfer Success activities.

The topics covered in this chapter include:

- Transfer Degrees
- Comprehensive Articulation Agreement (CAA)
- General Education Core
- Three Paths to Transfer
- Transferable Courses
- Pre-Major Guides
- A Transfer's Timeline
- Online Resources

At the end of this chapter, you will find the following documents:

- Required Activity: Strategic Plan for Transfer Success (3 parts)
- Associate in Arts Requirements
- Associate in Science Requirements
- Associate in Fine Arts Requirements
- Comprehensive Articulation Agreement Transfer Course List
- Pre-Major Associate in Arts Articulation Agreement: Business Administration, Accounting, Economics, Finance, and Marketing

Transfer Degrees

The Associate in Arts (AA), the Associate in Science (AS), and the Associate in Fine Arts (AFA) are intended for transfer.

The AA and AS degrees include 44 semester credit hours in general education courses in composition, humanities and fine arts, social and behavioral sciences, and natural sciences and mathematics. An additional 21 hours consist of elective courses, including this class, ACA. Not surprisingly, the AS requires more hours in science and math as well as higher-level math courses. Review the Associate in Arts, Science, and Fine Arts Requirements at the end of this chapter. These are also found in the college catalog.

How do you choose between the AA and the AS? Those interested in the following fields should consider earning an **Associate in Arts**:

- Anthropology
- Art Education
- Business Administration, Accounting, Economics, Finance, and Marketing
- Business Education and Marketing Education
- Communication/Communication Studies
- Computer Science
- Criminal Justice
- Elementary Education
- English
- English Education
- Geography
- Health Education
- History
- Information Systems
- Liberal Studies
- Mass Communication/Journalism
- Middle Grades Education and Special Education
- Nursing
- Physical Education
- Political Science
- Psychology
- Social Science Secondary Education
- Social Work
- Sociology
- Special Education

Those who want to pursue a career in the following fields should earn an **Associate in Science**:

- Biology and Biology Education
- Chemistry and Chemistry Education
- Engineering
- Mathematics
- Mathematics Education

The **Associate in Fine Arts** is intended for students seeking a bachelor's degree in these areas:

- Art
- Drama
- Music and Music Education

The AFA curriculum includes only 28 semester credit hours in general education courses. Therefore, AFA students who transfer must meet the general education requirements of the college or university they transfer to. This degree is designed to prepare students to meet the selective admission criteria for programs such as the Bachelor of Fine Arts.

However, this degree does not guarantee admission into a college or university art program. Many art programs at four-year schools require a portfolio or performance for admission. Transfer after one year of community college study is often recommended for fine arts majors.

Comprehensive Articulation Agreement (CAA)

The Comprehensive Articulation Agreement (CAA) is a formal agreement established in 1996 by the state legislature. The CAA standardized transfer procedures between the 58 North Carolina community colleges and 16 University of North Carolina institutions. The goal of the CAA is to simplify and unify transfer policies, in the process expanding access to higher education. The CAA gives you certain rights as a transfer student; these protections should facilitate your transfer and allow you to earn a bachelor's degree within a reasonable period of time—ideally, within two years of transfer. Not every state has an articulation agreement; students who attend community colleges in states that lack these agreements do not have the same rights and protections that you have as a North Carolina community college student. The CAA eases your transition to a UNC institution, so you spend less time and less money earning your bachelor's degree.

What is an *articulation agreement*? A *transferable* course is not necessarily an *articulated* course. A transferable course is accepted by the transfer institution: in other words, you will be able to count those credits toward your bachelor's degree. However, there is no guarantee that the course will actually be applied toward your major or toward the university's general education requirements. Will the university accept the English you took at the community college as meeting their English requirement, or will they give you three credits but still require you to repeat English at their school? In this scenario, you would receive three credits toward graduation, but you would have to retake courses at the university. Repeating courses in this way would certainly delay your graduation with a bachelor's degree. An articulation agreement helps you avoid this kind of needless repetition.

An *articulated* course is therefore not only guaranteed to transfer, but also to fulfill a specific requirement. Therefore, you do not have to repeat general education courses, and you can progress toward your bachelor's degree with fewer setbacks.

Any course that falls under the umbrella of the CAA is protected—as long as you have met the requirements on your end (see "Three Paths to Transfer").

Sixteen UNC institutions have signed onto this agreement:

- Appalachian State University
- UNC-Asheville
- Winston-Salem State University
- Western Carolina University
- UNC-Charlotte
- East Carolina University
- UNC-Wilmington
- UNC-Chapel Hill
- UNC-Greensboro
- NC Central University
- NC State University
- Fayetteville State University
- UNC-Pembroke
- Elizabeth City State University
- NC School of the Arts
- NC A&T University

Many private institutions in North Carolina endorse the Independent Comprehensive Articulation Agreement, which developed out of the CAA:

- Barton College
- Belmont Abbey College
- Bennett College
- Brevard College
- Campbell University
- Catawba College
- Chowan College
- Gardner-Webb University
- Johnson C. Smith University
- Livingstone College
- Louisburg College
- Mars Hill College
- Montreat College
- Mount Olive College
- North Carolina Wesleyan College
- Peace College
- Pfeiffer University
- Queens University of Charlotte
- St. Andrews Presbyterian College
- St. Augustine's College
- Shaw University
- Warren Wilson College
- Wingate University

If you plan to transfer to one of the institutions listed above, you are protected by this agreement as long as you meet the requirements outlined in the CAA. If you do not plan to transfer to one of these institutions, then your transcript will be evaluated on a course-by-course basis by the receiving institution, and you may have to repeat some courses. Contact the Admissions Office at your transfer institution to find out what courses you should take at Surry Community College.

■ General Education Core

The General Education Core equals at least 44 semester credit hours of courses in "general education": English composition, humanities and fine arts, social and behavioral sciences, and natural sciences and mathematics. Our educational system is based on the idea that all students, regardless of their major or program of study, should be educated in these general areas. In other words, an "educated" person is well-rounded, possessing some knowledge and skills in composition, math, the arts, humanities, social sciences, etc. To that end, our public colleges and universities require that students complete a certain number of semester credit hours in these general education categories before moving on to the more specialized, upper-level courses.

You can complete all general education, lower-division level courses at a community college. If you complete this 44-hour core and meet certain requirements (discussed later in this chapter), then UNC schools are obligated to accept these hours as a complete fulfillment of their general education requirements. Not having to take additional general education courses upon transfer means you can progress toward your bachelor's degree that much faster.

The specific general education requirements for the Associate in Arts and Associate in Science are outlined in the following table. To see a specific list of courses in each category, review the Associate in Arts and Associate in Science Requirements documents at the end of this chapter.

Remember, the AFA includes only 28 semester credit hours toward general education. Therefore, fine arts students who transfer must meet the general education requirements of the transfer institution.

	Associate in Arts	Associate in Science
English Composition Courses in this category include English 111, 112, 113, and 114. English 111 is a prerequisite for the other three courses.	6 semester credit hours	6 semester credit hours
Humanities/Fine Arts Courses in this category include art, drama, foreign languages, humanities, literature, music, philosophy, and religion.	12 semester credit hours: ■ Four courses must be selected from at least three different disciplines ■ One course must be a literature course	9 semester credit hours: ■ Three courses must be selected from at least three different disciplines ■ One course must be a literature course
Social/Behavioral Sciences Courses in this category include anthropology, economics, geography, history, political science, psychology, and sociology.	12 semester credit hours: ■ Four courses must be selected from at least three different disciplines ■ One course must be a history course	9 semester credit hours: ■ Three courses must be selected from three different disciplines ■ One course must be a history course
Natural Sciences/Mathematics Courses in this category include biology, chemistry, physics, math, and computer science.	8 semester credit hours in science; 6-8 hours in math.	20 semester credit hours in natural science/math, including: ■ A minimum two-course sequence in biology, chemistry, or physics ■ Two courses in math, starting with precalculus algebra ■ One of the math courses could be statistics, intro to computers, or intro to programming ■ An additional number of hours to total 20 may come from natural science or math Gen Ed courses

■ Three Paths to Transfer

You have three options for transfer to a UNC institution or private college that has endorsed the CAA:

1. **You can transfer before you finish the 44-hour Gen Ed core**. However, you are *not* protected under the CAA. Your transcript from Surry Community College will be evaluated on a course-by-course basis, and you will be required to meet your transfer institution's general education requirements.

2. **You can transfer after you finish the 44-hour Gen Ed core but before you earn an associate's degree**. You are considered a "non-graduate" at this point, though you have the option to receive a Transfer Core Diploma from Surry Community College. You are granted some protections from the CAA when you complete this 44-hour block of general education classes.

3. **You can transfer after you earn an associate's degree**. Doing so grants you all of the protections of the CAA.

The second option, transferring after finishing the 44-hour core but shy of the 65 credits needed for the associate's degree, does offer some protections. According to the CAA, non-graduates are "considered to have fulfilled the institution-wide, lower-division general education requirements of the receiving institution. To be eligible for inclusion in this policy, a student must have an overall GPA of at least 2.0 on a 4.0 scale at the time of transfer and a grade of 'C' or better in all core courses." The transfer institution agrees to accept these 44 hours as a fulfillment of all of its general education requirements. Therefore, when you transfer, you should be able to progress toward your bachelor's degree in a timely manner.

The third option, transferring after earning an associate's degree, provides the best protections, as long as you meet the following qualifications:

- Earned a grade of "C" or better in approved transfer courses
- Earned a GPA of at least 2.0 on a 4.0 scale

What are the protections?

- **You are assured admission to one of the 16 UNC institutions**. Admission is not assured to a specific campus, program, or major, and you must meet the judicial and application requirements at the transfer institution. You must also meet all application deadlines.
- **You will transfer with junior status**. At least 64 of your community college credits are guaranteed to transfer. If you take ACA 122 instead of ACA 111, then all 65 of your credits are guaranteed.
- **You will have fulfilled the transfer institution's general education requirements**. You must meet the transfer school's foreign language or physical education requirements before or after transfer. Universities are not allowed to place requirements on you that are not also required of their native junior-level students.
- **You can appeal if you think these protections have not been honored**. The CAA includes a grievance policy for transfer students.

If you decide to transfer to a school that does not endorse the North Carolina CAA, then your transcript will be evaluated on a course-by-course basis by the receiving institution. In other words, the institution is not obligated to accept your course credits from Surry Community College as a fulfillment of its general education requirements and can require you to repeat courses or take additional courses. The best plan is to contact the Admissions Office at your transfer school as soon as possible to find out what courses you should take.

■ Three Types of Transferable Courses Protected by the CAA

Three types of courses are transferable and articulated:

1. General Education Core

2. Pre-Major

3. Elective

If you look at the course descriptions in the college catalog, you will see that some course descriptions contain an italicized sentence as the last sentence. For **General Education Core** classes, it will read something like this sentence from ENG 111: *This class has been approved to satisfy the Comprehensive Articulation Agreement general education core requirement in English composition.* If you take ENG 111 and pass it with a "C" or better, it fulfills part of the Gen Ed requirement in English composition. If you meet the requirements outlined in the CAA, then UNC transfer institutions are obligated to count this course toward their English composition requirement, and you will not have to repeat it when you transfer as long as you earn a "C" or higher.

Pre-major and **elective** courses are approved for transfer under the CAA. They may not be used to fulfill general education requirements. However, general education courses may be used as electives. Course descriptions in the college catalog indicate pre-major and elective status in an italicized statement: *This course has been approved to satisfy the Comprehensive Articulation Agreement for transferability as a pre-major and/or elective course requirement.*

Review the "Comprehensive Articulation Agreement Transfer Course List" at the end of this chapter to see a complete list of courses offered at Surry Community College labeled as "Gen Ed" and "Pre-Major/Elective."

If you already know what you want to major in when you transfer, the pre-major guides give you the best options for meeting Gen Ed and elective requirements.

■ Pre-Major Guides

Pre-major guides are meant to be just that—guides. They were developed by university and community college faculty as "blueprints" to help you take the best courses for your intended major. If you know now what you intend to major in after you transfer, and you plan to transfer to an institution that has endorsed the CAA, then pre-major guides provide special guidance for you as you plan your course schedule at Surry Community College. The pre-major guide specifies which lower-division community college courses are the best options for your major upon transfer. The guides help you choose the best General Education and elective courses; you want the courses you take at Surry to go as far as they can when you transfer. For example, what is the best math class for your intended major? Should you take ENG 112, 113, or 114? Should you take EDU 216, Foundations of Education, as one of your electives? Should you take an economics class as one of your electives? Is a specific science recommended for your major? Is a foreign language recommended?

Example: Business Administration, Accounting, Economics, Finance, and Marketing Majors

Let's look at one example, the pre-major guide for Business Administration and related fields. This pre-major guide is included at the end of this chapter. If you are planning to transfer to a UNC institution to get a bachelor's degree in one of these fields, you should follow the guidelines when choosing your general education courses and "other required hours" (electives).

- **General Education Courses**: You want to make the best general education choices for your major. Notice that ECO 251 is required and can count as one of your general education courses in the social sciences. The guide also recommends that you choose two additional courses to fulfill this Gen Ed requirement: POL 120, PSY 150, and SOC 210 are the recommendations. Taking these courses not only fulfills part of the Gen Ed Core for the AA degree, but also puts you on the path toward fulfilling lower-division level requirements for your eventual major. When you transfer, you should be on par with the students who have been at the university all along. This way, you haven't wasted any time.
- **Elective Courses**: The pre-major guide also offers guidance on the elective courses you should take. To earn your AA, many, many courses qualify as electives. To narrow down the field to your best options, consult the pre-major guide. Business majors should take two accounting classes, a computer class, and another economics class. You should also take a statistics class. Now you know that your courses not only count toward your AA degree, but they also count toward your eventual bachelor's degree as they lay the groundwork for your major.

■ A Transfer's Timeline

1st semester:

- Focus on taking your General Education core classes (44 semester hours) first. If you know what your major is going to be when you transfer, get your hands on a *Pre-Major Guide* that more specifically shows you what courses to take while at SCC (these can be found in racks in the lobby of the H-Building [first and second floors], the T-Building, E-Building lobby, in Student Development, or online at http://www.surry.edu.
- 1)   In your SCC catalog, please review "Graduation Requirements," so you know what is expected right from the start.
  2)   Carefully follow the checklist for your Associate in Arts or Science Degree.
- Decide which college/university you wish to transfer to. You may also want to have a back-up college chosen and plan to apply there, too.
- Review that college's web site. (For addresses, see the following page.) On the site, you can usually access the academic catalog, a schedule for application deadlines, the application itself, the academic calendar, etc. **Read that academic catalog! It is important for you to know as soon as possible what requirements you will need to meet at the college you want to transfer to.** For example, will you need to satisfy a foreign language requirement? How many semesters will you need? What specific math courses are recommended? (Note: If you do not have access to the Internet at home, or aren't sure how to use it, see your faculty advisor or a counselor to get you started.) Many university sites

now have transfer web sites. Some even give you exactly what community college courses to take.

■ Attend College Day held each fall semester on the SCC Campus. Typically over fifty representatives are here to answer your questions.

■ Become familiar with the SCC Transfer Advising web page at http://www.surry.edu.

2nd Semester

■ Continue taking your general education core classes.

■ **Visit the Admissions Office of the colleges you are interested in attending** You should call ahead to schedule a tour; find the number on the web site. Also take your transcript and list of planned courses. Ask for feedback from their Admissions Counselor.

■ Sketch out your schedule for the rest of your time at SCC to make sure you have all the credits and classes you need to graduate on time. Follow the recommendations and requirements you were given during your university/college visit.

Summer

■ You may decide to get some courses out of the way during summer session.

■ **Visit the college you want to attend if you have not done so yet.**

3rd Semester

■ Apply to two or three colleges of your choice. (Note: The Academic Support Center encourages you to meet with a tutor to review your application essays. This is a free service of the college!)

4th Semester

■ If you are graduating in May, you must apply for your degree, diploma, or certificate. Dates will be advertised and posted around campus. All graduates must see a Counselor in Student Development to complete a checksheet and to complete the graduation application.

■ Once you have completed a checksheet, a graduation fee of $20.00 per degree, diploma, or certificate must be paid at the Cashiers Window in the Business Office.

■ Caps, gowns, and invitations will be ordered in random sizes and graduates pick those up and pay at the beginning of April in the College Bookstore. Graduation Announcements and Class Rings will also be available during this time. All marching graduates will receive a letter in the mail with more detailed instructions.

Note: All fall, spring, and summer graduates should apply no later than the March application deadline.

Transfer Websites

University	Link
ASU	http://www.admissions.appstate.edu/process/transfer.htm (Transfer Equivalencies are at the bottom of the page.)
ECU	http://www.ecu.edu/cs-acad/fyc/ccplans.cfm Additional link: http://www.ecu.edu/cs-acad/admissions/transfer.cfm
Gardner-Webb GOAL Program	http://www.goal.gardner-webb.edu
NC State	http://admissions.ncsu.edu/find-stuff/transfer-student/index.php http://www.ncsu.edu/registrar/curricula/ https://www.acs.ncsu.edu/scripts/ugadmiss/trnsfcrs.pl/2?instit=5656
UNC-Asheville	http://www.unca.edu/admissions/process/transfer.html
UNC-Chapel Hill	http://www.admissions.unc.edu/applying/transfer.htm Additional links: Course requirements for some specialized majors at UNC-CH http://advising.unc.edu/fortransferstudents
UNC-Charlotte	http://www.uncc.edu/admissions/transfer/College_Transfer_Guides.asp
UNC-Greensboro	http://www.uncg.edu/reg/TransferGuide/current/Curriculum/index.html http://www.uncg.edu/reg/transfer/
UNC-Pembroke	http://www.uncp.edu/admissions/undergraduate/transfer.asp
UNC-Wilmington	http://www.uncw.edu/admissions/admissionsTransfer.html http://www.uncw.edu/admissions/documents/transferguide_000.pdf
Western Carolina	http://admissions.wcu.edu/205.asp http://www.wcu.edu/WebFiles/PDFs/transferadmissions_2step.pdf
Winston-Salem State	http://www.wssu.edu/NR/rdonlyres/93A02F97-385F-43D0-A991-BB68CB47E9F8/0/ CommunityCollegeTransferCourseList.pdf http://www.wssu.edu/WSSU/About/Administration/Division+of+Student+Affairs /Office+of+Undergraduate+Admissions/Tranfer/ Additional link: Winston-Salem State Catalog
Articulation Agreement	http://www.northcarolina.edu/content.php/assessment/reports/student_info/caa.htm

■ Online Resources

Visit the Surry Community College site to find information about transferring: http://www.surry.edu. Look for "Transfer Information."

Visit the UNC system site to find all of the pre-major guides and other important transfer documents and information: http://www.northcarolina.edu/content.php/assessment/reports/student_info/caa.htm

Visit CollegeTransfer.net for information about successful transfer: http://www.collegetransfer.net

Read the complete *Comprehensive Articulation Agreement between the University of North Carolina and the North Carolina Community College System* at http://intranet.northcarolina.edu/docs/assessment/caa/2008/May/102.51CAA_Modified_Feb_2008.pdf

Name: _____ Date: _____

▌REQUIRED ACTIVITY: Strategic Plan for Transfer Success

As an ACA 122 student, you must complete a strategic plan for transfer in order to:

- ▊ Practice your research skills
- ▊ Improve your writing skills
- ▊ Improve your thinking skills
- ▊ Learn about your transfer institution
- ▊ Plan for transfer so you have a better chance to earn your bachelor's degree in a timely manner

You will complete this assignment in three parts:

I. Transfer Institution Profile
II. Transfer Timeline
III. Transfer Success Paper

Each assignment should be typed, double-spaced, in 12-point font. No cover page is necessary. Be **precise** (specific, detailed) and **clear** (understandable) in your wording, and make sure your explanations related to the CAA are **accurate**. Remember to proofread your plan to catch grammar, spelling, and typing errors—and avoid plagiarism!

Visit the Academic Support Center on the second floor of the library or call 386-3460 to make an appointment for free help with writing, typing, and formatting these assignments.

I. Transfer Institution Profile   **Maximum Points: 6**   **Due Date:_____**

Brainstorming Questions:

1. Where do you want to transfer? Why that particular school? Describe the transfer institution: What aspects of the school appeal to you? Why? (If you haven't decided where you want to transfer, you can list and explain the possibilities, or for this assignment you can choose one institution to research.)

2. What do you want to major in? If you haven't decided, list and explain the majors you are considering. Ensure those majors are offered at the school(s) of your choice.

3. How much does it cost to attend the transfer institution? Will you live on campus or commute from home? Research the relevant costs (tuition, books, fees, room and board, etc.).

UNC system schools: http://www.northcarolina.edu/content.php/assessment/reports/student_info.htm

Using your responses to the brainstorming questions, write a one-page profile of your transfer institution. Explain why you want to transfer to that college or university. Describe the transfer institution: its academic programs, costs, location, and any other aspects of the school that seem to suit your needs. Be sure to explain just how these aspects of the school fit your goals.

II. Transfer Timeline   **Maximum Points: 10**   Due Date:_____

Brainstorming Questions:

1. What is the Comprehensive Articulation Agreement (CAA)? Read the agreement at the website given below. Read Chapter 9 in your ACA textbook. Why is the CAA important for transfer students?

2. What are the benefits of completing the 44-hour General Education Core component? What are the benefits of earning the associate degree before transfer?
    a. Read Chapter 9 in your ACA textbook
    b. Read the CAA document (see link below)

3. What is your timeline for transferring? How many semesters will you complete at Surry Community College? Plan the schedule of classes you want to take at SCC that will be most beneficial for your intended major.
    a. Use the pre-major guide that fits your intended major
    b. Use the checklists at the end of Chapter 9
    c. Review the Example of a Student's Educational Plan in Chapter 1

Comprehensive Articulation Agreement: http://intranet.northcarolina.edu/docs/assessment/caa/2008/May/102.51CAA_Modified_Feb_2008.pdf

SCC Site: http://www.surry.edu. Find "Transfer Information."

UNC Transfer Site, including links to pre-major guides: http://www.northcarolina.edu/content.php/assessment/reports/student_info/caa.htm

Using your responses to the brainstorming questions, create a two-page timeline for transfer. In it, include a one-paragraph explanation of the CAA. Specifically, explain how it protects you as a transfer student. (If you are transferring to a non-CAA school, what do you need to know about transferring your SCC courses?) Explain when you will transfer: after the 44-hour core, after the associate's degree, etc. Then plot your schedule for the remainder of your time at Surry in a semester-by-semester timeline. *Check off the courses on the pre-major guide and associate degree checklist; attach the checklists to your timeline.* Include dates when you plan to visit the transfer institution and application and financial aid deadlines.

To summarize, your timeline should include the following:

1. Explanation of the CAA

2. Your Path to Transfer

3. Your Educational Plan (include checklists and important dates)

Note: If you copy any wording from the CAA, the college catalog, Chapter 9 in this textbook, or any of the websites you research, you must enclose that wording in quotation marks to indicate that the material is not conveyed in your words. If you put someone else's idea entirely in your words, you do not have to use quotation marks, but you do need to reference the source. Example: *According to the CAA . . .* For a good explanation of plagiarism, review Chapter 1 in your ACA textbook.

III. Transfer Success Paper   **Maximum Points: 6**   **Due Date:**_____

How is SCC preparing you to transition successfully to a four-year school? Explain how each of the following skills is necessary to ensure success when you transfer, and explain how SCC is helping you improve your performance in each:

1. Critical Thinking

2. Writing and Speaking (Communication Skills)

3. Reading Skills

4. Study and Test-Taking Skills

5. Time Management

6. Awareness of Learning Styles and Instructional Styles

Research www.collegetransfer.net to find out why you need these skills to be successful. Also, review the following chapters in your ACA textbook: Chapters 3, 4, 5, 6, and 7.

Write a one- to two-page explanation of the skills you need to develop to ensure a successful transfer. Explain how SCC is helping you achieve success in these skills.

ASSOCIATE IN ARTS (A10100) REQUIREMENTS
65 semester hours
See page 82 to insure minimum course requirements (MCR) are met.

Transfer Core Diploma - D10100 :
44 SHC (This Page Only)

English/Composition (6 SHC)
___ ENG 111 Expository Writing (3)

and one of the following:

___ ENG 112 Argument-based Research (3)
___ ENG 113 Literature-based Research (3)

Humanities/Fine Arts (12 SHC)
Select four courses from three different prefix areas. One must be Literature. See MCR language requirement.

___ ART 111 Art Appreciation (3)
___ ART 114 Art History Survey I (3)
___ ART 115 Art History Survey II (3)
___ ART 116 Survey of American Art (3)

___ COM 231 Public Speaking (3)

___ ENG 131 Intro to Literature (3)
___ ENG 231 American Literature I (3)
___ ENG 232 American Literature II (3)
___ ENG 233 Major American Writers (3)
___ ENG 241 British Literature I (3)
___ ENG 242 British Literature II (3)
___ ENG 243 Major British Writers (3)
___ ENG 261 World Literature I (3)
___ ENG 262 World Literature II (3)

___ HUM 110 Technology and Society (3)
___ HUM 115 Critical Thinking (3)
___ HUM 120 Cultural Studies (3)
___ HUM 121 Nature of America (3)
___ HUM 122 Southern Culture (3)
___ HUM 130 Myth in Human Culture (3)
___ HUM 160 Intro to Film (3)
___ HUM 220 Human Val & Meaning (3)

___ MUS 110 Music Appreciation (3)
___ MUS 112 Intro to Jazz (3)

___ PHI 215 Philosophical Issues (3)
___ PHI 240 Intro to Ethics (3)

___ REL 110 World Religions (3)
___ REL 211 Intro to Old Testament (3)

___ REL 212 Intro to New Testament (3)
___ REL 221 Religion in America (3)

___ FRE 111 Intro to French (2)
___ GER 111 Elementary German I (3)
___ JPN 111 Elementary Japanese I (3)
___ POR 111 Elementary Portugese I (3)

___ SPA 111 Elementary Spanish I (3)
___ SPA 112 Elementary Spanish II (3)
___ SPA 211 Intermediate Spanish I (3)
___ SPA 212 Intermediate Spanish II (3)

Social/Behavioral Science (12 SHC)
Select four courses from three different prefix areas. One must be HIS.

___ ANT 210 General Anthropology (3)
___ ANT 220 Cultural Anthropology (3)
___ ANT 221 Comparative Cultures (3)
___ ANT 240 Archaeology (3)

___ ECO 151 Survey of Economics (3)
___ ECO 251 Prin of Microeconomics (3)
___ ECO 252 Prin of Macroeconomics (3)

___ GEO 111 World Reg Geography (3)

___ HIS 121 Western Civilization I (3)
___ HIS 122 Western Civilization II (3)
___ HIS 131 American History I (3)
___ HIS 132 American History II (3)

___ POL 110 Intro Political Sci. (3)
___ POL 120 American Government (3)

___ PSY 150 General Psychology (3)
___ PSY 237 Social Psychology (3)
___ PSY 239 Psychology of Personality (3)
___ PSY 241 Developmental Psychology (3)
___ PSY 281 Abnormal Psychology (3)

___ SOC 210 Introduction to Sociology (3)
___ SOC 213 Sociology of the Family (3)
___ SOC 220 Social Problems (3)
___ SOC 225 Social Diversity (3)
___ SOC 230 Race & Ethnic Relations (3)
___ SOC 240 Social Psychology (3)

Natural Science (8 SHC)
Select two classes on advisement:

___ AST 151 Gen Astronomy I (4)
___ AST 152 Gen Astronomy II (4)
___ BIO 110 Principles of Biology (4)
___ BIO 111 General Biology I (4)
___ BIO 112 General Biology II (4)
___ BIO 120 Introductory Botany (4)
___ BIO 140 & 140A Enviro Bio & Lab (4)

___ CHM 131 Intro to Chemistry & Lab (4)
___ CHM 132 Organic & Biochemistry (4)
___ CHM 151 General Chemistry I (4)
___ CHM 152 General Chemistry II (4)

___ PHY 110 Conceptual Physics I (3)
___ PHY 110A Conceptual Physics Lab (1)
___ PHY 151 College Physics I (4)
___ PHY 152 College Physics II (4)
___ PHY 251 General Physics I (4)
___ PHY 252 General Physics II (4)

Mathematics (6-8 SHC)
Select one or both courses from the following:

___ *MAT 140 Survey of Mathematics (3)
___ MAT 141 Math Concepts I (3)
___ MAT 161 College Algebra (3)
___ MAT 162 College Trigonometry (3)
___ MAT 171 Precalculus Algebra (3)
___ MAT 172 Precalculus Trigonometry (3)
___ MAT 175 Precalculus (4)
___ MAT 263 Brief Calculus (3)
___ MAT 271 Calculus I (4)
___ MAT 272 Calculus II (4)

The second unit may be selected from the following:

___ *CIS 110 Intro to Computers (3)
___ CIS 115 Intro to Programming (3)

___ MAT 151 Statistics (3)
(RECOMMENDED OVER CIS)

*More math will typically be required after transfer if MAT 140 & CIS 110 are used to meet these requirements.

The general education core component (44 SHC), if completed successfully with a grade of "C" or better on each course, shall be portable and transferable as a block from Surry Community College to UNC institutions whether or not the student has earned the associate degree. Students who transfer the full general education core component shall be considered to have fulfilled the institution-wide, lower division requirements of the receiving institution. **However, graduates of the Associate in Arts or Associate in Science degree program (65 SHC) will be eligible to transfer to all constituent institutions of the University of North Carolina with junior status if admitted into the institution.**

ASSOCIATE IN ARTS   OTHER REQUIRED HOURS ("Electives"): 20-21 SHC
Select 20 hours from previous page or from following list:

___ + ACA 122 College Transfer Success (1) **(Required for degree)**
___ +ACA 120 Career Assessment (1)
___ ACC 120 Principles of Financial Accounting (4)
___ ACC 121 Principles of Managerial Accounting (4)
___ ANT 245 World Prehistory (3)
___ ART 113 Art Methods and Materials (3)
___ ART 121 Design I (3)
___ ART 131-132 Drawing I & II (3)
___ ART 240-241 Painting I & II (3)
___ ART 244 Watercolor (3)
___ ART 261 Photography I (3)
___ ART 283 Ceramics I (3)
___ ART 284 Ceramics II (3)
___ ART 285 Ceramics III (3)
___ ART 286 Ceramics IV (3)
___ ART 288 Studio (3)
___ BIO 143 Field Biology Minicourse (2)
___ BIO 146 Regional Natural History (4)
___ BIO 150 Genetics in Human Affairs (3)
___ BIO 155 Nutrition (3)
___ BIO 163 Basic Anatomy & Physiology (5)
___ BIO 168 Anatomy & Physiology I (4)
___ BIO 169 Anatomy & Physiology II (4)
___ BIO 173 Microbes in World Affairs (3)
___ BIO 223 Field Botany (3)
___ BIO 275 Microbiology (4)
___ BUS 110 Introduction to Business (3)
___ BUS 115 Business Law I (3)
___ BUS 137 Prin. of Management (3)
___ CHM 251 Organic Chemistry I (4)
___ CHM 252 Organic Chemistry II (4)
___ CJC 111 Introduction to Criminal Justice (3)
___ CJC 121 Law Enforcement Operations (3)
___ CJC 141 Corrections (3)
___ + COE 111 Co-op Work Experience I (1)
___ COM 233 Persuasive Speaking (3)
___ COM 251 Debate (3)
___ CSC 134 C++ Programming (3)
___ CSC 139 Visual BASIC Programming (3)
___ CSC 151 JAVA Programming (3)
___ CSC 239 Adv. Visual Basic (3)

___ DRA 111Theatre Appreciation (3)
___ +EDU 216 Foundations in Education (4)
___ EDU 221 Children with Exceptionalities (3)
___ ENG 125 Creative Writing I (3)
___ ENG 126 Creative Writing II (3)
___ ENG 132 Intro to Drama (3)
___ ENG 265 Thematic World Lit I (3)
___ ENG 266 Thematic World Lit II (3)
___ ENG 272 Southern Lit (3)
___ HEA 110 Personal Health/Wellness (3)
___ HEA 112 First Aid & CPR (2)
___ HEA 120 Community Health (3)
___ HIS 163 World Since 1945 (3)
___ HIS 221 African American History (3)
___ HIS 232 History of the Old West (3)
___ HIS 236 North Carolina History (3)
___ HIS 260 History of Africa (3)
___ HUM 230 Leadership Development (3)
___ JOU 110 Introduction to Journalism (3)
___ MAT 145 Analytical Math (3)
___ MAT 167 Discrete Math (3)
___ MAT 273 Calculus III (4)
___ MAT 280 Linear Algebra (3)
___ MAT 285 Differential Equations (3)
___ MUS 131-252 Music (1)
___ PED (All activity courses are acceptable)
___ PED 110 Fit and Well for Life (2)
___ POL 130 State & Local Government (3)
___ PSY 211 Psychology of Adjustment (3)
___ PSY 243 Child Psychology (3)
___ PSY 246 Adolescent Psychology (3)
___ PSY 259 Human Sexuality (3)
___ PSY 263 Educational Psychology (3)
___ PSY 271 Sports Psychology (3)
___ +RED 111 Critical Reading for College (3)
___ SOC 232 Social Context of Aging (3)
___ SPA 141, 161 Spanish Culture (3)
___ SPA 151 Hispanic Literature (3)
___ SPA 181-182 Spanish Lab I & II (1)
___ SPA 281-282 Spanish Lab III & IV (3)

STRONGLY RECOMMENDED: (Check as completed)
___Visit Admissions Offices of universities considered during first year.
___Meet and work with SCC Faculty Advisor each semester.
___Apply to universities in fall of sophomore year for admission following fall.

___Regularly use the SCC Trasnfer website for transfer information. *(http://depts.surry.edu/transfer/)*
___Apply for graduation in December for spring; June for summer; October for fall.

NOTES
1. *Students must meet the receiving institution's foreign language and/or heath & p.e. requirements, if applicable, prior to or after transfer.*
2. *1 SHC of Cooperative Education (+COE) may be included in the AS and AA as an elective.*
3. *See link below for a complete transfer list from NC Community Colleges to UNC/CAA private college.*
    http://intranet.northcarolina.edu/docs/assessment/caa/December%202005/132_Transfer_Course_List_11.16.05.pdf

In compliance with the Comprehensive Articulation Agreement, graduates of the Associate in Arts degree program as outlined here will be eligible to transfer to all constituent institutions of the University of North Carolina with junior status if admitted into the institution. To be considered for junior status, graduates must meet the same requirements set for native university students with respect to such things as grade point average and credit hours accumulated. Graduates will normally receive 64 SHC upon admission to a university. Admission to a university does not constitute admission to a particular school or a specific program within the university.

*All courses listed on this sheet (except those identified with a +) will transfer to all UNC institutions. These and other courses offered at SCC may transfer to selected public and private colleges and universities. **See your SCC advisor and contact an advisor at the college you wish to attend for additional information.***

ASSOCIATE IN SCIENCE (A10400) REQUIREMENTS
65 semester hours
See page 82 to insure minimum course requirements (MCR) are met.

Transfer Core Diploma - D10100:
44 SHC (This Page Only)

English/Composition (6 SHC)
___ ENG 111 Expository Writing (3)
and one of the following:
___ ENG 112 Argument-based Research (3)
___ ENG 113 Literature-based Research (3)

Humanities/Fine Arts (9 SHC)
Select three courses from three different pre-fix areas. One must be Literature. See MCR language requirement.
___ ART 111 Art Appreciation (3)
___ ART 114 Art History Survey I (3)
___ ART 115 Art History Survey II (3)
___ ART 116 Survey of American Art (3)

___ COM 231 Public Speaking (3)

___ ENG 131 Intro to Literature (3)
___ ENG 231 American Literature I (3)
___ ENG 232 American Literature II (3)
___ ENG 233 Major American Writers (3)
___ ENG 241 British Literature I (3)
___ ENG 242 British Literature II (3)
___ ENG 243 Major British Writers (3)
___ ENG 261 World Literature I (3)
___ ENG 262 World Literature II (3)

___ HUM 110 Technology and Society (3)
___ HUM 115 Critical Thinking (3)
___ HUM 120 Cultural Studies (3)
___ HUM 121 Nature of America (3)
___ HUM 122 Southern Culture (3)
___ HUM 160 Intro to Film (3)
___ HUM 220 Human Val & Meaning (3)

___ MUS 110 Music Appreciation (3)
___ MUS 112 Intro to Jazz (3)

___ PHI 215 Philosophical Issues (3)
___ PHI 240 Intro to Ethics (3)

___ REL 110 World Religions (3)
___ REL 211 Intro to Old Testament (3)
___ REL 212 Intro to New Testament (3)
___ REL 221 Religion in America (3)

___ FRE 111 Intro to French (2)
___ GER 111 Elementary German I (3)
___ JPN 111 Elementary Japanese I (3)
___ POR 111 Elementary Portugese I (3)

___ SPA 111 Elementary Spanish I (3)
___ SPA 112 Elementary Spanish II (3)
___ SPA 211 Intermediate Spanish I (3)
___ SPA 212 Intermediate Spanish II (3)

Social/Behavioral Science (9 SHC)
Select three courses from three different prefix areas. One must be HIS.
___ ANT 210 General Anthropology (3)
___ ANT 220 Cultural Anthropology (3)
___ ANT 221 Comparative Cultures (3)
___ ANT 240 Archaeology (3)

___ ECO 151 Survey of Economics (3)
___ ECO 251 Prin of Microeconomics (3)
___ ECO 252 Prin of Macroeconomics (3)

___ GEO 111 World Reg Geography (3)

___ HIS 121 Western Civilization I (3)
___ HIS 122 Western Civilization II (3)
___ HIS 131 American History I (3)
___ HIS 132 American History II (3)

___ POL 110 Intro Political Sci (3)
___ POL 120 American Government (3)

___ PSY 150 General Psychology (3)
___ PSY 237 Social Psychology (3)
___ PSY 239 Psychology of Personality (3)
___ PSY 241 Developmental Psychology (3)
___ PSY 281 Abnormal Psychology (3)

___ SOC 210 Introduction to Sociology (3)
___ SOC 213 Sociology of the Family (3)
___ SOC 220 Social Problems (3)
___ SOC 225 Social Diversity (3)
___ SOC 230 Race & Ethnic Relations (3)
___ SOC 240 Social Psychology (3)

Natural Sciences/Math *(20 SHC)
Natural Science (8 SHC)
A minimum two course sequence from:
___ BIO 111 General Biology I (4)
___ BIO 112 General Biology II (4)

___ CHM 151 General Chemistry I (4)
___ CHM 152 General Chemistry II (4)

___ PHY 151 College Physics I (4)
___ PHY 152 College Physics II (4)
___ PHY 251 General Physics I (4)
___ PHY 252 General Physics II (4)

Mathematics (6-8 SHC)
*Select one or both courses from the following: (Recommended to select both from this category)
___ MAT 171 Precalculus Algebra (3)
___ MAT 172 Precalculus Trig (3)
___ MAT 175 Precalculus (4)
___ MAT 252 Statistics II (3)
___ MAT 263 Brief Calculus (3)
___ MAT 271 Calculus I (4)
___ MAT 272 Calculus II (4)
___ MAT 273 Calculus III (4)

The second unit may be selected from the following:

___ CIS 110 Intro to Computers (3)
___ CIS 115 Intro to Programming (3)
___ MAT 151 Statistics (3)

Additional hours to total 20 may come from below courses, MAT courses on this page, or any from "GEN ED: Natural Science or Math" courses from list beginning on p. 83.

___ AST 151 Gen Astronomy I (4)
___ AST 152 Gen Astronomy II (4)
___ BIO 110 Principles of Biology (4)
___ BIO 120 Introductory Botany (4)
___ BIO 140 & 140A Enviro. Bio. & Lab (4)
___ CHM 131 Intro to Chemistry & Lab (4)
___ CHM 132 Organic & Biochemistry (4)
___ PHY 110 Conceptual Physics (4)

The general education core component (44 SHC), if completed successfully with a grade of "C" or better on each course, shall be portable and transferable as a block from Surry Community College to UNC institutions whether or not the student has earned the associate degree. Students who transfer the full general education core component shall be considered to have fulfilled the institution-wide, lower division requirements of the receiving institution. **However, graduates of the Associate in Arts or Associate in Science degree program (65 SHC) will be eligible to transfer to all constituent institutions of the University of North Carolina with junior status if admitted into the institution.**

ASSOCIATE IN SCIENCE   OTHER REQUIRED HOURS ("Electives") : 20-21 SHC

Required Courses: *Select 20 hours from previous page or from following list:* **(Of the elective hours, a minimum of 14 additional shc of college transfer courses in mathematics, natural sciences, or computer science is required.)**

___+ ACA 122 College Transfer Success (1) **(Required for degree)**
___+ACA 120 Career Assessment (1)
___ ACC 120 Principles of Financial Accounting (4)
___ ACC 121 Principles of Managerial Accounting (4)
___ ANT 245 World Prehistory (3)
___ ART 113 Art Methods and Materials (3)
___ ART 121 Design I (3)
___ ART 130 Basic Drawing (2)
___ ART 131-132 Drawing I & II (3)
___ ART 140 Basic Painting (2)
___ ART 240-241 Painting I & II (3)
___ ART 244 Watercolor (3)
___ ART 261 Photography I (3)
___ ART 283 Ceramics I (3)
___ ART 284 Ceramics II (3)
___ ART 285 Ceramics III (3)
___ ART 286 Ceramics IV (3)
___ ART 288 Studio (3)
___ BIO 143 Field Biology Minicourse (2)
___ BIO 146 Regional Natural History (4)
___ BIO 150 Genetics in Human Affairs (3)
___ BIO 155 Nutrition (3)
___ BIO 163 Basic Anatomy & Physiology (5)
___ BIO 168 Anatomy & Physiology I (4)
___ BIO 169 Anatomy & Physiology II (4)
___ BIO 173 Microbes in World Affairs (3)
___ BIO 223 Field Botony (3)
___ BIO 275 Microbiology (4)
___ BUS 110 Introduction to Business (3)
___ BUS 115 Business Law I (3)
___ BUS 137 Prin. of Management (3)
___ CHM 251 Organic Chemistry I (4)
___ CHM 252 Organic Chemistry II (4)
___ CJC 111 Introduction to Criminal Justice (3)
___ CJC 121 Law Enforcement Operations (3)
___ CJC 141 Corrections (3)
___+ COE 111 Co-op Work Experience I (1)
___ COM 233 Persuasive Speaking (3)
___ COM 251 Debate (3)
___ CSC 134 C++ Programming (3)

___ CSC 139 Visual BASIC Programming (3)
___ CSC 151 JAVA Programming (3)
___ CSC 239 Adv. Visual Basic (3)
___+EDU 216 Foundations in Education (4)
___ EDU 221 Children with Exceptionalities (3)
___ ENG 125 Creative Writing I (3)
___ ENG 126 Creative Writing II (3)
___ ENG 132 Intro to Drama (3)
___ ENG 265 Thematic World Lit I (3)
___ ENG 266 Thematic World Lit II (3)
___ ENG 272 Southern Lit (3)
___ ENV 110 Environmental Science (3)
___ HEA 110 Personal Health/Wellness (3)
___ HEA 112 First Aid & CPR (2)
___ HEA 120 Community Health (3)
___ HIS 163 World Since 1945 (3)
___ HIS 221 African American History (3)
___ HIS 232 History of the Old West (3)
___ HIS 236 North Carolina History (3)
___ HIS 260 History of Africa (3)
___ HUM 230 Leadership Development (3)
___ JOU 110 Introduction to Journalism (3)
___ MAT 161 College Algebra (3)
___ MAT 280 Linear Algebra (3)
___ MAT 285 Differential Equations (3)
___ MUS 131-252 Music (1)
___ PED (All activity courses are acceptable)
___ PED 110 Fit and Well for Life (2)
___ POL 130 State & Local Government (3)
___ PSY 239 Psychology of Personality (3)
___ PSY 243 Child Psychology (3)
___ PSY 246 Adolescent Psychology (3)
___ PSY 259 Human Sexuality (3)
___ PSY 263 Educational Psychology (3)
___ PSY 271 Sports Psychology (3)
___+RED 111 Critical Reading for College (3)
___ SOC 232 Social Context of Aging (3)
___ SPA 141, 161 Spanish Culture (3)
___ SPA 181-182 Spanish Lab I & II (1)
___ SPA 281-282 Spanish Lab III & IV (3)

STRONGLY RECOMMENDED: (Check as completed)
___Visit Admissions Offices of universities considered during first year.
___Meet and work with SCC Faculty Advisor each semester.
___Apply to universities in fall of sophomore year for following fall.

___Regularly use the SCC Transfer website for transfer information. *(http://depts.surry.edu/transfer/)*
___Apply for graduation in December for spring; June for summer; October for fall.

NOTES:
1. *Students must meet the receiving institution's foreign language and/or heath & p.e. requirements, if applicable, prior to or after transfer.*
2. *1 SHC of Cooperative Education (+COE) may be included in the AS and AA as an elective.*
3. *See link below for a complete transfer list from NC Community Colleges to UNC/CAA private college.*
    http://intranet.northcarolina.edu/docs/assessment/caa/December%202005/132_Transfer_Course_List_11.16.05.pdf

In compliance with the Comprehensive Articulation Agreement, graduates of the Associate in Science degree program as outlined here will be eligible to transfer to all constituent institutions of the University of North Carolina with junior status if admitted into the institution. To be considered for junior status, graduates must meet the same requirements set for native university students with respect to such things as grade point average and credit hours accumulated. Graduates will normally receive 64 SHC upon admission to a university. Admission to a university does not constitute admission to a particular school or a specific program within the university.

All courses listed on this sheet (except those identified with a +) will transfer to all UNC institutions. These and other courses offered at SCC may transfer to selected public and private colleges and universities. **See your SCC advisor and contact an advisor at the college you wish to attend for additional information.**

ASSOCIATE IN FINE ARTS (A10200) REQUIREMENTS
65 semester hours
Program/Degree Description:

Upon admission to another public two-year institution or to a public university, a community college student who was enrolled in an associate in fine arts degree program and who satisfactorily completed with a grade of "C" or better all courses that are designated for college transfer (general education, elective, or pre-major) will receive credit for those courses. The receiving institution will determine whether the course will count as general education, major, or elective credit. Because the AFA curriculum standard includes only 28 SHC for general education, AFA students who transfer must meet the general education requirements of the receiving institution.

While this degree is designed to prepare students to meet selective admission criteria for programs such as the Bachelor of Fine Arts, this degree does not guarantee automatic admission into a college or university art

1st Semester		Credit	Contact
ENG 111	Expository Writing	3	3
ART 121	Design I	3	6
ART 131	Drawing I	3	6
MAT 161	College Algebra	3	3
ACA 122	College Transfer Success	1	1
ART 111	Art Appreciation	3	3
		16	22

2nd Semester			
ENG 112	Argument-Based Research or		
ENG 113	Literature-Based Research	3	3
ART 122	Design II	3	6
ART 261	Photography I	3	6
CHM 131/131A	Intro. To Chemistry/Lab or		
BIO 111		4	6
PSY 150	General Psychology	3	3
		16	24

3rd Semester			
ART 114	Art History Survey I	3	3
ART 283	Ceramics I	3	6
ART 116	Survey of American Art	3	3
ENG 131	Intro to Lit.	3	3
HIS 131	American History	3	3
	Art Elective	3	6
		18	24

4th Semester			
ART 115	Art History Survey II	3	3
ART 284	Ceramics II	3	6
	Art Elective	3	6
SOC/ANT/POL	Elective	3	3
ART 288	Studio	3	5
		15	23

	Total Hours:	65	93

ART ELECTIVES:

ART 113	Art Methods & Materials (3shc)
ART 132	Drawing II (3shc)
ART 240	Painting I (3shc)
ART 241	Painting II (3shc)
ART 244	Watercolor (3shc)
ART 262	Photography II (3shc)
ART 264	Digital Photography I (3shc)
ART 265	Digital Photography II (3shc)
ART 281	Sculpture I (3shc)
ART 285	Ceramics III (3shc)
ART 286	Ceramics IV (3shc)

COMPREHENSIVE ARTICULATION AGREEMENT TRANSFER COURSE LIST

COURSE	TITLE	UNIVERSITY REQUIREMENT SATISFIED
ACC 120	Principles of Financial Accounting	Pre-Major/Elective
ACC 121	Principles of Managerial Accounting	Pre-Major/Elective
ANT 210	General Anthropology	GEN ED: Social/Behavioral Science
ANT 220	Cultural Anthropology	GEN ED: Social/Behavioral Science
ANT 240	Archaeology	GEN ED: Social/Behavioral Science
ART 111	Art Appreciation	GEN ED: Humanities/Fine Arts
ART 114	Art History Survey I	GEN ED: Humanities/Fine Arts
ART 115	Art History Survey II	GEN ED: Humanities/Fine Arts
ART 116	Survey of American Art	GEN ED: Humanities/Fine Arts
ART 121	Design I	Pre-Major/Elective
ART 122	Design II	Pre-Major/Elective
ART 130	Basic Drawing	Pre-Major/Elective
ART 131	Drawing I	Pre-Major/Elective
ART 132	Drawing II	Pre-Major/Elective
ART 135	Figure Drawing I	Pre-Major/Elective
ART 140	Basic Painting	Pre-Major/Elective
ART 212	Gallery Assistantship I	Pre-Major/Elective
ART 222	Wood Design I	Pre-Major/Elective
ART 223	Wood Design II	Pre-Major/Elective
ART 240	Painting I	Pre-Major/Elective
ART 241	Painting II	Pre-Major/Elective
ART 244	Watercolor	Pre-Major/Elective
ART 261	Photography I	Pre-Major/Elective
ART 264	Digital Photography I	Pre-Major/Elective
ART 265	Digital Photography II	Pre-Major/Elective
ART 281	Sculpture I	Pre-Major/Elective
ART 283	Ceramics I	Pre-Major/Elective
ART 284	Ceramics II	Pre-Major/Elective
ART 285	Ceramics III	Pre-Major/Elective
ART 286	Ceramics IV	Pre-Major/Elective
BIO 110	Principles of Biology	GEN ED: Natural Science
BIO 111	General Biology I	GEN ED: Natural Science
BIO 112	General Biology II	GEN ED: Natural Science
BIO 120	Introductory Botany	GEN ED: Natural Science
BIO 130	Introductory Zoology	GEN ED: Natural Science
BIO 140	Environmental Biology	GEN ED: Natural Science
BIO 140A	Environmental Biology Lab	GEN ED: Natural Science
BIO 143	Field Biology Minicourse	Pre-Major/Elective
BIO 145	Ecology	Pre-Major/Elective
BIO 146	Regional Natural History	Pre-Major/Elective
BIO 150	Genetics in Human Affairs	Pre-Major/Elective
BIO 155	Nutrition	Pre-Major/Elective
BIO 163	Basic Anat & Physiology	Pre-Major/Elective
BIO 168	Anatomy and Physiology I	Pre-Major/Elective
BIO 169	Anatomy and Physiology II	Pre-Major/Elective
BIO 173	Microbes in World Affairs	Pre-Major/Elective
BIO 175	General Microbiology	Pre-Major/Elective
BIO 223	Field Botany	Pre-Major/Elective
BIO 224	Local Flora Spring	Pre-Major/Elective
BIO 225	Local Flora Summer	Pre-Major/Elective
BIO 226	Local Flora Fall	Pre-Major/Elective
BIO 227	Winter Plant ID	Pre-Major/Elective
BIO 235	Orinthology	Pre-Major/Elective
BUS 110	Introduction to Business	Pre-Major/Elective
BUS 115	Business Law I	Pre-Major/Elective
BUS 137	Principles of Management	Pre-Major/Elective
CHM 131	Introduction to Chemistry	GEN ED: Natural Science
CHM 131A	Introduction to Chemistry Lab	GEN ED: Natural Science

COMPREHENSIVE ARTICULATION AGREEMENT TRANSFER COURSE LIST (Continued)

CHM 132	Organic and Biochemistry	GEN ED: Natural Science
CHM 151	General Chemistry I	GEN ED: Natural Science
CHM 152	General Chemistry II	GEN ED: Natural Science
CHM 251	Organic Chemistry I	Pre-Major/Elective
CHM 252	Organic Chemistry II	Pre-Major/Elective
CIS 110	Introduction to Computers	GEN ED: Mathematics (quantitative option)
CIS 115	Intro to Programming and Logic	GEN ED: Mathematics (quantitative option)
CJC 111	Introduction to Criminal Justice	Pre-Major/Elective
CJC 121	Law Enforcement Operations	Pre-Major/Elective
CJC 141	Corrections	Pre-Major/Elective
COM 231	Public Speaking	GEN ED: Humanities/Fine Arts (substitute)
COM 233	Persuasive Speaking	Pre-Major/Elective
COM 251	Debate I	Pre-Major/Elective
CSC 134	C++ Programming	Pre-Major/Elective
CSC 139	Visual BASIC Prog	Pre-Major/Elective
CSC 148	JAVA Programming	Pre-Major/Elective
CSC 151	JAVA Programming	Pre-Major/Elective
CSC 239	Adv Visual BASIC Prog	Pre-Major/Elective
DFT 170	Engineering Graphics	Pre-Major/Elective
DRA 111	Theatre Appreciation	GEN ED: Humanities/Fine Arts
DRA 115	Theatre Criticism	GEN ED: Humanities/Fine Arts
ECO 151	Survey of Economics	GEN ED: Social and Behavioral Science
ECO 251	Principles of Microeconomics	GED ED: Social and Behavioral Science
ECO 252	Principles of Macroeconomics	GEN ED: Social and Behavioral Science
EDU 216	Foundations in Education	*Pre-Major/Elective at select institutions only
ENG 111	Expository Writing	GEN ED: English Composition
ENG 112	Argument-Based Research	GEN ED: English Composition
ENG 113	Literature-Based Research	GEN ED: English Composition
ENG 114	Professional Research and Reporting	GEN ED: English Composition
ENG 125	Creative Writing I	Pre-Major/Elective
ENG 126	Creative Writing II	Pre-Major/Elective
ENG 131	Introduction to Literature	GEN ED: Humanities/Fine Arts
ENG 132	Introduction to Drama	Pre-Major/Elective
ENG 231	American Literature I	GEN ED: Humanities/Fine Arts
ENG 232	American Literature II	GEN ED: Humanities/Fine Arts
ENG 233	Major American Writers	GEN ED: Humanities/Fine Arts
ENG 241	British Literature I	GEN ED: Humanities/Fine Arts
ENG 242	British Literature II	GEN ED: Humanities/Fine Arts
ENG 243	Major British Writers	GEN ED: Humanities/Fine Arts
ENG 253	The Bible as Literature	Pre-Major/Elective
ENG 261	World Literature I	GEN ED: Humanities/Fine Arts
ENG 262	World Literature II	GEN ED: Humanities/Fine Arts
ENG 265	Thematic World Lit I.	Pre-Major/Elective
ENG 266	Thematic World Lit II	Pre-Major/Elective
ENG 272	Southern Literature	Pre-Major/Elective
FRE 111	Elementary French I	GEN ED: Humanities/Fine Arts
GEO 111	World Regional Geography	GED ED: Social Behavioral Science
GEL 120	Physical Geology	GEN ED: Natural Science
GER 111	Elementary German I	GEN ED: Humanities/Fine Arts
HEA 110	Personal Health and Wellness	Pre-Major/Elective
HEA 112	First Aid and CPR	Pre-Major/Elective
HEA 120	Community Health	Pre-Major/Elective
HIS 121	Western Civilizations I	GEN ED: Social/Behavioral Science
HIS 122	Western Civilizations II	GEN ED: Social/Behavioral Science
HIS 131	American History I	GEN ED: Social/Behavioral Science
HIS 132	American History II	GEN ED: Social/Behavioral Science
HIS 141	Genealogy & Local History	Pre-Major/Elective
HIS 162	Women and History	Pre-Major/Elective
HIS 163	The World Since 1945	Pre-Major/Elective
HIS 221	African-American History	Pre-Major/Elective

COMPREHENSIVE ARTICULATION AGREEMENT TRANSFER COURSE LIST (Continued)

HIS 226	The Civil War	Pre-Major/Elective
HIS 232	History of the Old West	Pre-Major/Elective
HIS 236	North Carolina History	Pre-Major/Elective
HIS 260	History of Africa	Pre-Major/Elective
HUM 110	Technology and Society	GEN ED: Humanities/Fine Arts
HUM 115	Critical Thinking	GEN ED: Humanities/Fine Arts
HUM 120	Cultural Studies	GEN ED: Humanities/Fine Arts
HUM 121	The Nature of America	GEN ED: Humanities/Fine Arts
HUM 122	Southern Culture	GEN ED: Humanities/Fine Arts
HUM 123	Appalachian Culture	Pre-Major/Elective
HUM 130	Myth in Human Culture	GEN ED: Humanities/Fine Arts
HUM 160	Introduction to Film	GEN ED: Humanities/Fine Arts
HUM 220	Human Values and Meaning	GEN ED: Humanities/Fine Arts
JOU 110	Intro to Journalism	Pre-Major/Elective
JPN 111	Elementary Japanese I	GEN ED: Humanities/Fine Arts
MAT 140	Survey of Mathematics	GEN ED: Mathematics
MAT 141	Math Concepts I	Pre-Major/Elective
MAT 142	Math Concepts II	Pre-Major/Elective
MAT 145	Analytical Math	Pre-Major/Elective
MAT 151	Statistics I	GEN ED: Mathematics (quantitative option)
MAT 151A	Statistics I Lab	Pre-Major/Elective
MAT 155	Statistical Analysis	GEN ED: Mathematics
MAT 155A	Statistical Analysis Lab	Pre-Major/Elective
MAT 161	College Algebra	GEN ED: Mathematics
MAT 162	College Trigonometry	GEN ED: Mathematics
MAT 167	Discrete Math	Pre-Major/Elective
MAT 171	Precalculus Algebra	GEN ED: Mathematics
MAT 172	Precalculus Trigonometry	GEN ED: Mathematics
MAT 175	Precalculus	GEN ED: Mathematics
MAT 252	Statistics II	Pre-Major/Elective
MAT 263	Brief Calculus	GEN ED: Mathematics
MAT 271	Calculus I	GEN ED: Mathematics
MAT 272	Calculus II	GEN ED: Mathematics
MAT 273	Calculus III	GEN ED: Mathematics
MAT 280	Linear Algebra	Pre-Major/Elective
MAT 285	Differential Equations	Pre-Major/Elective
MUS 110	Music Appreciation	GEN ED: Humanities/Fine Arts
MUS 112	Introduction to Jazz	GEN ED: Humanities/Fine Arts
MUS 113	American Music	GEN ED: Humanities/Fine Arts
MUS 131	Chorus I	Pre-Major/Elective
MUS 132	Chorus II	Pre-Major/Elective
MUS 151	Class Music I	Pre-Major/Elective
MUS 152	Class Music II	Pre-Major/Elective
MUS 161	Applied Music I	Pre-Major/Elective
MUS 162	Applied Music II	Pre-Major/Elective
MUS 210	History of Rock & Roll	Pre-Major/Elective
MUS 231	Chorus III	Pre-Major/Elective
MUS 232	Chorus IV	Pre-Major/Elective
MUS 251	Class Music III	Pre-Major/Elective
MUS 252	Class Music IV	Pre-Major/Elective
PED	All PED courses	Pre-Major/Elective
PHI 215	Philosophical Issues	GEN ED: Humanities/Fine Arts
PHI 240	Introduction to Ethics	GEN ED: Humanities/Fine Arts
PHY 151	College Physics I	GEN ED: Natural Science
PHY 152	College Physics II	GEN ED: Natural Science
PHY 251	General Physics I	GEN ED: Natural Science
PHY 252	General Physics II	GEN ED: Natural Science
POL 110	Intro Political Science	GEN ED: Social/Behavioral Science
POL 120	American Government	GEN ED: Social/Behavioral Science
POL 130	State & Local Government	Pre-Major/Elective

COMPREHENSIVE ARTICULATION AGREEMENT TRANSFER COURSE LIST (Continued)

POR 111	Elementary Portugese I	GEN ED: Humanities/Fine Arts
PSY 150	General Psychology	GEN ED: Social/Behavioral Science
PSY 211	Psychology of Adjustment	Pre-Major/Elective
PSY 237	Social Psychology	GEN ED: Social/Behavioral Science
PSY 239	Psychology of Personality	GEN ED: Social/Behavioral Science
PSY 241	Developmental Psychology	GEN ED: Social/Behavioral Science
PSY 243	Child Psychology	Pre-Major/Elective
PSY 246	Adolescent Psychology	Pre-Major/Elective
PSY 247	Psychology of Adulthood	Pre-Major/Elective
PSY 249	Psychology of Aging	Pre-Major/Elective
PSY 259	Human Sexuality	Pre-Major/Elective
PSY 263	Educational Psychology	Pre-Major/Elective
PSY 271	Sports Psychology	Pre-Major/Elective
PSY 281	Abnormal Psychology	GEN ED: Social/Behavioral Science
REL 110	World Religions	GEN ED: Humanities/Fine Arts
REL 211	Introduction to Old Testament	GEN ED: Humanities/Fine Arts
REL 212	Introduction to New Testament	GEN ED: Humanities/Fine Arts
REL 221	Religion in America	GEN ED: Humanities/Fine Arts
SOC 210	Introduction to Sociology	GEN ED: Social/Behavioral Science
SOC 213	Sociology of the Family	GEN ED: Social/Behavioral Science
SOC 220	Social Problems	GEN ED: Social/Behavioral Science
SOC 225	Social Diversity	GEN ED: Social/Behavioral Science
SOC 230	Race and Ethnic Relations	GEN ED: Social/Behavioral Science
SOC 232	Social Context of Aging	Pre-Major/Elective
SOC 234	Sociology of Gender	Pre-Major/Elective
SOC 240	Social Psychology	GEN ED: Social/Behavioral Science
SOC 244	Soc of Death & Dying	Pre-Major/Elective
SPA 111	Elementary Spanish I	GEN ED: Humanities/Fine Arts
SPA 112	Elementary Spanish II	GEN ED: Humanities/Fine Arts
SPA 141	Culture and Civilization	Pre-Major/Elective
SPA 151	Hispanic Literature	Pre-Major/Elective
SPA 161	Cultural Immersion	Pre-Major/Elective
SPA 181	Spanish Lab I	Pre-Major/Elective
SPA 182	Spanish Lab II	Pre-Major/Elective
SPA 211	Intermediate Spanish I	GEN ED: Humanities/Fine Arts
SPA 212	Intermediate Spanish II	GEN ED: Humanities/Fine Arts
SPA 221	Spanish Conversation	Pre-Major/Elective
SPA 231	Reading and Composition	Pre-Major/Elective
SPA 281	Spanish Lab 3	Pre-Major/Elective
SPA 282	Spanish Lab 4	Pre-Major/Elective

NOTE: *This list includes courses that are currently transferrable under the CAA. Under this agreement, students who complete the AA or AS degree or who complete the 44-hour core will, upon acceptance to a university, meet the institution's general education requirements. Students who do not complete the degree or the 44-hour core will receive general education or elective credit for courses at the discretion of the university.*

Pre-Major Associate in Arts Articulation Agreement: Business Administration, Accounting, Economics, Finance, and Marketing (A1010B)

This template has been developed by university and community college faculty as a blueprint for guiding community colleges in developing programs for students who intend to major in Business Administration, Accounting, Economics, Finance or Marketing. Students who successfully complete this course of study and who meet the requirements for admission to the university may be eligible to apply for admission to the major with junior standing.

All colleges will not offer all pre-major programs and course selections may vary. Check college catalogs for course and program offerings.

General Education Core (44 SHC)* Forty-four semester hours of credit in general education core courses are required as outlined on the NCCCS Curriculum Standards for Associate in Arts degree programs. The general education core includes study in the areas of humanities and fine arts, social and behavioral sciences, natural sciences and mathematics, and English composition.

English Composition (6 SHC) *Two English composition courses are required.*
- English 111, Expository Writing, is required as the first composition course.
- The second composition course must be selected from the following:
ENG 112	Argument-Based Research	(3 SHC)
ENG 113	Literature-Based Research	(3 SHC)
ENG 114	Professional Research and Reporting	(3 SHC)

Humanities/Fine Arts (12 SHC**) *Four courses from three discipline areas are required.*
- One course must be a literature course.
- Three additional courses from the following discipline areas are required: art, dance, drama, foreign languages, interdisciplinary humanities, literature, music, philosophy, and religion.

Social/Behavioral Sciences (12 SHC) *Four courses from three discipline areas are required.*
- One course must be a history course
- The following course is required (3 SHC):
ECO 251	Principles of Microeconomics	(3 SHC)
- Two additional courses from the following discipline areas are required: anthropology, economics, geography, history, political science, psychology, and sociology.
  The following courses are recommended:
POL 120	American Government	(3 SHC)
PSY 150	General Psychology	(3 SHC)
SOC 210	Introduction to Sociology	(3 SHC)

Natural Sciences/Mathematics (14-16 SHC)

Natural Sciences (8 SHC): Two courses from the biological and physical science disciplines, including accompanying laboratory work, are required.

Mathematics (6-8 SHC):
- The following courses are required:

  choose one:
MAT 161	College Algebra (3 SHC) *or*	
MAT 171	Pre-calculus Algebra (3 SHC) *or*	
MAT 175	Pre-calculus (4 SHC)	

  choose one:
MAT 263	Brief Calculus (3 SHC) *or*	
MAT 271	Calculus I (4 SHC)	

A college may award a diploma under the A1010B for completion of the entire general education core, as outlined, with a grade of ìCî or better in each course.

Other Required Hours (20 SHC)* One semester hour of credit may be included in a sixty-five semester hour credit associate in arts program. The transfer of the 65th hour is not guaranteed.

- The following courses are required (14 SHC):
  - ACC 120   Principles of Financial Accounting (4 SHC)
  - ACC 121   Principles of Managerial Accounting (4 SHC)
  - CIS 110   Introduction to Computers (3 SHC)
  - ECO 252   Principles of Macroeconomics (3 SHC)
- One of the following is required (3 SHC):
  - BUS 228   Business Statistics (3 SHC) *or*
  - MAT 151   Statistics I (3 SHC) *or*
  - MAT 155   Statistical Analysis (3 SHC)

- Three additional hours of approved college transfer courses are required.

Total Semester Hours Credit (SHC) in Program: 64-65

*   **Students must meet the receiving universityís foreign language and/or health and physical education requirements, if applicable, prior to or after transfer to the senior institution.**

**   **3 SHC in Speech/Communication may be substituted for 3 SHC in Humanities/Fine Arts. Speech/Communication may not substitute for the literature requirement.**

Application to a University

Admission application deadlines vary; students must meet the deadline for the university to which they plan to transfer. Upon successful completion of the associate degree, students who meet the requirements outlined in this pre-major articulation agreement will be eligible to be considered for admission as juniors to the universities offering the baccalaureate degree as listed at www.northcarolina.edu/content.php/aa/planning/traditional.htm. Students are encouraged to contact the senior institution to confirm degree offerings.

Admission to the Major

Grade point average requirements vary and admission is competitive across the several programs in Business Administration.